THE POETICS OF NOVELS

The Poetics of Novels

Fiction and its Execution

Mark Axelrod

Professor, Comparative Literature and English
Chapman University
Orange, California

BEAVER COLLEGE LIBRARY
GLENSIDE, PA 19038

Published by PALGRAVE
Houndmills, Basingstoke, Hampshire RG21 6XS and
175 Fifth Avenue, New York, N. Y. 10010
Companies and representatives throughout the world

PALGRAVE is the new global academic imprint of
St. Martin's Press LLC Scholarly and Reference Division and
Palgrave Publishers Ltd (formerly Macmillan Press Ltd).

Outside North America
ISBN 0–333–68957–7

In North America
ISBN 0–312–17724–0

This book is printed on paper suitable for recycling and
made from fully managed and sustained forest sources.

A catalogue record for this book is available from the British Library.

Library of Congress Cataloging-in-Publication Data
Transnational corporations and the global economy / edited by Richard
Kozul-Wright and Robert Rowthorn.
p.   cm.
A collection of papers "originally presented at a conference sponsored
by WIDER at King's College, Cambridge, in September 1995"–
–Pref.
Includes bibliographical references and index.
ISBN 0–312–17724–0 (cloth)
1. International finance—Congresses.   2. International business
enterprises—Finance—Congresses.   3. Investment, Foreign—Congresses.
I. Kozul-Wright, Richard, 1959–   II. Rowthorn, Bob
HG3881.T6533   1997
332'.042—DC21   97–22917
                                                 CIP

10   9   8   7   6   5   4   3   2
08   07   06   05   04   03   02   01

Printed and bound in Great Britain by
Antony Rowe Ltd, Chippenham, Wiltshire

As always, to Camila, Alicia and Matías

Contents

List of Figures

Acknowledgements

I'd like to thank both Chapman University for affording me a sabbatical leave, and the University of East Anglia and the Leverhulme Trust for affording me the workspace and the fellowship all of which allowed me the time to complete much of the manuscript.

Speaking on behalf of Charles and Emma Bovary, I would also like to acknowledge Dimitri Radoyce for his graphic contributions

A Poetics Foreword

These are the truly stupid things: 1. literary criticism, whatever it may be, good or bad; 2. The Temperance Society; 3. the Montyon Prize; 4. a man who vaunts the human species – a donkey eulogising long ears.

From Flaubert's *Intimate Notebook, 1840–1841*

'It has taken me five days to write one page...'

Flaubert's letter to Louise Colet, 15 January 1853

Tzvetan Todorov begins his *The Poetics of Prose* by stating, 'My undertaking is epitomized by Valéry's remark which I shall try to make both exemplary and explicit: 'Literature is and cannot be anything but, a kind of extension and application of certain properties of language' (Todorov, p. 19). He then cautiously follows that with 'I propose to indicate here, apropos of literary prose, several points where the relationship between language and literature seems particularly noticeable. Of course, because of the present state of our knowledge in this field, I shall limit myself to remarks of a general nature, without the slightest claim to *"exhausting the subject"*' (my emphasis) (Todorov, pp. 20–1). The first quote is, of course, a plea to a literary authority (Valéry), the literary heresiarch who continues the sacred synecdochal lines of Baudelaire and Verlaine and Rimbaud a plea to which I ascribe. The second quote essentially offers Todorov a 'back door' from his thesis – if needed. Recalling McHale's exordium about multiple postmodernisms it is easy to see that what Todorov is perhaps doing is allowing himself a reasonably honourable escape. Todorov speaks of Shklovsky's Formalists who located it (poetics) between 'the devices of style and the procedures of narrative organisation' (Todorov, p. 21). What one finds curious about these suggestions is the apparent 'anxiety of influence' we find in literary criticism in general and poetics in particular. As Christine Brooke-Rose (p. 287) has so aptly stated:

Something remains, then, when critical fashions pass. It may seem strange, looking back on the days of structuralism, that so many should have made such great reputations on models that were so clearly or turned out so rapidly to be unusable, or on merely translating into mathematical or logical formulas what could have easily or had already been said, on the opposite page, much more readably in discourse. But these were 'representations', just like fictions. And quick jettisoning can hardly be a reproach in a highly consumerist society where 99% of both criticism and artistic production also gets jettisoned after barely a decade. The few models that survived, on the contrary, became so necessary, their codes and categories leaping to the naked eye in a sad, professional deformation of reading for pleasure, to which indeed the chief protagonists of structuralism later turned with a sigh of relief.

Todorov finally gets to a definition of poetics on page 33 where he states that what poetics studies 'is not poetry or literature but "poeticity" or "literariness". The individual work is not an ultimate goal for poetics; if it pauses over one work rather than another, it is because such a work reveals more distinctly the properties of literary discourse. Poetics will have to study not the already existing literary forms but, starting from them, a sum of possible forms: what literature can be rather than what it is'. Of course, such a notion begs numerous questions. Such as: What is literariness? Literary discourse? Why can't poetics study existing literary forms especially if they are more pauseworthy than what is being written? And how does one study a possible form especially if some of the most innovative forms either have been lost to literary letters, are too original and hence not cost effective to produce, have poor distribution or have only been recently published? As, for example, *The Memoirs of the Extraordinary Life, Works and Discoveries of Martinus Scriblerus*, or the works of B. S. Johnson, or Ronald Sukenick, or Raymond Federman, or Steve Katz, or Doug Rice or Fowles' *Mantissa* or even Axelrod's *Cloud Castles*.

For Benjamin Hrushovski, poetics is 'the systematic study of literature as literature. It deals with the question "What is literature?" and with all possible questions developed from it, such as What is art in language? What are the forms and kinds of literature? What is the nature of one literary genre or trend? What is the system of a particular poet's "art" or "language"? How is a story made? What are the specific aspects of works of literature? How are they constituted? How do literary texts embody "non-literary" phenomena? etc' (Rimmon-Kenan, p. 2). Traditionally, poetics was a systematic theory or doctrine of poetry. It defined poetry and its various branches and subdivisions, forms and technical resources, and discussed the principles that governed it and that distinguished it from other creative activities. The term itself is derived from the title of Aristotle's work 'on poetic art' which is the foundation and prototype for all later poetics. (Preminger, p. 636) Aristotle defined his poetics as dealing with 'poetry itself and its kinds and the specific power of each, the way in which the plot is to be constructed if the poem is to be beautiful, of how many and of what parts it is composed and anything else that falls within the same inquiry' (Preminger, p. 636). The relations of literary criticism to poetics are manifold and complex. The main concern is usually with the evaluation and analysis of the work, but this evaluation logically implies standards of judgment which have their root in an aesthetic or poetic of some kind. (Preminger, p. 638).

So if one then talks about a poetics of novels, what then are we talking about? Poetics 'does not claim to name the meaning of a work, but it seeks to be much more rigorous than critical meditation' (Todorov, p. 34). And Todorov continues by saying, 'The object of poetics will be constituted by literary "devices" – which is to say, by concepts which describe the functioning of literary discourse' (Todorov, p. 236). But he does not actually enumerate what those devices are. So without Todorov's help (or anyone else's for that matter) one needs a framework for a poetics of novels. In other words, what definition can one use since one can only get from Todorov that 'Poetics must offer a systematic understanding of literary discourse as that which comprehends its individual manifestations and it must understand in systematic fashion its own discourse in literature' (Todorov, p. ix). But that does not really help. What does help is what he says poetics is not; that being 'descriptions of the particular work, the designation of meaning, but the establishment of general laws of which the particular text is the product' (Todorov, p. ix). In other words, there are principles that are inherent in the production of novels and those principles constitute a kind of poetics. Each individual author creates a paradigm for his/her work. The paradigm sets the boundaries of the fiction and it is up to the individual author to satisfy the requirements of the boundaries. The boundaries, then, constitute the mechanizations of the poetics of the individual text and those poetics enable us to understand better what texts may 'mean' both diachronically and synchronically.

But then one is still left asking the question, 'What is poetics?'. Personally, I am inclined towards Roman Jakobson's definition of poetics which I find sweetly succinct: 'Poetics deals primarily with the question, What makes a verbal message a work of art? Because the main subject of poetics is the *differentia specifica* of verbal art in relation to other arts and in relation to other kinds of verbal behavior, poetics is entitled to the leading place in literary studies' (Sebeok, p. 350). It is a definition that is clearly in line with Aristotle's *peri poetikes* – on the poetic art – and not out of line with Valéry's admonition regarding execution. For what makes a verbal message a work of art is not so much the content of the species, but the manner in which it is presented and the execution of its manner. One is reminded of Tomashevsky's contention in the 'Thematics' which asserts that the unifying principle in a text is a general thought or theme and, by extension, how that theme is executed through an infrastructure to reflect a pervasive *Weltanshaaung*.

But what one should be asking at this point is that since no two novels are alike is a poetics totally applicable? In other words, are all textual compositions equal? In what constitutional order are they presented? Is the paradigm the author creates unified? So one has already run into a problem with this kind of methodology since what we naturally find is no two novels are exactly alike in terms of poetics though some may be measurably more like one than another. In other words, we may have a novel that exists on a logical order and another that appears to exist on an illogical order. The poetics of some novels are composed in a seemingly orderly, harmonious way (for example, *Le Père Goriot*, *Fathers & Sons*) and others are seemingly chaotic (for example, *Hour of the Star*, *Company*) and some rest in between (for example, *The Posthumous Memoirs of Braz Cubas*). The question arises: Why the difference? And can we apply one method of poetics to works that are seemingly so dissimilar?

One knows the origin of a poetics ostensibly comes from Aristotle. His was the first poetics that really came to terms with methods of composition in poetry and drama. His emphasis, however, was on plot, character, chronological and linear development of incidents, an emphasis on a structure that rigidly adheres to a 'systematized aesthetics' and is unified with a clearly defined beginning, middle and end; adherence to characters who are relate-able and who comply with a veracity of the representational spirit. In contradistinction, there are non- Aristotelian texts that tend to undermine those notions on all levels so it appears that there are two separate kind of texts: Aristotelian ones and non-Aristotelian ones. One can visualize this better if one takes what Herbert Read has defined as organic and abstract forms: An 'organic form: a work of art which has its own inherent laws, originating with its very invention and fusing in one vital unity both structure and content, then the resulting form may be described as organic' (Orr, p. 15). An 'abstract form: an organic form is stabilized and repeated as a pattern and the intention of the artist is no longer related to the inherent dynamism of an inventive act, but seeks to adapt content to predetermined structure, then the resulting form may be described as abstract' (Orr, p. 15). What these two forms tend to do is establish a difference between notions of inventiveness, ori-ginality and derivativeness. In other words, for a work of art to be organic it must adhere to its own rules, those rules develop through an agitation of the spirit and not necessarily by an adaptation of the spirit which is what abstract form designates. To those ends one could use Balzac as one standard and Beckett as another.

In the same light one sees there is an internal and an external poetics at work; a poetics of the text as text and a poetics of the text as content. Many critics believe and have believed that form is inseparable from content, but few ever look at the form as content. To that extent we are working in new territory and a poetics of novels must address the form as content as well.

In his *Critique of Judgement*, Kant writes that 'aesthetic pleasure is a contemplative state which joins the cognitive faculties into a peace-ful unity or harmony free of any appetite, desire for the object, emotional or personal relation, or practical considerations of the object financial gain or worth, utilitarian goals'. (Orr, p. 16) But that aesthetic pleasure was presumably for the reader and the wri-ter, disinterested in writing for consumption, could direct his/her attention to the text at hand. But as the writing process became more and more a product, something to be marketed, the consumptive qualities increased. To that extent, certain forms became more mar-ketable than others. Not coincidentally those were often the abstract forms we talked about. This form became commodified to such an extent that it became the standard by which other novels were judged. When that happens we have a form that appeals to a broad spectrum of marketable readers who want 'comfortability' and writers who want to 'cash in' on that comfortability. To that extent, why is one form more redeemable than another? In other words, why has one form 'evolved' into a form of choice among readers?

The reason appears to lie in a homeostatic quality of certain works that gives balance and symmetry to the whole. That is, certain forms tend to stabilize the chaos around us in a representational way and bring to the foreground a semblance of harmony, of 'reality'. Though the harmony is obviously illusory, it situates in us the requisite feeling for order in our lives and as we turn the page we are, in a way, in control of the order the writer has written for us. In other words, the writer has presented an orderly universe which somehow mimics the one with which we are familiar. At the same time, the mere act of turning a page or closing the book, gives us certain control over the universe that has been presented to us.

But this is merely an appearance of order, of control. In actuality, we live in a constant state of chaos and this state of chaos synchronises with notions of poetics. In Rudolf Arnheim's essay *Entropy and Art*, he writes: 'Order is a prerequisite for survival; therefore the impulse to produce orderly arrangements is inbred by evolution' (Arnheim, p. 3). He also writes that 'Order is a necessary condition for anything the human mind is to understand...Order makes it possible to focus on what is alike and what is different, what belongs together and what is segregated...For the purposes of structure, regularity is a mainstay of order and this order is the basic requirement for any adequate information about structural things' (Arnheim, p. 18). To this end there is an extraordinary relationship between entropy and art.

Entropy is the quantitative measure of the degree of disorder in a system. The Second Law of Thermodynamics states that the entropy of the world strives towards the maximum; that is, is subject to the laws of dissipation and degradation, in other words, it moves towards chaos. The structures of literary Realism, strive towards order. So what one sees is two phenomena diametrically opposed to each other: entropy, the movement towards dissipation; realism, the movement towards harmony; one deals with the dissolution of form; the other with the propenstly for precise form. 'Physicists speak of entropy as a tendency towards disorder when they have their minds set on the catabolic (crumbling, rusting, etc.) destruction of form' (Arnheim, p. 29). Literary critics speak of a realistic approach to writing as something that implies an order, a distinct beginning, middle and end, something that unifies. 'The more remote the arrangement is from a random distribution, the lower will be its entropy and the higher its level of order' (Arnheim, p. 19). 'Man imposes orderliness on his activities because it is so useful, cognitively and technologically, in a society, a household, a discourse, or a machine' (Arnheim, p. 34). In physiological terms, this orderliness translates to a kind of homeostasis which indeed takes care of the mundane activities of daily life in order to free the body and mind for higher activities.

It is not coincidental, I think, that the notion of chaos is a scientific notion. It has been considered along with quantum physics and relativity as the third revolution in modern physics. 'Relativity eliminated the Newtonian illusion of absolute space and time; quantum theory eliminated the Newtonian dream of a controllable measurement process; and chaos eliminates the Laplacian fantasy of deterministic predictability. Of the three, the revolution in chaos applies to the universe we see and touch, to objects at a human scale. Everyday experience and real pictures of the world have become legitimate targets for inquiry [as have literary texts]' (Gleick, p. 6). In other words, chaos is dynamics freed of order and predictability and anything that deviates from order and predictability could be very uncomfortable. As Prigogine and Stengers have stated in *Order out of Chaos*, 'We find ourselves in a world in which reversibility and determinism apply only to limiting simple cases, while irreversibility and randomness are the rules' (Prigogine and Stengers, p. 8).

What one sees here in terms of the physical universe is a human's attempt at striving for order while living in a state of entropy. It is not coincidental that the discovery of entropy and the rise of literary realism were both nineteenth-century phenomena. On the one hand we have a discovery that there is a constant movement towards degradation, dissolution, chaos. On the other, a poetics of realism that moves towards a notion of orderliness and harmony. Is it merely coincidental? And would this movement towards a state of stasis be more advantageous than a movement towards instability?

'Orderliness comes from the maximum of tension reduction obtainable for a given pattern of constraints. When more constraints are removed, tension reduction can proceed further until it reaches homogeneity and homogeneity is the simplest possible level of order because it is the most elementary structural scheme that can be subjected to ordering' (Arnheim, p. 51). If we add to that notion Kenneth Burke's comment that 'Form in literature is an arousing and fulfilment of desires. A work has form in so far as one part of it leads a reader to anticipate another part, to be gratified by the sequence' (Burke, p. xx) we clearly have the makings of a text that is unifying in form and function. The apparent absurdities of the human condition, of the fact that we, and the entire universe, are in a constant state of chaos becomes adumbrated to the point that we perceive a harmony and, against nature, force a harmony on a condition that is clearly in a state of decomposition.

But writers and artists have continually attempted to deal with the disharmony, with the lack of reason in the world and attempted to convince us that all is well in the world, that plots can be easily conceived and easily resolved, that the only disturbance there is is in our imagination. Henry James in his *Art of Fiction* claims that a novel is 'a living thing, all one and continuous', but James overlooked the fact that all living things eventually die and not all that is one is necessarily continuous in the manner of Aristotle.

So one comes back again to the notion of poetics and I will attempt to approach the follows novels with this type of methodology in mind: that there is not one type of novel, but a number of types and that each novel demands scrutiny on its own terms. We may apply a set of criteria to one novel and the same set to another, but not without understanding the novel itself presents its own parameters for study. The approach is a study in the poetics of novels, not in the poetics of the novel. Some criteria will be directly applicable, others will not. One discovers that one kind of novel, among all other novels, tends to get the most critical attention: realistic novels. And one discovers that realistic novels are often those novels that enjoy the most popularity in terms of form and content.

In a discussion of poetics it is clear that what constitutes one critic's notion of poetics from another's is as variable as one's notion of the cosmos. Perhaps that is why I tend to see an evolution in poetics in the novel that is coterminous with the devolution of the novel form. From Cervantes to Beckett, from the majestic to the minimal, from broad canvases to small frames there is that seemingly inherent motion towards entropy. I have chosen these authors based on the notion of that relation between entropy and poetics, of that movement from the seemingly harmonious to the seemingly chaotic that becomes the frame of *Don Quixote* and *Company*. One may react to such a collection of writers as seemingly disparate as Austen and Beckett, but in dealing with notions of poetics and entropy they are, in a way, very harmonious especially in a work like *Northanger Abbey* which is clearly a pre-postmodern work that not only engages stylistically, but, by virtue of the form, calls attention to the fact that notions of what is novel as well as what is 'real' must be taken into account. In that sense, the gap between Austen and Beckett, at least in those texts, is not nearly as wide as one might presume. The fractionation is not necessarily gender specific either as we see not only in Austen, but again in Lispector and Smart; not only in Machado de Assis but again in writers such as Robert Coover and Beckett. From early-eighteenth-century England to late-twentieth-century Canada, from nineteenth-century Brazil to twentieth-century North America, there are major admonitions being made in the poetics of these novelists which, even on a subconscious level, parallel that entropic movement. This is not to say that lengthy novels have not been written in a post-entropic climate. *Gravity's Rainbow, One Hundred Years of Solitude, The Name of the Rose, Hopscotch* are all entropic novels in terms of how they manipulate the chaos to make it appear harmonious. Curiously, Prigogine and Stengers believe that 'under certain conditions, entropy itself becomes the progenitor of order' (Prigogine and Stegners, p. xxi) and one only need read Beckett to understand that on a sub-macroscopic level.

Like the notion of 'postmodernism', there is a kind of enigma to the notion of 'poetics'. To an understanding of poetics; to a poetics of novel notions: a cacophony of phonetics, semantics, semiotics, linguistics *et al*. Forms that often undermine the Aristotelian notion of fair game, fair play, of what Leonard Orr writes of as 'Aristotelian novels' versus 'non-Aristotelian' ones; of a seemingly corporeal harmony for Socrates, placating Peripatetic wanderings. Just as we are left pondering Brian McHale's question 'whose postmodernism is it anyway?' when he writes 'we can discriminate among constructions of postmodernism, none of them any less "true" or less fictional than the others, since all of them are finally fictions. Thus, there is John Barth's postmodernism, the literature of replenishment; Charles Newman's postmodernism, the literature of inflationary economy; Jean-François Lyotard's postmodernism, a general condition of knowledge in the contemporary informational regime; Ihab Hassan's postmodernism, a stage on the road to the spiritual unification of humankind; and so on. There is even Kermode's construction of postmodernism, which in effect constructs it right out of existence' (McHale, p. 4) we have to ask, 'whose poetics is it anyway?' Shklovsky's? Wellek's? Warren's? Fryés? Said's? Todorov's? Hutcheon's? (who even labels hers 'postmodern'). And what is this thing called poetics? Presumably it is the method of their madness. Those fools who protest too much; those deceivers who actually know the difference between windmills and giants, but execute their own game; those fabricators of labyrinths and manufacturers of such and such and so on and so on. It is their vision that disembowels the genie to perform the Herculean feats of transmogrifying the intangible, the inchoate, to that which incises into some fleshless archive called 'craft' or 'art'. To work on the notion of a poetics is to work on a disputational system of erecting monomyths in order to destroy them. Yet there must be a method to the mania (whether Aristotelian or not) that enables the writer to satisfy the expedients of the fissures of the soul in order to mollify the anguish which disturbs one, perturbs one, to write. In addressing the notion of 'the arduous labor of style', Barthes writes of Flaubert that 'the dimension of this agony is altogether different; the labor of style is for him an unspeakable suffering (even if he speaks it quite often), an almost expiatory ordeal for which he acknowledges no compensation of a magical (i.e. aleatory) order, as the sentiment of inspiration might be for many writers: style, for Flaubert, is absolute suffering, infinite suffering, useless suffering ... it requires an "irrevocable farewell to life," a pitiless sequestration' (Barthes, p. 69). And for Beckett, writing was 'the only thing left for [me] to do' (Axelrod, Interview). This notion is not new as Barthes alludes to in his mention of Antoine Albalat's, *Le travail du style, enseigné par les corrections manuscrites des grands écrivains* (1913), but for some the 'act of literature' is something that seems to happen *au passant*.

For example, Derrida, in his 'Laguna Beach Interviews', has said that 'deep down I have probably never drawn any great enjoyment from fiction, from reading novels, for example, beyond the pleasure taken in analyzing the play of writing, or else certain naive movements of identification' (Derrida, p. 39). 'The play of writing?' Apologies to Beckett, *et al.* and Flaubert of whose work we read in Albalat that 'Le travail du style fut chez Flaubert une vraie maladie. Sa sévérité devint puérile à force d'être minutieuse. La moindre

assonance l'effarouchait. Passionne d'harmonie, il proscrivait les
hiatus et voulait qu'on rythmât la prose comme les vers. Il haïssait
surtout le style, cliché, banal composé d'expressions toutes faites,
comme: "La tristesse régnait sur son visage. La mélancolie était
peinte sur ses traits. Prêter une oreille... Verser des larmes... As-
siége d'inquiétudes..."' (Albalat, p. 67). Perhaps there is no
method for Derrida which would satisfy his apparent need for
the epiphany of a transcendent reading, a kind of orgasmicreading.
So without any 'direction' suggested even from the guru of decon-
struction, what then is the method of poetics? Or are there methods? Are there approaches that coexist with the verities of the
script? From whatever storehouse of methodologies that exist?
Can there be a 'poetics of the novel' at all? Or merely 'poetics of
novels'? Is there a way to apply the standards of a 'poetics of the
novel' to texts as disparate as *Don Quixote* and *Hunger, Les Liaisons
Dangereuses* and *Braz Cubas, Hour of the Star* and *Company?* Can we
take Henry James seriously when he writes in his 'The Art of
Fiction' that 'The only reason for the existence of a novel is that it
does attempt to represent life. When it relinquishes this attempt,
the same attempt that we see on the canvas of the painter, it
will have arrived at a very strange pass?' (James, p. 5). Actually,
no. Theories of the novel from Lukács to Leavis, Lubbock to
Stevick, the art of fiction from James to Kundera all tend to
homogenize the beast into a senescent organism capable of
'swallowing its own'. What motivates an individual writer to
write his/her way is a mélange of ascendencies. A carnival of a
different colour which absorbs a writer in the exploration of the
finiteness of his/her ability. Balzac, even in his majestic sloppiness,
is equal to Beckett in the respect given to his signature on the page.
Most of the time.

    The Poetics of Novels will engage the heretofore unengageable. Or
at least the heretofore unmanageable. An awkward notion in light of
the panoply of scientific discourses from French and German scho-
larship. That is, to return to those thrilling days of Shklovksy,
Tomashevsky, Eichenbaum and Robbe-Grillet, to minimize archaeo-
logies of knowledge and vials of semiosis and return to the archi-
tectonics of the texts themselves, because in the final analysis one is
merely left with two things: the text qua text and the person who
wrote it. As Ronald Sukenick has written: 'The truth of the page is
that there's a writer sitting there writing the page...' and the reader
'is forced to recognize the reality of the reading situation as the

writer points to the reality of the writing situation, and the work, instead of allowing him to escape the truth of his own life, keeps returning him to it but, one hopes, with his own imagination activated and revitalised'. (Sukenick, p. 25). This is not to say the politics in the text is less important than the politics of the text; it is meant to say in dealing with notions of poetics the content will pay homage to its parent structure and implied in the structure is a politics that may even transcend the content. As Valéry has written: 'The art of literature, derived from language and by which, in turn, language is influenced, is thus, of all the arts . . . the one which engages and utilizes the greatest number of independent parts (sound, sense, syntactic forms, concepts, images . . .). Its study . . . is basically . . . an analysis of the mind executed with a particular intention' (Hytier, p. 224). To that end, writers exist in the text whether we critics want to accept that or not.

There are numerous approaches to the composition of novels and to reading them. Regardless of claims by critics such as Hélène Cixous that writing said to be feminine 'revels in open-ended textuality' (Moi, p. 109) there is a distinctly cohesive format in texts as seemingly open-ended as, for example, Lispector's *The Hour of the Star*, Sarraute's *Tropisms* and Smart's *By Grand Central Station I Sat Down and Wept* that tends to undermine that notion. The apparently chaotic vagaries of Beckett are truly that, apparent not real, and the seemingly chaotic nature of a novel such as Cortázar's *Rayuela* is clearly meant to undermine the fabric of realistically represented novels, while paying homage to a clarified chaos of composition.

We find that poetics can involve a number of aspects devoted to the novel, but in order to deal with these on multiple planes, from different angles of reading, as Breton might have said in referring to *Nadja*, we have to acknowledge the approaches to each of these novels will be both the same, yet different. What will be similar is the presumption, a presumption hedged in the formulation that writers write to say something (whatever that something may be) and execute it in a particular way. Though the mania of multiple readings perpetuates there is no mistaking the 'meaning' by which an individual writer structures his/her work. That compositional poetics may be based upon a clearly defined social, economic or political perspective that may be 'reflected' in the manner of the madness or as a way of placating the madness, there is no question. From the cartographic journeys of *Quixote* to the epidermal ones of *Braz Cubas* to the suspicious autobiographical 'ramblings' of

Company's voice, the poetics of novels seek to reify a particular structure suitable to the behaviour of the text and the person executing it.

In Walter Benjamin's essay *The Work of Art in the Age of Mechanical Reproduction* he writes, 'The authenticity of a thing is the essence of all that is transmissible from its beginning, ranging from its substantive duration to its testimony to the history which it has experienced ... And what is really jeopardized when the historical testimony is affected is the authority of the object. One might subsume the eliminated element in the term "aura". and go on to say: that which withers in the age of mechanical reproduction is the aura of the work of art' (Benjamin, p. 221). Perhaps it is to that end that this work will try to maintain the authority of the aura and the poetics of the novels in question.

1

The Poetics of the Quest in Cervantes' *Don Quixote*

Regardless of what might be said about the pre-postmodern posture of the 'ingenious gentleman Don Quixote de la Mancha' and about his ingenious host, Cervantes was very much concerned with both edification and entertainment and, to a great extent, entertainment came first. As a matter of fact, 'entertainment, Cervantes plainly implies, is the first duty of prose fiction' (Riley, p. 84) and to that extent, Cervantes was a proponent of the Golden Age dictum: 'satisfy an audience'. The Golden Age writers made a distinction between the *discretos* and the *vulgo*, a distinction which 'stood for the accepted if artificial division between enlightened and discerning, and unenlightened and foolish, readers' (Riley, p. 108); and though, for Cervantes, the *vulgo* was the 'conventional anonymous enemy, to which he rarely refers without dislike and contempt' (Riley, p. 108), he was, indeed, concerned with satisfying as many readers as possible. *Don Quixote* was both a work of art and a bestseller, a station which is rarely the occurrence today yet Balbuena asserts: 'Who would cook for everybody? If I write for the wise and the discriminating, I shall leave unsatisfied the majority of the public, which is not included among these. If I write for the crowd and no more, there is neither pleasure nor profit to be had from what is very trite and common' (Cervantes, DQ II, p. 3). 'Yet "cooking for everybody" was the summit of Cervantes' literary aspirations, at least with every novel after the *Galatea*, and it would be rash to assert positively that it was not the case there also' (Riley, p. 115). So one realizes that regardless of the brilliance of text, the artistry of the text, Cervantes wanted, in no small measure, 'to communicate with as wide a public as possible without sacrificing his standards to the lowest tastes of its members' (Riley, p. 115). In short, the notion of entertaining held an esteemed position for Cervantes, but it was not merely entertainment for an audience that was important for Cervantes. In the process of entertaining there was also a process of self-discovery as a writer, a quest as a

1

writer, which clearly parallels the quest that Don Quixote himself is on. It is in this unique inter-relationship between and among entertainment, self-discovery and notions of truth that the majesty of *Don Quixote* lies.

The object of entertainment is simply the act of holding or maintaining interest, an audience's interest, a reader's interest. To that degree, one must look at *Don Quixote* as an object that appeals to common interests and which 'affords mental relaxation, distraction, "escape"' (Riley, p. 84). Without that ability to appeal to and maintain common interest, the novel would not entertain and that would have presented a conundrum for Cervantes who keenly felt an obligation to reconcile the marvellously 'admirable' with the notion of verisimilitude (Riley, p. 89). In other words, in Cervantes' time it was expected that a work of art elicit a kind of *admiratio* in the reader, and that state of *admiratio* not only meant admiration for the work, but also something akin to '"pleasurable surprise", "astonishment", "wonder" and "awe"' (Riley, p. 89). With that in mind one sees a clear relationship between the act of entertainment and the notion of adventure. What better way to hold or maintain an audience's interest if not in the realm of adventure, those escapades seemingly happen to a character by chance, by fortune. So what Cervantes attempts to do with the *Quixote* is to write a novel whose main character 'appears' to have things happen to him without design, that seem aleatory, yet are astonishing, that advocate an allegiance to verisimilitude and, at the same time, create a form that not only extends the boundaries of the three most prevalent forms of fiction of the time (the chivalric romance, the picaresque and the pastoral), but also manifest something mystical. It is mysticism, 'the most romantic of adventures, from one point of view the art of arts, their source and also their end, finds naturally enough its closest correspondences in the most purely artistic and most deeply significant of all forms of expression' (Underhill, p. 76).

Cervantes accomplishes that aim by taking advantage of what was wrong with the chivalresque, the picaresque, and the pastoral: the fact that they had been (or would be) produced *en masse* for a mass public whose collective mind was habituated to – and, indeed, saturated with – the simple patterns of their fiction. By cleverly and mischievously bringing them together in a single narrative, he would 'invent' not only 'in' the innumerable printed romances he himself had read, but, more importantly, 'in' the very minds of his readers' (Gilman, p. 91). And so one has a work of fiction that sets out to be entertaining by using a form modelled on other popular forms yet incorporates the new, the novel, and the new is most obvious in the treatment of the Prologue for in terms of adventure and innovation the Prologue is a poetic passage that demands as much scrutiny as any other passage in the text. The Prologue lays the foundation not only for Don Quixote's quest as a character, but for Cervantes' quest as a writer.

In Hans Ulrich Gumbrecht's '*Eccentricities: On Prologues in Some Fourteenth-Century Castilian Texts*' he writes that 'prologues can be regarded as an *eccentric* from of commentary. Their generic eccentricity, however, is part of a mild paradox: in most cases, prologues have the status of *intrinsic* commentaries. Articulating the voices of authors, they are forms of textual self-reference' (Gumbrecht, p. 891). Cervantes' *Prólogo* is no different. It is, quite clearly, a kind of eccentric commentary which 'lays bare the device'. Cervantes begins, 'Idle reader, you may believe me, without my having to swear, that I would have liked this book, as it is the child of my brain, to be the fairest, gayest, and cleverest that could be imagined. But I could not counteract Nature's law that everything shall beget its like; and what, then, could this dry, sterile, uncultivated wit of mine beget but the story of a dry, shriveled, eccentric offspring, full of thoughts of all sorts and such as never came into any other imagination...' (Cervantes, p. 9). ['Desocupado lector: sin juramento me podrás creer que quisiera que este libro, como higo del entendimiento, fuera el más hermoso, el más gallardo y más discreto que pudiera imaginarse. Pero no he podido yo contravenir al orden de naturaleza; que en ella cade cosa engendra su semejante. Y así, ¿qué podrá engendrar el estéril y mal cultivado ingenio mío sino la historia de un hijo seco, avellanado, antojadizo y lleno de pensamientos varios y nunca imaginados de otro alguna'] (Cervantes, p. 19). The novel begins (and the Prologue begins the novel) and continues with a kind of allegiance to self-deprecation, a notion that not only disenfranchises the narrator from the text, but, in addition, disenfranchises the writer from the written word. And yet one knows that the Prologue is clearly Cervantes' prologue. There is no implied author here as the title of the novel is the same title as the copyright privilege signed by the King and in the dedication to the Duke of Bejar. No pretence is fashioned, yet Cervantes clearly wants to distance himself from the work and works hard at obscuring or making ambiguous the author of the Quixote. 'I, however – for though I pass for the father, I am the stepfather of Don Quixote – have no desire to go with the current of custom or to implore you, dearest reader, almost with tears in my eyes, as other do, to pardon or excuse the defects you may perceive in this child of mine' (Cervantes, p. 9). ['Pero yo, que, aunque parezco padre, soy padrastro de don Quijote, no quiero irme con la corriente del uso, ni suplicarte casi con las lágrimas en los ojos, como otros hacen, lector carísimo, que perdones o disimules las faltas que en este mi hijo vieres'] (Cervantes, p. 19).

Cervantes makes the feeble attempt to distance himself from the text by stating clearly that he is not the *father* of Quixote, but the *step-father* and step-fathers have no genetic relationship with their offspring, hence they cannot be responsible for any of the 'errors' one may find in the substance of the text nor in the character of Quixote himself. The technique of distancing and disenfranchising himself from any responsibility for the character's character in the text lends a certain amount of verisimilitude to the text, an approach that is generally in keeping with what Cervantes wanted to accomplish in combining that which was 'realistic' and that which was 'remarkable' and, at the same time, offer a tongue-in-cheek apology if the novel didn't work out. The disenfranchisement tends to add a kind of credibility to the text as if the mediation of time and possession has rendered the novel more believable regardless of the substance. One finds the same kind of disenfranchisement in Voltaire's *Candide*, in Cortázar's *Rayuela* and in countless Borgesian stories among others.

Cervantes continues, 'My wish would be simply to present it to you plain and unadorned, without the embellishment of a prologue or the lengthy catalogue of the usual sonnets, epigrams, and eulogies, such as are commonly put at the beginning of books. For I can tell you, though composing it cost me considerable effort, I found nothing harder than the making of this prologue you are now reading. Many times I took up my pen to write it, and many I laid it down again, not knowing what to write' (Cervantes, p. 9). ['Sólo quisiera dártela monda y desnuda, sin el ornato de prólogo, ni de la inumerabilidad y catálogo de los acostumbrados sonetos, epigramas y elogios que al principio de los libros suelen ponerse. Porque te sé decir que, aunque me costó algún trabajo componerla, ninguno tuve por mayor que hacer esta prefación que vas leyendo. Muchas veces tomé la pluma

para escribille, y mucahs la dejé, por no saber lo que escribiría']
(Cervantes, p. 20).

Of course, what follows the *Prólogo* and precedes Part I and
which is often excluded in many translations of *Don Quixote* is
the exact thing he includes: *elogios* and *sonetos*. For Cervantes only
states that he would have *wished* to present the text without
those items, but he does not say why he would have wished to
do so and what made him not do so. In fact, he is doing this
because he is already giving us a Prologue as he writes it. He
continues with: 'For, how could you expect me not to feel uneasy
about what that ancient lawgiver they call the Public will say when
it seems me, after slumbering so many years in the silence of
oblivion, coming out now with all my years upon my back, and
with a book as dry as a bone, devoid of invention, meager in
style, poor in conceits, wholly wanting in learning and doctrine,
without quotations in the margin or annotations at the end, after
the fashion of other books I see, which, though on fictious and
profane subjects, are so full of maxims from Aristotle and Plato
and whole herd of philosophers that they fill readers with amazement and convince them that the authors are men of learning,
erudition, and eloquence' (Cervantes, p. 10). ['Porque¿ como quer-
éis vos que no me tenga confuso el qué dirá el antiguo legislador
que llaman vulgo cuando vea que, al cabo de tantos años como
ha que duermo en el silencio del olvido, salgo ahora, con todos
mis años a cuestas, con una leyenda seca como un esparto, ajena de
invención, menguada de estilo, pobre de concetos y falta de
toda erudición y doctrina, sin acotaciones en las márgenes y sin
anotaciones en el fin del libro, como veo que están otros libros,
aunque, sean fabulosos y profanos, tan llenos de sentencias de
Aristóteles, de Platón y de toda la caterva de filósofos, que admiran
a los leyentes y tienen a sus autores por hombres leídos, eruditos y
elocuentes?'] (Cervantes, p. 20).

One sees that Cervantes is executing exactly what he says he
is not executing which is a measure of his ironic genius. The
narrator's nameless 'friend' (un amigo quien es el otro Cervantes)
says 'Pay attention to me, and you will see how, in the opening
and shutting of an eye, I sweep away all your difficulties and
supply all those deficiencies which you say check and discourage
you from bringing before the world the story of your famous
Don Quixote, the light and mirror of all knight-errantry'
(Cervantes, p. 11). In order to do that his friend goes to some

length in offering suggestions to solve that dilemma. Those suggestions include the following:

1. In the matter of sonnets, epigrams and complimentary verses and 'which you lack for the beginning and which ought to be by persons of importance and rank' the problem can be alleviated by writing them 'yourself' and then attributing them to someone else.
2. In the matter of 'references in the margins and authors from whom you take the maxims and sayings you put into your story' just utilize any Latin phrases that are known by heart or else those that can be easily looked up. Such uses may take others to think him a scholar
3. In the matter of annotations at the end of the book use a giant such as Goliath so you it will be familiar to everyone. In the matter of proving oneself a 'man of erudition in polite literature and a cosmographer' mention the Tagus; if robbers, use Cacus, etc. 'In short, all you have to do is to manage to quote these names or refer to these stories I have mentioned, *and leave it to me to insert the annotations and quotations* (my emphasis), and I swear by all that's good to fill your margins and use up four sheets at the end of the book' (Cervantes, p. 12). In other words, be derivative and his friend will take it upon himself to include notes and quotes at the end.
4. In the matter of references to authors that are needed, merely 'look up some book that quotes them all, from A to Z as you say yourself, and then insert the very same list in your book, and though the deception may be obvious, because you had so little need to make use of them, that is no matter; there will probably be some stupid enough to believe that you have made use of them all in this simple, straightforward story of yours' (Cervantes, p. 13). Besides, no one will try to verify them anyway.
5. In the matter of readability, 'the melancholy may be moved to laughter, and the merry made merrier still; that the simple shall not be wearied, that the judicious shall admire the invention, that the grave shall not despise it, or the wise fail to praise it.'
6. In the matter of undermining the chivalric novel, 'keep your aim fixed on the destruction of that ill-founded edifice of books of chivalry, hated by so many yet praised by many more; for if you succeed in this you will have achieved no small success' (Cervantes, p. 13).

In this bit of fabulizing the fabulation, the 'suggestions' of 'the friend' are all contingent on the notion of 'deception' and the deception is clearly meant for the reader since the writer is not deceiving himself in the composition of deceiving. In the first instance, writing the material himself and attributing it to someone else is not only deception, but fiction; in the second instance, the use of marginalia is meant to deceive the reader into believing the writer is a 'grammarian'; in the third instance, the use of known material and the willingness of the friend to *insert the annotations and quotations* himself not only is meant to deceive the reader, but the friend's willingness to participate in the charade only adds to the deception of whose work is it anyway?; in the fourth instance, the notion of deception is clearly manifest; in the fifth and sixth instances, the notion of entertainment is readily apparent. And though Cervantes' use of deception is transparent, he really does not need to implement these things since his Prologue is also an invective against books of chivalry, which do not drift with the current of custom. The friend also says 'Nor do the niceties of truth come within the scope of its fabulous narrative.' To that end, Cervantes is clearly establishing a paradigm of what constitutes truth and the entire notion of truth is called into question. So what Cervantes has achieved in the Prologue is to prepare the reader for what is to follow. He has established what he would like to have done (in other words, present the story without ornament of Prologue and customary fancies which he says he must do) he cannot do. But he has. He has situated himself as a purveyor of history (and history is a presumed truth), but has acknowledged that there is a flood of deception surrounding the text, a text that has been influenced, in no small measure, by the advice of his nameless friend.

Subsequent to the Prologue one is given both the 'Preliminary Verses' and a 'Table of Chapters' before leading to Chapter I *Which Treats of the Character and Pursuits of the Famous Gentleman Don Quixote of La Mancha.* The chapter is critical because, as an obligatory chapter, it not only gives the reader some insight into the province of La Mancha, but establishes that the hero is from a nameless place in La Mancha. The reader is also informed of his diet: stew, hash, bacon and eggs, lentils, pigeon and that seventy-five percent of his income goes to food with the remainder going to clothing. He introduces a small cast of characters: a housekeeper, a niece, a servant, none of whom are detailed, but, presumably, each one is maintained by him through some unacknowledged source of income. One also knows that the hero is verging on 50 an age to which the narrator attributes little significance, but which is of great importance in that it was and is a crucial age in the quest of the human spirit.

The hero is referred to as Quixada or Quesada, though there is a difference on this point, but 'reasonable conjectures tend to show he was called Quexana' (Cervantes, p. 25). If a conjecture is a conclusion as to facts drawn from appearances, that begs the question: Why the clear establishment of an ambiguity only to obviate the ambiguity with yet another ambiguity? Not only does it tend to call truth into question, but it clearly calls reason into question as one sees when he says: 'But this scarcely affects our story; it will be enough not to stray a hair's breadth from the truth in telling it' (Cervantes, p. 25). What is clear about the ambiguity is that there is no authentic name, which raises the more philosophical question: Does one exist without a name? If so, what is the person's designation? If not, how does one relate to the issue? Don Quixote exists because of his name. But his true name is in question and the fact there is no true name, brings into question whether the existence of Don Quixote and his travels were actual or metaphorical.

When he has nothing to do (which is most of the year) he buys books and reads books on knight errantry which, presumably, allows him to escape the mundane things in life. One discovers his interest in books of Feliciano de Silva whom he admired 'for their lucidity of style and complicated conceits [which] were as pearls in his sight, particularly when in his reading he came upon outpourings of adulation and courtly challenges. There he often found passages like "the reason of the unreason with which my reason is afflicted so weakens my reason that with reason I complain of your beauty;" or again, "the high heavens, that of your divinity divinely fortify you with the stars, render you deserving of the desert your greatness deserves"' (Cervantes, p. 25–6) ['la razón de la sinrazón que a mi razón se hace, de tal manera mi razón enflaquece, que con razón me quejo de la vuestra fermosura. Y también cuando leía:... los altos cielos que de vuestra divinidad divinamente con las estrellas os fortifican, y os hacen merecedora del merecimiento que merece a vuestra grandeza'] (Cervantes, p. 37).

These examples from Feliciano de Silva allegedly drive the poor knight out of his wits, and though he admires de Silva, 'many a time he felt the urge to take up his pen and finish it, just as its author had promised. He would, no doubt, have done so, and succeeded with it too, had he not been occupied with greater and more absorbing thoughts' (Cervantes, p. 26). [...'y muchas veces le vino deseo de tomar la pluma y dalle fin al pie de la letra, como allí se promete; y sin duda alguna lo hiciera, y aun, saliera con ello, si otros mayores y continuos pensamientos no se lo estorbaran'] (Cervantes, p. 37). Further on one reads that he read so much 'his brain shriveled up and he lost his wits' (Cervantes, p. 26) or that 'in a word, his wits being quite gone, he hit upon the strangest notion that ever madman in this world hit upon' (Cervantes, p. 27). So what Cervantes is executing in relation to Quixote's character is that the books have clearly driven Don Quixote out of his 'wits', wits, in this case, being the faculty of thinking and reasoning in general, one's mental capacity, one's ability to understand. This 'madness', of course, motivates him to fancy 'it was right and requisite, no less for his own greater renown than in the service of his country, that he should make a knight-errant of himself, roaming the world over in full armor and on horseback in quest of adventures...righting every king of wrong, and exposing himself to peril and danger from which he would emerge to reap eternal fame and glory' (Cervantes, p. 27). [...'y fue que le pareció convenible y necesario, así para el servicio de su...'república, hacerse caballero andante, y irse por todo el mundo con sus armas y caballo a buscar las aventuras ...andantes se ejercitaban, deshaciendo todo género de agravio, y poniéndose en ocasiones y peligros donde, acabándolos, cobrase eterno nombre y fama'] (Cervantes, p. 38).

Not only does this mental state establish Don Quixote's motive, but it also establishes Cervantes' motive. One needs to get Don Quixote on the journey to self-discovery, but one also needs to get Cervantes on his own journey. But one also needs to get him on the quest with a reason. But what is the reason? The mediating reason seems to be that Don Quixote is bored with life; that Quixote is in the 'twilight of his life' (verging on 50)[1] may be motivation enough for him to embark on the final quest of his life. To that extent, not only are the preparations he makes significant, but so too is the manner in which he makes those preparations since they are not made serendipitously, but with a measured manner all of which brings the notion of his madness as well as Cervantes' method into question. 'The earthly artist, because perception brings with it the imperative longing for expression, tries to give us in

colour, sound or words a hint of his ecstasy, his glimpse of truth'
(Underhill, p. 76).

The sallies that Quixote makes certainly parallel the movements
that the Sufi poet Attar describes in his mystical poem, 'The Collo-
quy of Birds' in which he describes a quest through Seven Valleys.
'The lapwing, having been asked by other birds what is the length
of the road which leads to the hidden Palace of the King, replies
that there are Seven Valleys through which every traveller must
pass: but since none who attain the End ever come back to describe
their adventures, no one knows the length of the way' (Underhill,
p. 131). These seven valleys are important in Quixote's quest as
well and they include:

1. the Valley of the Quest where the traveller must strip himself of
   all earthly things, become poor, bare and desolate;
2. the Valley of Love or the mystic life, the onset of Illumination;
3. the Valley of Knowledge or Enligtenment where each finds in
   communion with the Truth the place that belongs to him;
4. the Valley of Detachment where duty is seen to be in all;
5. the Valley of Unity, where the naked Godhead is the one object
   of contemplation;
6. the Valley of Amazement, where the Vision, far transcending the
   traveller's receptive power, appears to be taken from him and he
   is plunged into darkness and bewilderment; and
7. the Valley of Annihilation of Self, the supreme degree of union
   in which the self is utterly merged in Divine Love.

'Through all of these metaphors of pilgrimage to a goal – of a road
followed, distance overpassed, fatigue endured – there runs the
definite idea that the travelling self in undertaking the journey is
fulfilling a destiny, a law of the transcendental life; obeying an
imperative need' (Underhill, p. 132). Though a detailed account of
all the valleys Quixote traverses is beyond the scope of this
chapter, certainly the journey Quixote takes is clearly one of self-
enlightenment which one can see as he prepares himself for such
a journey.

The first thing Quixote does is clean his armour, a procedure that
would be executed by someone in his 'right' mind as well, but the
key item here is the method he uses to clean his helmet. And
though he cleans it as best as he could 'the one great defect he
saw in it was that it had no closed helmet, nothing but a simple

morion' (Cervantes, p. 27). Without a complete visor Quixote has the wherewithal to fashion a half-visor which gives the appearance of a complete head-piece. 'This deficiency, however, his ingenuity made good, for he contrived a kind of half-helmet of pasteboard which, fitted on to the morion, looked like a whole one' (Cervantes, p. 27) ['mas a esto suplió su industria, porque de cartones hizo un modo de media celada, que, encajada con el morrión, hacían una apariencia de celada entera'] (Cervantes, p. 39). Technically, the visor is the front of the helmet covering the face, but providing holes or openings to permit seeing and breathing and capable of being raised and lowered. But in a figurative context, a visor is an outward appearance or show under which something different is hidden, a mask or a disguise. Of course this leads one to believe that the visor was only partially effective since the appearance of a complete headpiece *is not* a complete headpiece. Nor is a cardboard visor the same as a metal one. 'Appearances are deceiving' and once again one is confronted with notions of truth and deception not only at the literal level, but at the figurative level as well. He tests the visor for strength which results in its demolition, then he recasts the visor with metal strips to satisfy himself that it is functional; however, he does not retest it, but 'accept[s] and commission[s] it as a helmet of the most perfect construction' (Cervantes, p. 28).

Quixote then inspects his horse. 'He strove to find something that would indicate what it had been before belonging to a knight-errant, and what it had now become. It was only reasonable that it should be given a new name to match the new career adopted by its master, and that the name should be a distinguished and full-sounding one, befitting the new order and calling it was about to follow. And so, after having composed, struck out, rejected, added to, unmade, and remade a multitude of names out of his memory and fancy, he decided upon calling it Rocinante' (Cervantes, p. 28). ['y ansí, procuraba acomodársele de manera, que declarase quién había sido antes que fuese de caballero andante, y lo que era entonces; pues estaba muy puesto en razón que, mudando su señor estado, mudaseél...convenía a su nueva orden y nuevo ejercicio que ya profesaba; y así, después de muchos nombres que formó, borró y quitó, añadió, deshizo y tornó a hacer en su memoria e imaginación, al fin le vino a llamar *Rocinante*...] (Cervantes, p. 39). But a 'hack' is not a charger and the use of the word is double-fisted: (1) though it is a horse let out for hire, it is also, deprecatively, a worn-out horse; and (2) anything that is in indiscriminate and everyday use is 'hackneyed' or deprived of novelty. The irony here is that by calling the horse Rocinate Cervantes privileges what the horse was and still is, a *rocín*, a hack.

After four days of deciding on the horse's name, Quixote then spends eight days contemplting a name for himself before coming up with Don Quijote de la Mancha. The allusion to the creation of the heavens and earth is apparent. The word 'quijote' means 'the piece of armor that protects the thigh' (Cervantes, p. 28), but the word can also be a portmanteau in which case the name is composed of *Qui*(a)–surely not; *jot*(ajot)*[e]* as in [no saber (una) jota; that is, to be completely ignorant]): surely not completely ignorant. The naming process is no less ambiguous than is the historical veracity of the man himself for Cervantes writes: 'At last he made up his mind to call himself Don Quixote – which, as stated above, led the authors of this veracious history to infer that his name quite assuredly must have been Quixada, and not Quesada as others would have it' (Cervantes, p. 28). [. . . 'y al cabo se vino a llamar *don Quijote*; de donde, com queda dicho, tomaron ocasión los autores desta tan verdadera historia que, sin duda, de debía d llamar Quijada, y no Quesada, como otros quisieron decir'] (Cervantes, p. 40).

Lastly, he selects a lady – Aldona Lorenzo – to be enamoured of and calls her Dulcinea del Toboso (Dulcinea – sweetheart, ideal; el toboso – of the limestone region). 'To his way of thinking, the name was musical, uncommon, and significant, like all those he had bestowed upon himself and his belongings' (Cervantes, p.29). [. . . 'nombre, a su parecer, músico y peregrino y significativo, como todos los demás que a él a sus cosas había puesto'] (Cervantes, p. 41). So in a rather methodical and self-conscious way, Quixote has prepared himself to embark on a quest as this 'veracious history' would lead a reader to believe. But such a history must be questioned as well since the word 'historia' not only means history, but also 'story,' 'tale,' 'fable' and this relationship between history and story, especially in relation to notions of reason is significant in that it undermines what shall become the foundation of Hegelian reason.

The sole thought which philosophy bring to the treatment of history is the simple concept of *Reason*: that Reason is the law of the world and that, therefore, in world history, things have come about rationally . . . Through its speculative reflection philosophy has demonstrated that Reason – and this term may be accepted here without closer examination of its relation to God – is both *substance and infinite power*, in itself the infinite material of all natural and spiritual life as well as the *infinite form*, the actualization of itself as content' (Hegel, p. 11).

With Chapter II, *Which Treats of the First Sally the Ingenious Don Quixote Made From Home*, Don Quixote puts his reason into effect, 'for he was afflicted by the thought of how much the world would suffer because of his tardiness. Many were the wrongs that had to be righted, grievances redressed, injustices made good, abuses removed, and duties discharged' (Cervantes, p. 29). The fact that the indications for his initial sally are founded in a deeply moral and ethical constitution would beg the questions: Are these the visions of a madman? What other madmen have had these visions and what might that mean? The fact that he tells no one of his intentions and that no one saw him leave is a clear indication that all of these preparations were made by someone with a clear and thoughtful purpose whose reasoning ran against the grain of current thought.

And so, putting 'on his suit of armor, [he] mounted Rocinante with his patched-up helmet on, grasped his shield, took his lance, and by the back door of the yard sallied forth upon the plain. It gave him immense pleasure and satisfaction to see with what ease he had inaugurated his great purpose' (Cervantes, p. 29). The fact that Cervantes has Quixote leave through the 'back door' of his yard is a brilliant literary manœuver and is an insightful exhibition of the machinations involved in the peripatetics of the quest since the greatest of adventures all begin the same way: passing out or through something as mundane as a gate or door. This is clearly Quixote's 'call to adventure' and this call to adventure, as Campbell writes, 'may sound the call to some high historical undertaking. Or it may mark the dawn of religious illumination. As apprehended by the mystic, it marks what has been termed "the awakening of the self"' (Campbell, p. 51). It appears to be that Quixote's quest is an awakening of the self which could be construed as an element of madness but a type of madness that is not 'unreasonable'. Quixote's madness is not the madness about which Foucault discusses in which the alienated sensibilities of the insane were likened to beasts. As Foucault writes, 'Beginning with the seventeenth century, unreason in the most general sense no longer had much instructive

value' (Foucault, p. 78). To that end, Quixote must appear to be
mad, but, at the same time, must be proceeding in a reasonable
path towards a kind of enlightenment that is clearly part of the
mystic way. 'For classical man, madness was not the natural condition, the human and psychological root of unreason; it was only
unreason's empirical form; and the madman, tracing the course of
human degradation to the frenzied nadir of animality, disclosed
that underlying realm of unreason which threatens man and en-
velops – at a tremendous distance – all the forms of his natural
existence' (Foucault, p. 83). Quixote's madness is a madness of
'reasonable unreason' or mystical proportions with the notions of
unreason being linked with the perspectives of what one would
consider normal behaviour of the mundane. But in the awakening
of the self, this behaviour takes on an altogether different perspective. 'It is a disturbance of the equilibrium of the self, which results
in the shifting of the field of consciousness from lower to higher
levels, with a consequent removal of the centre of interest from the
subject to the object now brought into view: the necessary beginning of any process of transcendence' (Underhill, p. 176). It is that
appearance of madness that one must address to see how Cervantes manipulates that appearance in light of the decisions Quixote makes. To say only that 'The *Quijote* began and begins as a
satire of the Amadís and its progeny, just as *Joseph Andrews* began
and begins as a satire of Pamela written "in the manner of Cervantes"'' (Gilman, p. 142) would only be partially true. The examples of a quest beyond the parodic are both numerous and
methodic and relate as much to Quixote's path to enlightenment
as it does for Cervantes' journey as a writer.

One of the first problems Quixote must resolve is that of the
'honor of knighthood' since 'it occurred to him that he had not been
dubbed a knight and that according to the law of chivalry he
neither could nor ought to bear arms against any knight.... These
reflections made him waver in his purpose, but his craziness being
stronger than any reasoning ['Estos pensamientos le hicieron titu-
bear en su propósito; mas, pudiendo más su locura que otra razón
alguna'], he made up his mind to have himself dubbed a knight by
the first one he came across' (Cervantes, p. 30). In this instance
there is the recognition of an element of authority. Yet his 'craziness being stronger than any reasoning' calls into question the
relative state of madness *vis-à-vis* Quixote's journey as a whole. In
his apparent madness, Quixote still acknowledges that he needs

sanctions to do what he feels he must do as a knight and the allusions to the chivalric texts are merely pretexts for his alleged insanity to get both he and Cervantes on their way.

The fact that Rocinante chooses the path which will ultimately be the road of Montiel (mountain-like, passage of mountains) is clearly a statement of the 'road less travelled'. But as Quixote talks to his future chronicler (sage enchanter) who may chronicle this 'strange history' both notions of history and mysticism are clear. 'As our new-fledged adventurer paced along, he kept talking to himself [How would the narrator know this?] "Who knows," he said, "whether in time to come, when the veracious history of my famous deeds is made known, the sage [*el sabio*] who writes it, when he has to set forth my first sally in the early morning, may not do it after this fashion?"... And thou, O sage magician [*sabio encantador*], whoever thou art, to whom it shall fall to be the chronicler of this wondrous history, forget not, I entreat thee, my good Rocinante, the constant companion of my ways and wanderings' (Cervantes, p. 30). Not only does the narrator then write the history in the manner of how he would like the history written, but the fact it is Quixote who recognizes how the instrument of his journey should be written belies the apparent madness implicit in a rendering of that *historía*. In short, Don Quixote is *el sabio* and if that is not clear in substance then it should be clear in the similarities in both Cervantes' discourse and Quixote's discourse, which, ironically, is imbedded in Cervantes' discourse, and which has the grammar and syntax of someone clearly of sound mind.

The allusion to other 'authors' and to the differences of opinion regarding the first adventure merely prepare the way for Quixote's future journeys. Though some accounts say it occured at the Puerto Lápice (lapiz-pencil), and others at the windmills (molinos de viento), according to what he had found written in the annals of La Mancha the first adventure *really* took place at the inn. Quixote 'perceived not far out of his way an inn. It was as welcome as a star guiding him to the portals, if not the palaces, of his redemption...' (Cervantes, p. 31). ['que fue como si viera una estrella que, no a los portales, sino a los alcázare; de su redención le encaminaba] (Cervantes, p. 43). The selection of words is important in that the first adventure of the first sally does not occur at the Puerto Lápice nor at the windmills, but at the inn which pre-figures as the gateway to Quixote's redemption. But the notion of redemption is a rather curious one in relation to the exploits of a madman. It certainly begs for an explanation what is meant by 'redemption' and for what it is needed since the variety of redemptory choices is reductive: either deliverance from sin and its consequences by the atonement of Jesus Christ or the action of freeing, delivering or restoring in some way. The former seems notwithstanding (unless one uses the model of Jesus Christ as a model of mystical redemptive value), while the latter is clearly an action coterminous with the kind of spiritual rite of passage that Quixote would be on.

The chapter concludes with the entrance of the swinegelder who sounds his reed pipe as he arrives and 'Don Quixote, consequently, became completely convinced that he was in some famous castle, and that they were regaling him with music, and that the codfish was trout, and the bread the whitest, the wenches ladies, and the landlord the castellan of the castle. In view of all this, he concluded that his resolve and sortie had been to some avail' (Cervantes, p. 34). ['con lo cual acabó de confirmar don Quijote que estaba en algún famoso castillo, y que le servían con música, y que el abadejo eran truchas, el pan candeal y las rameras damas, y el ventero castellano del castillo, y con esto daba por bien empleada su determinación y salida'] (Cervantes, p. 47). The conclusion brings up the interesting proposition of whether Quixote became convinced or convinced himself. The Spanish is clear in that he was convinced of the situation which presupposes a kind of intentionality on his part to be involved in the fictionalization of the place which is much different than being convinced of its authenticity. Curiously it is the music which engenders the vision and music has, for centuries, been linked with the mystical adventure. 'The significance of music among the ancients was intimately bound up with the mythical intimations of the *Harmony of the Spheres*' and was 'seen as part of the terrestrial blueprint, as the foundation of the world, even as the world soul itself' (Hamel, p. 93).

But one of the more interesting aspects of Quixote's madness comes in Chapter IV *Of What Happened to Our Knight When He Left the Inn* when he approaches a boy being whipped for what he claims are wages not paid him. Don Quixote orders that they be paid and the farmer (Juan Haldudo [haldudo – *flying skirts*] of Quintana[r] [*country house; fever occuring every fifth day*]) pays 63 reals less for shoes and blood-lettings. Quixote's response is 'But let the shoes and the blood-lettings stand as compensation for the blows you have given him without any cause. For if he ruined the hide of the shoes you paid for, you have damaged that of his body, and if the barber took blood from him when he was sick, you have drawn it when he was sound. So on that score he owes you nothing' (Cervantes, p. 40). ['pero quédense los zapatos y las sangrías por loz azotes que sin culpa le habéis dado; que si él rompió el cuero de los zapatos que vos pagastes, vos le habéis rompido el de su cuerpo; y si le sacó el barbero sangre estando enfermo, vos en sanidad se la habéis sacado: ainsí que, por esta parte, no os debe nada'] (Cervantes, p. 56). What is revealing about the statement is that it clearly does not imply madness unless it be the the madness of a Shakespearian fool since Quixote's reasoning is syllogistically sound. When Quixote leaves the boy is soundly beaten, but Quixote believes he has redressed that wrong. Quixote deals with the situation in a reasonable manner. By the time we get to Hegel reason has become cosmic, but here, prior to the Enlightenment, we have the 'mad' Quixote dealing reasonably with the farmer who, for whatever reason, accepts Quixote's reasoning at least while he is there. The fact he continues to flog the boy after Quixote has left has no bearing on the manner in which Quixote approaches the ethics of the problem.

When Quixote comes upon merchants they talk disparingly about Dulcinea. 'The traders halted at the sound of this language and the sight of the strange figure that uttered it, and from both figure and language they at once guessed the craziness of their owner. They wish to find out, however, just what sort of avowal was being demanded...' (Cervantes, p. 42). ['Paráronse los mercaderes al son destas razones y a ver la estraña figura del que las decía; y por la figura y por las razones luego echaron de ver la locura de su dueño; mas quisieron ver despacio en qué paraba aquella confesión que se les pedía...'] (Cervantes, p. 59). One notices from this passage that although each one of them perceives Quixote as mad, they play along with him. This mutuality *vis-à-vis* madness is a curious phenomenon because it calls into question the whole notion of madness. If Quixote is perceived as mad and one deals with him on those terms, what does that say about the perceiver? If Quixote is not mad, but appears mad, and is dealt with on those terms, then who, in fact, is mad? The chapter concludes with the muleteer, one who is not interested in playing the game, beating Quixote badly: 'Coming up to him he seized his lance, broke it in pieces, and with one piece began so to belabour our Don Quixote that, notwithstanding and in spite of his armor, he milled him like a measure of wheat' (Cervantes, p. 43). Yet, 'however battered in body as he was, to rise was beyond his power' (Cervantes, p. 44).

Which leads into Chapter V *In Which the Narrative of our Knight's Mishap is Continued*. Quixote is discovered by Pedro Alonzo who says, ' "Señor Quixada," he said (so he appears to have been called when he was in his senses and had not yet changed from a quiet country gentleman into a knight-errant), "who has brought your worship to this pass?" ' (Cervantes, p. 45). The fact that there has been a change in the name implies self-consciousness about the name change, and farther along when Pedro Alonzo exclaims that he is not Don Rodrigo de Narváez and that Quixote is not Quixote, but Quixoda, he replies unequivocally, 'I know who I am, replied Don Quixote, "and I know that I may be not only those I have named, but all twelve Peers of France and even all the Nine Worthies, since my achievements surpass all that they have done all together and each of them on his own account" ' (Cervantes, p. 46) [' "Yo sé quién soy" – respondío don Quijote, 'y sé que puedo ser no sólo los que he dicho, sino todos los doce Pares de Francia, y aun todos los nueve de la Fama, pues a todas las hazañas que ellos todos juntos y cada uno por sí hicieron, se aventajarán las mías" '] (Cervantes, pp. 63–4). The inference is clear from both 'yo sé quien soy' and 'sé que puedo ser' that he knows who he is and knows that he can be whomever he chooses to be. Quixote is returned, but Pedro keeps away until it is dark enough for him to enter. That delay gives the reader the opportunity to hear what the housekeeper, the niece and the priest have to say about him. Curiously, the peasant finds him 'the good man removed as well as he could the breastplate and backpiece to see if Don Quixote had any wound, but he could perceive no blood or any mark whatever' (Cervantes, p. 45) which clearly begs the question of assault.

Chapter VI *Of the Diverting and Important Scrutiny Which the Priest and the Barber Made in the Library of our Ingenious Gentleman* sheds more light on Quixote's apparent madness. The priest shows up the next day with the barber and condemns to the flames all of Quixote's books. They peruse each book and as they come upon certain books, they pause to reflect. The priest, for example, wants to burn *Amádis of Gaul*, but the Barber intervenes and saves it. The choice of the main arbiter is not serendipitous. In the Middle Ages, there was no clear distinction between aesthetic, scientific and moral discourse as they were all considered the same so it was the clerics who were considered the guardians of moral law. The same held in

Cervantes' time as well and so the moral authority of choosing what was burned or not remained the cleric's decision. As the barber quotes the book titles, the cleric comments on them then passes sentence before handing them to the housekeeper who tosses them into the yard. Yet through the entire decision-making process there are the constant allusions to style and substance. At one point the priest says in relation a work of translation that 'He robbed him of a great deal of his natural force, and so do all those who try to turn books written in verse into another language. With all the pains they take and all the cleverness they show, they can never reach the level attained in the original language' (Cervantes, p. 50). This opinion was certinly a warning to all translators of Cervantes as well since the use of an almost-right-word undermines the fabric of the fiction. They continue choosing books to burn until they come upon the only one they decide to salvage: Cervantes' *Galatea*. They agree on that one. The priest says, 'That Cervantes has been for many years a great friend of mine, and to my knowledge he has had more experience in reverses than in verses. His book is not without imagination; it presents us with something but brings nothing to a conclusion. We must wait for the Second Part he promised; perhaps it will show enough improvement to win the unrestricted praise that is now denied it. In the meantime, my good friend, keep it shut up in your own quarters' (Cervantes, p. 54). ['Muchos años ha que es grande amigo mío ese Cervantes, y sé que es más versado en desdichas que en versos. Su libro tiene algo de buena invención; propone algo, y no concluye nada: es menester esperar le segunda parte que promete; quizá con la enmienda alcanzará del todo misericordia que ahora se le niega; y entre tanto que esto se ve, tenedle recluso en vuesta posada, señor compadre'] (Cervantes, p. 75). This kind of self-consciousness in writing is doubtless striking for the time, but it also comments on several other issues as well. 'In the prologue to the *Galatea* Cervantes paid his tribute to the Spanish language for the opportunity it offered for displaying that diversity of *conceptos* that came so naturally to its writers.... Spanish was held to be peculiarly suited to all forms of word-play, equivocation and conceit.... In accordance with these definitions, Don Quixote says, "the pen is the tongue of the mind; [one's] writings will correspond to whatever conceits are engendered there" II, 16' (Gilman, pp. 149–50). But that particular volume is not only part of Quixote's collection, but one that is not burned. Why is it not burned? Do they believe it has not influenced Quixote or that it has not been influential on the *Quixote*? To both questions the answer is, 'yes'.

During the course of Quixote's recovery he remains home for fifteen days during which time, 'The priest sometimes contradicted him and sometimes agreed with him, for had he not observed this precaution he would have been unable to bring him to reason' (Cervantes, p. 56). Which obviously begs the question, If one is mad, then what good would it do to reason with a madman? How does one negotiate reasonably with a madman? The clear implication is that Quixote is not mad at all. That Sancho Panza is introduced as someone without 'much salt in his brain-pan' and whom Quixote convinces to go with him based on the assumption that Quixote will make him governor of his own isle only shows how clear-minded Quixote is since it is the potential for material gain, not noble causes that intrigues Panza and Quixote knows that. But it is Chapter VIII *Of the Good Fortune Which the Valiant Don Quixote Had in the Terrible and Undreamed of Adventure of the Windmills, With Other Occurrences Worthy to be Fitly Recorded* that reveals Quixote's 'true nature' and fully establishes his *raison d'être* for embarking on the quest upon which he has set out. At the opening of the chapter they see thirty or forty windmills which Quixote recognizes as giants. When Sancho Panza counters with the fact they are windmills Quixote replies very matter-of-factly, 'It is easy to see,' replied Don Quixote, 'that you are not used to this business of adventures. Those are giants, and if you are afraid, away with you out of here and betake yourself to prayer, while I engage in them in fierce and unequal combat' (Cervantes, p. 59) [– 'Bien parece' – respondió Don Quixote – '*que no estás cursado en esto de las aventuras* [my italics]: ellos son gigantes; y si tienes miedo, quítate de ahí, y ponte en oración en el espacio que yo voy a entrar con ellos en fiera y desigual batalla'] (Cervantes, p. 82). Quixote says that Sancho Panza is not experienced or skilled in *adventures*. In Sancho Panza we have the prototypical 'realist', the man who sees what is ther to be seen: the essentialist, the literalist. He is, of course, counterpoint to Quixote who is not only the fabulist, but the mystic. The fact is, Quixote knows they are windmills, but chooses to see them as something else. Sancho Panza is not skilled in adventures neither of the mundane nor of the imaginary. 'This intuition of the Real lying at the root of the visible world and sustaining its life, is present in a modified form in the arts; perhaps it were better to say, *must* be present if these arts are to justify themselves as heightened forms of experience. It is this which gives to them that peculiar vitality, that strange power of communicating a poignant emotion, half torment and half joy, which baffle their more rational interpreters' (Underhill, p. 74). To that end, there is no amount of suffering that would discourage Quixote from his quest and those who cannot perceive that vision are not only not skilled in the adventures, but in the quest for enlightenment.

When they approach a coach carrying two Benedictine monks and a lady, Quixote says they are enchanters bearing off a princess. Sancho, predictably, says no they aren't. 'I have told you already, Sancho,' replied Don Quixote, 'that on the subject of adventures you know very little. What I say is the truth, as you shall see presently' (Cervantes, p. 62). [– 'Ya te he dicho, Sancho' – respondió don Quijote, 'que sabes poco de achaque de aventuras; lo que yo digo es verdad, y ahora lo verás'] (Cervantes, p. 85). In Spanish he says '*que sabes poco de achaque de aventuras*'. It is the use of the word '*achaque*' that is significant. The immediate and seemingly obvious assumption is that Quixote is mad, yet the polarization Cervantes is presenting is the conflict between the imagination of a fabulator and one who merely reacts to what is represented to him as 'reality'. It is the conflict between one who perceives reality as a literal representation of events and one who is exploring the possibilities of 'reality'. The word '*achaque*' can be translated as 'subject', but it can also be translated as an 'ailment of older people.' If one translates it as the latter, then the implication of the phrase is entirely different and lends credence to the fact that Quixote is clearly knowledgable about what he is doing regardless of the apparent threat to life and limb.

In the middle of the fight with the Basque, the narrator breaks off with the reason that 'But at this point of crisis, the author of the history leaves the battle in suspense, spoiling the whole episode. The excuse he offers is that he could find nothing more written about these achievements of Don Quixotes than what has already been told. It is true the second author of this work was unwilling to believe that so interesting a history could have been allowed to lapse into oblivion, or that the learned persons in La Mancha could have been so undiscerning as not to preserve in their archives or registries some documents referring to this famous knight. Since such was his conviction, he did not despair of discovering the conclusion of this pleasant history. He did this, heaven favouring him, in a way related in the Second Part' (Cervantes, p. 64). Thus ends the first part, though the second part, although titled *The Second Part of the Ingenious Gentleman Don Quixote of La Mancha* doesn't begin with Chapter I, but continues with Chapter IX.

The narrator supposedly continues with the Basque story. But he does not. He presumably digresses and this presents the reader with something altogether new, that is the poetics of fictional digression. The narrator tells how he came upon discovering the sequel to the story of the Basque and the Manchegan knight and he also attempts to make perfectly clear that this is a 'history'. A delightful history, a gallant history, a modern history, but a history through and through.

Then the narrator says, 'I know well, nevertheless, that if Heaven, chance, and good fortune had not helped me, the world would have remained deprived of an entertainment and pleasure that may well occupy the attentive reader for a couple of hours or so' (Cervantes, p. 66). What is truly original about this line is, of course, its self-reflexive nature and that self-reflexive writing calls attention to itself as being artifice, the *sine qua non* of postmodern writing. But there is also the narrator's continued interest in entertainment and the significance that entertainment plays and one must entertain the notion of who the narrator is. In other words, at this point one must ask, 'Who is the "I" of the story?' Is it really Cervantes or is it someone else? The I tries to discover the sequel and travels to Toledo where he serendipitously buys a manuscript written in Arabic (which he cannot read), gives it to a Moor, who can, and who translates it from Arabic into Castilian which reads *The History of Don Quixote De La Mancha*, written by Cide Hamete Benengeli, Arabic historian. The narrator buys the rest of the parchments and the Moor translates everything that has to do with Don Quixote. The narrator pays him (50 pounds of raisins and two bushels of wheat) and the Moor promises to 'translate them well, faithfully and very quickly' which takes 6 weeks. What he translates reveals a life-like picture of Quixotes's fight with the Basque whose name is Don Sancho de Azpeitia. 'Some other trifling particulars might be mentioned, but they are all of slight importance and have nothing to do with the faithful telling of the story, and no story can be bad so long as it is true' (Cervantes, p. 67).

The narrator says that if any objection about the truth of the history can be made it would be that the narrator was an Arab and those of that nation are 'ready liars'. That translation then might be problematic because 'This is ill done and worse contrived, for it is the business and duty of historians to be exact, truthful, and wholly free from passion. Neither interest nor fear, hatred nor love, should make them swerve from the path of truth, whose mother is history, rival of time, storehouse of deeds, witness for the past, example and counsel for the present, and warning for the future. In this I know will be found all the entertainment that can be desired, and if any good quality is lacking, I maintain it is the fault of its hound of an author and not of the subject' (Cervantes, p. 68).

He then concludes the story which he began. But one must ask: Whose story is it at this point? It is the account of an untrustworthy Arab historian, translated from Arabic into Castillan, by a Moor, recounted by the narrator. If in fact we have the 'truth' at the level of originality, then, like the process of dissipation, the truth dissipates and we are left with the following scheme:

1. THE TRUTH – assuming the truth does exist – followed by
2. an Arabic commentary on the truth followed by
3. a Moorish translation of the Arabic commentary followed by
4. a Spanish narration of the Moorish translation followed by
5. An English translation of the novel at the level of our study

If one then reads the remainder of the story which begins with 'To be brief, its Second Part, according to the translation, began in this way' (which is the beginning of Cide's text) and then return and read the last paragraph of the story prior to the digression one finds absolutely no difference in style. To that degree one can posit a notion related to a Cervantean notions of poetics. One knows that what he does to the reader he does in the text. Just as the reader is rather bemused by what is truth and what is fiction, the text itself lends itself to the same kind of ambiguity. In Cervantes' theory of fiction he is concerned with the nature of truth in literary fiction. Where does the truth lie? In the tale or in the telling? He addresses problems of unity and bases his poetics on poetics of the time (Aristotle, Horace, Plato), communication with other writers, what he read and wrote. When he attributes to Cide Hamete we see the deception and that he recognizes that the world, in essence, is paradoxical and that an ambivalent, if not ambiguous, attitude alone can grasp its contradictory totality.

An in-depth exploration of the notion of the quest at both the textual and authorial levels is beyond the scope of this chapter, but the genuine nature of Don Quixote's quest is made apparent if one takes a look at the last two chapters of the *Second Part of Don Quixote de La Mancha* (which is not to be confused with the *Second Part of the Ingenious Gentleman Don Quixote de La Mancha*) which includes *Of the omens Don Quixote had as he entered his own village, and other incidents that embellish and give a color to this great history* and *Of how Don Quixote fell sick, and of the will he made, and how he died.* In Arnold van Gennep's *Les rites de passage*, van Gennep associated these rites of passage with what he calls 'life crises' and 'he pointed out that, when the activities associated with such ceremonies were examined in terms of their order and content, it was possible to distinguish three major phases: separation (*séparation*), transition (*marge*), and incorporation (*agrégation*). Considered as a whole, he labelled these the '*schéma*' of '*rites de passage*' (van Gennep, p. vii). These three *passages* or *transitions* as van Gennep would have preferred to call them, and written in 1908, predate and run parallel to the three stages that Campbell has talked about in terms of myth; namely, separation, initiation and return. 'The examination of any life-crisis ceremony will quickly establish the validity of the threefold classification of separation, transition and incorporation' (van Gennep, p. vii). In a very clear way, we see these transitions made in Don Quixote's quest from the *separation* of the first sally (First Part, Chapter II) through the *initiation/transition* (everything up to, but not including) the *return/incorporation* (Second Part, Chapters LXXIII and LXXIV). In that sense, there is a homage paid to the mystico–religious aspect of the quest and in a metaphorical sense a sacrifice to be made. 'The typical series of rites of passage (separation, transition, and incorporation) furnished the pattern for ceremonies of sacrifice, and in this connection it was systemized down to the last detail in ancient Hindu and Jewish rituals, as well as sometimes in the pilgrimage and the *devotio*. It is known that the Catholic pilgrim must follow a certain number of rules of preliminary sanctification before his departure, so that he can be removed from the profane world and incorporated into the sacred world' (van Gennep, p. 184). And certainly Cide Hamete Benengeli would have been aware that 'among Moslems the pilgrim who has pledged to go to Mecca is in a special state called *ihram* from the moment he enters the limits of the sacred territory [Mecca and Medina]. But, according to the ancient custom, he was invested with sacredness, with *ihram*, as soon as he left home, so that every pilgrim, from the time of his departure until his return, was outside ordinary life and in a transitional state' (van Gennep, pp. 184–5).

It is with that grounding that one can look at the last two chapters of the Don Quixote's quest with reasonable assurance that a) Don Quixote has been on a quest from the beginning of the novel and b) that Don Quixote has been cognizant of everything he has done through during the transitional phases of the quest. It is no coincidence, then, that it is according to Cide Hamete that Chapter LXXIII opens. The chapter hinges on two evil omens: (1) the statement by the boy that 'You'll never see it again as long as you live' (relating to a cage of crickets) and (2) the hare being hunted by the hounds. Both indicate to Don Quixote that, in fact, he shall never see Dulcinea again. To try to annul the omens, Sancho pays for both the crickets and the hare and by doing so says, 'There, señor! There are the omens broken and destroyed, and they have no more to do with our affairs, to my thinking, fool that I am, than with last year's clouds' (Cervantes, p. 822). Sancho thinks correctly, by his way of thinking, but his approach to solving the problem is similar to what Frazer talks about in variations of sympathetic magic in which 'the effect is to circumvent destiny by substituting a mock calamity for a real one' (Frazer, p. 42) with the difference being that Sancho believes he has circumvented Don Quixote's destiny by merely purchasing the objects that serve to issue the omen. Clearly, it is the *omen* Don Quixote perceives and no presumed remedy can alter the meaning of the prophetic sign. The fact that Don Quixote equates the hare with never seeing Dulcinea again is not an arbitrary relationship. In Greek mythology the hare is associated with Hecate ('she who has power far off'), presumed daughter of Perses and Asteria, and considered a triple goddess associated with the moon, Luna, the earth, Diana, and the underworld, Persephone. As representing the darkness and terror of the night, Hecate haunted the crossroads, graveyards, and was the goddess of sorcery and witchcraft (Zimmerman, p. 278). But a feminine character is inseparable from the fundamental symbolization of the hare and for Don Quixote to see the hare and relate it to Dulcinea would not appear to be an unnatural one.

Don Quixote explains to the bachelor and the priest of 'how he planned to become a shepherd for that year and spend his time in the solitude of the fields, where he could follow with perfect freedom, give range to his thoughts of love while he followed the virtuous pastoral calling' (Cervantes, p. 823). Quixote's new proposition is, quite clearly, a measure of his spiritual sanity and a continuation of the quest. In response to the arguments posited against such a decision by both his niece and the housekeeper, Quixote replies: 'Hold your peace, my daughters,' said Don Quixote. 'I know very well what my duty is; help me to bed, for I don't feel very well; and rest assured that, knight-errant now or wandering shepherd to be, I shall never fail to care for your needs, as you will see by my actions' (Cervantes, p. 825). ['Callad, hijas' les respondió don Quijote 'que yo sé bien lo que me cumple. Llevadme al lecho, que parece que no estoy muy bueno, y tened por cierto que, ahora sea caballero andante, o pastor por andar, no dejaré siempre de acudir a lo que hubiéredes menester, como lo veréis por la obra'] (Cervantes, pp. 1061–2). The comment of 'yo sé' is a refrain that one reads at various times throughout Quixote's quest. Not only does he know what he's doing he is also cognizant of his responsibility to both his niece and his housekeeper.

Though his illness seems suddenly acute, the expectancy of it is chronic. He has been experiencing the 'illness' of the human condition for some time and the omens merely reflect that which leads us to the final chapter which begins with: 'Since human affairs are not eternal but all tend ever downwards from their beginning to end, and above all man's life, and as Don Quixote's enjoyed no special dispensation from heaven to slow its course, its end and close came when he least expected it' (Cervantes, p. 825). There is, of course, a difference between a physical and a spiritual illness; of the former he may not have been aware; of the latter, there is little doubt. After his six hour sleep, Quixote awakes by saying: 'Blessed be Almighty God, who has shown me such goodness. In truth his mercies are boundless, and the sins of men can neither limit them nor keep them back!' (Cervantes, p. 826). After which time he tells his niece that his 'reason is free and clear' and later one reads that 'They looked at one another, amazed at Don Quixote's words; but, though uncertain, they were inclined to believe him, and one of the signs by which they concluded that he was dying was this sudden and complete return to his senses after having been mad; for to the words already quoted he added much more, so well expressed, so devout, and so rational, as to banish all doubt and convince them that he was sound of mind' (Cervantes, p. 827). Yet the notion of madness is clearly one that is perceived by the receiver of the message. At bottom there is little in the way of an alteration in Quixote's discourse itself, merely in the way it is presented and one even hears Sancho encouraging him to get out of bed since 'Perhaps behind some bush we'll find the lady Dulcinea disenchanted, as fine as fine can be' (Cervantes, p. 828) which is the truest measure of the influence that Quixote's 'madness' has had on 'normal, reasonable' people. There is nothing in the discourse itself that would indicate reason restored since Quixote has, to a great extent, been reasonable throughout the quest. At the end of his life, the quest done, he appeals to God much in the way a mystic would appeal to God. 'The mystic knows that destiny. It is laid bare to his lucid vision, as our puzzling world of form and colour is to normal sight. He is the "hidden child" of the eternal order, an initiate of the secret plan. Hence, whilst, "all creation groaneth and travaileth", slowly moving under the spur of blind desire towards that consummation in which it alone can have rest, he runs eagerly along the pathway to reality. He is the pioneer of Life on its age-long voyage to the One; and shows us, in his attainment, the meaning and value of that life' (Underhill, p. 447).

After finalizing his will, one reads the clearest statement of Cervantes' poetic quest as Cide Hamete writes 'Beware, ye cowards, stay your hands! Let it be touched by none. *For this adventure, O good king, Was meant for me alone*' [my italics] (Cervantes, p. 830) [Tate, tate, folloncicos! De ninguno sea tocada; porque esta empresa, buen rey, para mí estaba guardada' (Cervantes, p. 1068). Cide Hamete then closes the quest with 'And I shall remain satisfied and proud to have been the first who has ever enjoyed the fruit of his writings as fully as he could desire; for my desire has been no other than to cause mankind to abhor the false and foolish tales of the books of chivalry, which, thanks to that of my true Don Quixote, are even now tottering and doubtless doomed to fall for ever. Farewell' (Cervantes, p. 830). Clearly, Don Quixote's quest is Cervantes' quest on both spiritual and poetic levels, as both the character and the writer, the source of 'fictional wisdom' and the authority of that fictional wisdom. In the words of Pascal 'Men are mad so unavoidably that not to be mad would constitute one a madman of another order of madness'.

2

The Poetics of (P)ostmode(r)n(e) Parody in Austen's *Northanger Abbey*

What is considered Austen's 'juvenilia' period, dating from 1787 to 1793 and which contains 'principaly burlesque narratives that parody the fictional modes of her time' (Lauber, p. 11) is clearly the same period in which her significant 'experimental' modes are being written. The foundation for *Northanger Abbey* lay in the text *Susan* written in 1798–99 (her pre-postmodern-post-juvenilia phase) a time which also post-dates drafts she was writing of *Pride and Prejudice* in 1796. The novel, with the same title, was sold to Crosbie & Company in 1803 for £10, but was never published. Austen writes on 5 April 1809: 'Gentlemen, In the spring of the year 1803 a MS. Novel in 2 vol. entitled Susan was sold to you by a Gentleman of the name of Seymour, & the purchase money £10, recd at the same time. Six years have passed, & this work of which I am myself the Authoress, has never to the best of my knowledge, appeared in print, tho' an early publication was stipulated for at the time of sale. I can only account for such an extraordinary circumstance by supposing the MS. by some carelessness to have been lost; & if that was the case, *am willing to supply you with another copy if you are disposed to avail yourselves of it* [my italics], & will engage for no farther delay when it comes into your hands. It will not be in my power from particular circumstances to command this copy before the Month of August, but then, if you accept my proposal, you may depend on receiving it. Be so good as to send me a line in answer as soon as possible, as my stay in this place will not exceed a few days. Should no notice be taken of this address, I shall feel myself at liberty to secure the publication of my work, *by applying elsewhere* [my italics], I am Gentlemen &c. &c.' (Chapman, p. 263). This letter was answered by Richard Crosby on 8 April 1809 in which he answers by saying that they paid for the manuscript titled *Susan* the sum of £10 'for which we have his stamped receipt as a full consideration, but there was not any time stipulated for its publication, neither are we bound to publish it, Should you or anyone else [sic] we shall take proceedings to stop the sale. The MS. shall be yours for the same as we paid for it' (Chapman, p. 264). No mention of the novel is made again until 13 March 1817 in which she writes 'Miss Catherine is put upon the Shelve for the present, and I do not know that she will ever come out' (Chapman, p. 484). And that is basically the end of it.

When the work was finally published, albeit posthumously, we hear Austen, in her own voice, writing: 'This little work was finished in the year 1803, and intended for immediate publication. It was disposed of to a bookseller, it was even advertized, and why the business proceeded no farther, the author has never been able to learn. That any bookseller should think it worth-while to purchase what he did not think it worth-while to publish seems extraordinary. But with this, neither the author nor the public have any other concern than as some observation is necessary upon those parts of the work which thirteen years have made comparatively obsolete. The public are entreated to bear in mind that thirteen years have passed since it was finished, many more since it was begun, and that during that period, places, manners, books and opinions have undergone considerable changes' (Austen, Advertisement by the Authoress). As in introductory passages by other writers this introduction is noteworthy since it not only comments implicitly on that mysteriously fragile relationship between novelist and publisher (one which still exists and is purposefully exacerbated by that most nefarious of intermediaries, 'the literary agent'), but also highlights Austen's rather fragile apologetic tone. It is clear from her prose that because the publisher did nothing with the work and because it languished for years unseen and unread Austen was demonstrably peeved. And though she makes what reads as an apology to her readers, none was really needed. 'Those parts of the work which thirteen years have made comparatively obsolete' are actually those parts of the novel that make it so imaginative especially regarding period, books and opinions of which more will be said later. What is foremost is that Austen is sincerely interested in getting the work published. Not only is she willing to supply another copy to Crosbie, but firmly indicates that she feels at liberty to seek out other publishers should Crosbie be disinterested. Crosbie, in a response that is diachronically absolute in the publisher–writer diastalsis, is presumably chaffed by her comment regarding why a publisher would buy a book and not publish it.

Somehow, though, it is not surprising that after holding the book for six years the publisher did nothing with it because in 1803, barely a scratch into the nineteenth century, a novel such as *Northanger Abbey* may not have pleased publishing sensibilities at the time since the cult of the Gothic was still very much a fertile ground for publishers and a parody of the cult may have been deemed not in Crosbie's interest to publish it. 'Literary history marks a conventional ending for the cult of the Gothick at about 1820. The posthumous publication of *Northanger Abbey* in 1818, despite the fact that *Frankenstein* was published in the same year, contributes strongly to the sense of an historical watershed, the wit of Jane Austen's novel perhaps matching the feeling of the times that the literary cult of terror and the sublime has a touch of the grand guignol about it' (Sage, pp. 18–19). Certainly Radcliffe's *The Mysteries of Udolpho* (1794) was enjoying immense popularity at the time Austen tried to publish *Northanger Abbey* and that may have played some part in its rejection. Radcliffe received great sums of money for her books: £500 for *Udolpho*, £600 for *The Italian* in contrast to the meager £10 Austen received for *Northanger Abbey*. And Crosbie may have sensed that even such a meager investment of £10 may not have been worth the publication of a novel the publication of which might result in limited returns.

As Ian Watt has written in *The Rise of the Novel*, books were very expensive at the time and 'the high cost of books in the eighteenth century emphasizes the severity of economic factors in restricting the reading public' (Watt, p. 42). Coterminous with the high cost of reading (according to Watt, the price of a novel could have fed a family for a week or two) came the social significance of reading. 'The distribution of leisure in the period supports and amplifies the picture already given of the composition of the reading public; and it also supplies the best evidence available to explain the increasing part in it played by women readers' (Watt, p. 45). Given those parameters, one might speculate that a publisher would either reject outright or covertly reject Austen's novel based on the cost-effective issues of the day. Why publish a novel that parodies an enormously popular book that is predominately sold to women? Might such a publication offend the sensibilities of the predominately female reading public? And might that result in a kind of backlash against the publisher of such a novel? Certainly one must question (along with Austen) crosbie's intention to buy the book only to ignore it.

To some extent, *Northanger Abbey* may still not please publishing sensibilities especially in relation to texts deemed 'realistic', for the poetics of *Northanger Abbey* are not the same poetics as *Pride and Prejudice* or *Sense and Sensibility* or *Persuasion* or *Emma* all of which have been glamorized into television dramas or feature films. On the contrary, *Northanger Abbey* remains on the margins. In its own way, *Northanger Abbey* is the gothic equivalent to *Tristram Shandy* (1760–67) which was 'not so much a novel as a parody of a novel' (Watt, p. 303). Without arguing whether a parody of a novel is or is not a novel in its own right (though Fielding must also chafe at that proposition), one can see how the notion of the *parodic* becomes somewhat pejorative and as such tends to undermine the original-ity of the work.

Much of the criticism leveled at *Northanger Abbey* is because the work has been somehow *relegated* to the station of a 'burlesque' or a 'parody' (which were considered the same thing in the seven-teenth-century), both of which, as Lauber addresses, seem to be part of one's 'maturing' process as a writer and, in that context, somehow makes the work something less than 'artistic'. Obviously it is not. But it is precisely this post-juvenilia writing which marks Austen's brilliance as a novelist and which establishes *Northanger Abbey* as a work which needs to be considered as a poetic instru-ment equal to, though separate from, such works as *Pride and Prejudice* and *Sense and Sensibility*. To that extent, one is clearly puzzled by Leavis' suggestion when he writes, 'This at least is clear, that Miss Austen was not an inspired amateur who had scribbled in childhood and then lightly tossed off masterpieces between callers' (Leavis, p. 4), then goes on to say 'while another [novel] *Northanger Abbey* was so immature that she despaired of doing anything with it' (Leavis, p. 4). Leavis calls *Northanger Abbey* 'a "family joke" or a "sport", in its relation to the Gothic novels' (Leavis, p. 4), but such assertions clearly beg the question: Why, then, would Austen, who *was not* an 'inspired amateur', find it worth her time to write a family joke? Why would she feel deeply about publishing it, about sending another manuscript which would have necessitated the unenviable task of hand-writing another copy? Austen herself writes to her sister Cassandra (17 November 1798), that 'an artist cannot do anything slovenly' (Chapman, p. 30) and again to Cassandra (24 January 1809), 'I am

gratified by her [Fanny] having pleasure in what I write – but I
wish the knowledge of my being exposed to her discerning Criticism, may not hurt my stile, by inducing too great a solicitude. I
begin already to weigh my words and sentences more than I did,
and am looking about for a sentiment, an illustration or a metaphor
in every corner of the room' (Chapman, p. 256). Certainly, Austen's
artistic sensibilities are not staggered and her notions of style and
rigour were already grounded at a very young age. A better question to ask might be: Why did Austen write *Northanger Abbey* in the
first place? By 1809, Austen had already undertaken the manuscript of *Sense and Sensibility* (1811) so why, if she felt, as Leavis
assumes, *Northanger Abbey* was such a disaster, would she still
want it published? The answer must lie in the style of the novel
itself and what she was doing in terms of abrogating current trends
in popular novel writing.

After Furetière one reads that one speaks of a burlesque style in
prose, when one uses words which are spoken in pure pleasantries,
and would hardly be suffered in serious speech. Johnson slightly
modifies that to be 'something jocular which tends to arouse laughter by unnatural or unsuitable language or images'. Johnson then
speaks of 'parody' as 'a kind of writing, in which the words of
an author or his thoughts are taken, and by a slight change adapted
to some new purpose'. So too was burlesque divided between a
'high' and a 'low' style as Addison points out in No. 249 of
the *Spectator* in 1711 and a division which gained credence
throughout the rest of the eighteenth century. Certainly if those
are the parameters that critics have imposed on *Northanger Abbey*
one is likely to agree with them as it being a parcel of 'immature'
writing, but parody is not the rather facile device that they presumed it to be. In '*Literary Parody, Remarks on its Method and Function*', Tuvia Shlonsky writes that 'to subordinate parody to satire is
to undermine its literary exclusiveness in which resides its particular power, function and effect' (Rose, p. 44). Likewise, Tynjanov
writes that 'the essence of parody lies in its mechanization of a
certain device, where this mechanization is naturally only to be
noticed when the device which it "mechanizes" is known. In
this way parody fulfils a double task: 1) the mechanization of
a certain device and 2) the organization of new material to
which the old mechanized device also belongs' (Rose, p. 164).
To that extent, just as Cervantes transfigured the chivalric
mode through parody and Sterne transfigured Cervantes, Austen

transfigures Radcliffe, thereby regenerating the target text and creating a new one.

Certainly if one takes a twentieth-century approach to parody and the poetics of parody what one is left with is a kind of post-juvenilia meta-fiction for much of what Austen does in *Northanger Abbey* is equivalent to what Bakhtin addresses in Dostoevsky's poetics when he writes 'To introduce a parodic and polemical element into the narration is to make it more multi- voiced, more interruption-prone...' (Bakhtin, p. 226). So what is seen in *Northanger Abbey* is clearly the foundation of what will follow in terms of parody and postmodern fiction. This notion is clearly advanced by Hutcheon when she writes that 'parody – often called ironic quotation, pastiche, appropriation or intertextuality – is usually considered central to postmodernism, both by its detractors and defenders' (Hutcheon, p. 91).

Which brings one back again to Austen's 'juvenilia' writing precisely because *Northanger Abbey* has been linked with its predecessor, *Susan*. One must be puzzled by such a categorization since it too begs the question: What makes it juvenilia? Is it the writing itself in relation to the more 'mature' works such as *Pride and Prejudice* or *Sense and Sensibility* or the fact she wrote it at such a young age? Perhaps in terms of content one might consider *Northanger Abbey* to be the stuff of juvenilia, but in terms of a poetics, of a novel poetics, it is clearly in the category of pre- postmodern works (what Hassan has called 'jocose prepostmodernism') such as *Tom Jones* and *Tristram Shandy*, DeMaistre's *Un Voyage Autour de Ma Chambre* and Machado de Assis's *The Posthumous Memoirs of Braz Cubas*. And if one then categorizes *Northanger Abbey* in that fashion, then the poetics of the novel are certainly as innovative as anything written before *Northanger Abbey* or after it.

What one discovers about *Northanger Abbey* is that it is really a tripartite novel: on one level, it is a very stylistic novel that parodies the gothic novel made popular in the late eighteenth century by Walpole and Radcliffe, the latter of whom is mentioned directly and whose characters are alluded to; on another level we have a *Bildungsroman* about Catherine Morland, a heroine who is about as anti-heroic and pedestrian as any heroine in literary letters can be; and on yet another level we have a novel that is clearly intent on undermining both the reader's expectations of what a novel is supposed to look and read like and a novel that undermines Catherine's own expectations as a reader of her own story. So the text is operating on several different planes and yet co-mingles each of them in a skillfully laconic way.

Chapter I opens simply with the line, 'No one who had ever seen Catherine Morland in her infancy would have supposed her born to be an heroine' (Austen, p. 9). What this line does in the way of formulating a structure for the entire novel is that it puts the reader on notice that this is not going to be a usual heroine and, by extension, it will not be a usual novel. In the great realistic tradition, Austen starts to sketch our heroine by writing, 'She had a thin awkward figure, a sallow skin without color, dark lank hair, and strong features – so much for her person; and not less unpropitious for heroism seemed her mind. She was fond of all boy's plays, and greatly preferred cricket not merely to dolls, but to the more heroic enjoyments of infancy, nursing a dormouse, feeding a canary-bird, or watering a rose-bush' (Austen, p. 9). And more: 'But from fifteen to seventeen she was in training for a heroine; she read all such works as heroines must read to supply their memories with those quotations which are so serviceable and so soothing in the vicissitudes of their eventful lives' (Austen, p. 11). What such a presentation establishes is that the notion of a heroine, as she was so characterized at the time, was being undermined. The line 'so much for her person' is in direct contrast to the process of characterization popularly employed at the time. In other words, the extradiegetic approach Austen takes is clearly differentiated from a diegetic approach one might find in Scott.

As Austen continues to write, a number of quotes, all of which relate to the Austenian notion of what a heroine (at least this kind of heroine) is supposed to be, manifest themselves:

From Pope, she learnt to censure those who
   'bear about the mockery of woe'.
From Gray, that
   'Many a flower is born to blush unseen;
   And waste its fragrance on the desert air'.
From Thompson, that
   'It is a delightful task
   To teach the young idea how to shoot'.
And from Shakespeare she gained a great store of information – amongst the rest, that
   'Trifles light as air,

Are, to the jealous, confirmation strong,
　As proofs of Holy Writ'.
That
　'The poor beetle, which we tread upon,
　In corporal sufferance feels a pang as great
　As when a giant dies'.
And that a young woman in love always looks
　'like Patience on a monument
　Smiling at Grief'

(Austen, pp. 11–12)

The quotes (even though the Gray and Thompson are misquotes) all tend to shape the direction of the story in terms of its plot, as well as its structure. From Pope, expect to make a mockery of woe; to expect things to happen; from Gray, expect discouragement; from Thompson, expect experience to ensure a loss of innocence; from Shakespeare, expect to be talked about through rumour; from the beetle, expect suffering; and from a young woman, expect the sorrows of love. In a way, the quotations act as plot precursors (similar to what Lispector does in *The Hour of Star*); namely, the prefabrication of the plot of the story, the quest of its heroine, is alluded to in the subtext of the quotes she uses prior to the commencement of the primary 'storyline'. With the line, 'But when a young lady is to be a heroine, the perverseness of forty surrounding families cannot prevent her. Something must and will happen to throw a hero in her way' (Austen, p. 12) one detects the extradiegetic Austen directing the reader towards Catherine's experiences with a potential suitor.

But these things will not necessarily happen through a natural causality, rather, through a kind of contrived causality which Austen baldly manipulates and announces in precise, self-reflexive, extradiegetic terms; and the difference between a natural causality and a contrived causality is one of the major differences between 'realistic' fiction and 'postmodern' fiction. 'In evoking the expectations of an audience for the imitation of a certain work only to "disappoint" or shock the reader with another text, parody has also enabled the author to attack reader expectations for imitative or representational works. And through such parody, criticism of representational art has hence often been related to the social historical context of the reader's world' (Rose, p.185).

In Chapter II, new postures develop relative to the structure and the narrator takes significant steps to be a part of the story. This happens from the outset with 'In addition to what has been already said of Catherine Morland's personal and mental endowments, when about to be launched into all the difficulties and dangers of a six weeks' residence in Bath, it may be stated, for the reader's more certain information, lest the following pages should otherwise fail of giving any idea of what her character is meant to be, that her heart was affectionate; her disposition cheerful and open, without conceit or affectation of any kind – her manners just removed from the awkwardness and shyness of a girl; her person pleasing, and, when in good looks, pretty – and her mind about as ignorant and uninformed as the female mind at seventeen usually is' (Austen, p.13).

Austen constantly supports this incursion with such lines as: 'supposed to be'; 'must, of course'; plus the use of authorial plot queries such as 'Who would not think so?' The Shklovskian directive of 'laying bare the device' (which was a response to Sterne's *Tristram Shandy*) allows Austen to address the reader and by so doing undermines the alleged objectivity of the text. For what does it mean for her to use such phrases as 'supposed to be' or 'must, of course'? These would not be spoken in a novel that was taking itself seriously; but since Austen is writing something that attempts to undermine that kind of novel, the allusion only tends to augment the undermining. As David Lodge has pointed out in his essay 'Jane Austen's Novels: Form and Structure', 'In *Northanger Abbey*, Jane Austen played a delightful (and risky) double game with both the conventions of the sentimental novel and the conventions of traditional romance that were beginning to re-invade it through the contemporary cult of the gothic' (Grey 167–8).

As early as the first chapter the reader is put on notice that s/he will constantly be denied an expected passage of time, an expected development of the main character, an expected 'reading' of the text. In short, a proper *expectation* of what alleges to be a novel. Iser has written that 'Whenever we analyse a text, we never deal with a text pure and simple, but inevitably apply a frame of reference specifically chosen for our analysis' (Iser, p. 53). That 'frame of reference', Iser goes on to say, is 'the basic and misleading assumption [is] that fiction is an antonym of reality' (Iser, p. 53). But if fiction is not the opposite of reality, but a means of telling us something about reality, then why is a specific type of text see-mingly valorized above all others? In other words, just as there is a syntagmatic approach to the sentence, there seems to be a syntag-matic approach to plot. That is to say, the plot moves through the 'successive arousal, and selective satisfaction, of literary expecta-tions' (Lerner, p. 50). These expectations are 'aroused' by previous readings of previous texts which have also gone by the name 'novel' but in which case something did, in fact, happen. But if one's expectations are constantly denied, what, then, does that do to the text at hand?

In Chapter II Austen writes: 'Under these unpromising auspices, the parting took place, and the journey began. It was performed with suitable quietness and uneventful safety. Neither robbers nor tempests befriended them, nor one lucky overturn to introduce them to the hero. Nothing more alarming occurred than a fear on Mrs. Allen's side, of having once left her clogs behind her at an inn, and that fortunately proved to be groundless' (Austen, p. 14). So the utilization of what one might expect to happen has been once again been undermined and the reader is left in doubt as to whether anything *will* happen at all in the entire novel. Austen continues with an obligatory description of Mrs. Allen and the balance of the chapter moves towards a climax at a dance during which, of course, nothing eventful happens. So what Austen is clearly composing here relative to the novel she's writing and to the novels to which she is alluding is that she sets up situations 'intentionally' (no fallacy intended) to undermine them which makes the novel a thoroughly pre-postmodern text in that 'it does seem to deny the reader any sure ground for interpretation and discrimination and to make explicit the impossibility of getting the world into a book' (Grey, p. 168).

This process continues until we get to page 23 when the narrator writes 'Whether she thought of him so much, while she drank her warm wine and water, and prepared herself for bed, as to dream of him when there, *cannot be ascertained* [my emphasis]; but I hope it was no more than in a slight slumber, or a morning doze at most' (Austen, p. 23) gives the pretence of objectivity since it issues a pose of ignorance (i.e. 'cannot be ascertained' and 'I hope it was no more...'). Both statements assume a stature of presumed uncer-tainty which, given their relative posture in relation to the extra-diegetic pose already taken by Austen, are virtually dispelled in Chapter V.

By the time we reach Chapter IV, the pattern of *expectation denied* has been clearly foregrounded. 'With more than usual eagerness did Catherine hasten to the Pump-room the next day, secure within herself of seeing Mr. Tilney there before the morning were over, and ready to meet him with a smile – but no smile was demanded – Mr. Tilney did not appear' (Austen, p. 23). The chapter continues to characterize both Mrs. Allen as the philistine she is and the characters of the Thorpes before concluding with 'This brief account of the family is intended to supersede the necessity of a long and minute detail from Mrs. Thorpe herself, of her past adventures and sufferings, which might otherwise be expected to occupy the three or four following chapters; in which the worthlessness of lord and attornies might be set forth, and conversations, which had passed twenty years before, be minutely repeated' (Austen, pp. 26–7). This particular passage is a brilliant bit of self-reflexive artifice that masquerades as summary and challenges what Leavis assumes to be a kind of immature writing. What Austen issues here is clearly an assault, albeit minor at this point, on the 'fundamentals' of novel-writing and, specifically, on character development in the Realist mode, a mode formulated and commodified by Scott. But Austen is entirely in control of her material and is obviously capable of doing the exact thing she wishes to abrogate.

The abrogation turns into something much different in Chapter V, but not before the *expectation denied* continues for one discovers Catherine once again searching Bath for Tilney, but 'He was no where to be met with; every search for him was equally unsuccessful, in morning lounges or evening assemblies; neither at the upper nor lower rooms, at dressed or undressed balls, was he perceivable; nor among the walkers, the horsemen, or the curricle-drivers of the morning. His name was not in the Pump-room book, and curiosity could do no more. He must be gone from Bath' (Austen, pp. 27–8). The reader's undeniable thirst for a kind of completion, at least temporary satisfaction, is once again denied, deviated, if you will, and this 'deviation is bound up with the expectations of the reader' (Iser, p. 89). In addressing what he calls 'expectation norms', Iser speaks of a repertoire of social norms and literary references that supply the background against which the text is to be reconstituted by the reader (Iser, p. 89). If these expectations are denied they will inevitably produce a kind of tension in the reader and, in some cases, a hostility towards the text. It is not coincidental that these denials of expectation come prior to one of the clearest examples of authorial self- consciousness in English literature.

In Chapter V Austen continues with some rather vapid conversation 'for Mrs. Thorpe talked chiefly of her children, and Mrs. Allen of her gowns' (Austen, p. 28) as a kind of prelude to addressing the intimate relationship between Catherine and Isabella and how their friendship was defined so much so that 'they were still resolute in meeting in defiance of wet and dirt, and shut themselves up, to read novels together' (Austen, p. 29). And here, at length, is where Austen's major abrogation begins:

Yes, novels – for I will not adopt that ungenerous and impolitic custom so common with novel writers, of degrading by their contemptuous censure the very performances, to the number of which they are themselves adding – joining with their greatest enemies in bestowing the harshest epithets on such works, and scarcely ever permitting them to be read by their own heroine, who, if she accidentally take up a novel, is sure to turn over its insipid pages with disgust. Alas! if the heroine of one novel be not patronized by the heroine of another, from whom can she expect protection and regard? I cannot approve of it. Let us leave it to the Reviewers to abuse such effusions of fancy at their leisure, and over every new novel to talk in threadbare strains of the trash with which the now groans. Let us not desert one another; we are an injured body. Although our productions have afforded more extensive and unaffected pleasure than those of any other literary corporation in the world, no species of composition has been so much decried. From pride, ignorance, or fashion, our foes are almost as many as our readers. And while the abilities of the nine-hundredth abridger of the History of England, or of the man who collects and publishes in a volume some dozen lines of Milton, Pope, and Prior, with a paper from the Spectator, and a chapter from Sterne, are eulogized by a thousand pens, – there seems almost a general wish of decrying the capacity and undervaluing the labour of the novelist, and of slighting the performances which have only genius, wit, and taste to recommend them. 'I am no novel reader – I seldom look into novels – Do not imagine that *I* often read novels – It is really awful well for a novel.' – Such is the common cant. – 'And what are you reading, Miss —?' Oh! it is only a novel!' replies the young lady; while she lays down her book with affected indifference, or momentary shame. – 'It is only Cecilia, or Camilla, or Belinda'; or, in short, only some work in which the greatest powers of the mind are displayed, in which the most thorough knowledge of human nature, the happiest delineation of its varieties, the liveliest effusions of wit and humour are conveyed to the world in the best chosen language. Now, had the same young lady been engaged with a volume of the Spectator, instead of such a work, how proudly would she have produced the book, and told its name; though the chances must be against her being occupied by any part of the voluminous publication, of which either the matter or manner would not disgust a young person of taste: the substance of its papers so often consisting in the statement of improbable circumstances, unnatural characters, and topics of conversation, which no longer concern any one living; and their language, too, frequently so coarse as to give no very favourable idea of the age that could endure it'.

And so ends what must be called 'the diatribe' albeit controlled. One must not be lead into believing the myth of the implied author here. This excerpt is more than mere fictional prose, but, in its own way, is Austen's manifesto about the novel, if not novel writing. 'That no species of composition has been so much decried' is not the mockery of a writer set on writing a family joke. There is no irony in this excerpt; Austen is not poking self-referential fun at herself. She is devoutly taking a stand for the 'sorority' of novelists and that '[we] should not desert one another; [since] we are an injured body'. She addresses 'our production', 'our readers', 'our foes', the 'labour of the novelist', and his/her ability to display 'the most thorough knowledge of human nature, the happiest delineation of its varieties, the liveliest effusions of wit and humour'. Nothing in this excerpt is lacquer for the prose poseur or for one simply intent on writing 'chop-shop' fiction. Not coincidentally, 'Radcliffe too aims to challenge the relegation of the romance or novel to the realm of low culture by her imitations of the Odes of Collins, and other "graveyard" poets, which are interspersed through the texts of all her works' (Radcliffe, *Sicilian*, p. xiii). In that sense, if no other, Austen and Radcliffe are sisters. But what Austen does here in a way relates to the Advertisement addressed at the outset of the novel. For it does, outrageously, suggest and distinguish a difference between 'us' and 'them', between the 'labour of the novelist' and the appositeness of those (for example, publishers) who might want to deny them.

In a very revealing letter written to Anna Austen (10 August 1814), Austen writes, 'Your Aunt C[assandra] does not like desultory novels, & is rather fearful yours will be too much so, that there will be too frequent a change from one set of people to another, & that circumstances will be sometimes introduced of apparent consequences, which will lead to nothing – It will not be so great an objection to *me*, if it does. I allow much more Latitude than she does...' (Chapman, p. 396). And apparently so she did. The abrogation comes at a point in the chapter that takes the reader clearly by surprise coming as it does *in medias res* and ends abruptly with no allusion to what has preceded it (i.e. the Catherine–Isabella relationship) and no apology for having written it. In that way, it is very much like another abrogation written a century-and-a-half later by yet another resident of Lyme Regis: 'You may think novelists always have fixed plans to which they work, so that the future predicted by Chapter One is always inexorably the actuality of Chapter Thirteen. But novelists write for countless different reasons: for money, for fame, for reviewers, for parents, for friends, for amusement... Only one same reason is shared by all of us: *we wish to create worlds as real as, but other than the world that is*' (Fowles, p. 98). The similarities between these two excerpts are notable in that Austen has knowingly undermined the linear progression of the novel just as Fowles was to have done in *The French Lieutenant's Woman*. Austen has acknowledged the artifice of the novel from the first sentence of the first chapter, but clearly registers a self-reflexive posture in Chapter Five that not only denies the reader's expectation, but repositions the state of the novel in a uniquely different way.

From that moment on, the reader can *expect* nothing in the way of what one might expect to expect and Austen makes that clear in almost every subsequent chapter. When Chapter VI begins there is not even a hint of the diatribe written in Chapter V. She picks up the thread of the narrative where she left off prior to the diatribe and maintains the mode of *expectation denied* or, in contrast, *unexpectation met*, throughout. For example, Catherine *unexpectedly* meets her brother, James, in Bath; when she first meets Tilney he *does not* dance with her; on a carriage ride with Thorpe, 'they went in the quietest manner imaginable, without a plunge or a caper, or any thing like one' (Austen, IX); a trip to

Blaize Castle is *unremarkable; expecting* to see Miss Tilney at her window, Catherine *sees no one;* and finally we read in Chapter XIV that, 'The Tilneys called for her at the appointed time; and no new difficulty arising, no sudden recollection, no unexpected summons, no impertinent intrusion to disconcert their measures, my heroine was most unnaturally able to fulfill her engagement, though it was made with the hero himself' (Austen, XIV). In short, whatever one might expect to happen to our heroine, it does not.

Finally, after six weeks in Bath (which, coincidentally, is where Radcliffe spent much of her youth) and after 115 pages (or over half the novel) Northanger Abbey is finally mentioned in the context of Catherine's visit. 'Northanger Abbey! – These were the thrilling words, and wound up Catherine's feelings to the highest point of ecstasy' (Austen, p. 115). And with the invitation comes Catherine's inevitable expectations about the abbey itself. 'With all the chances against her of house, hall, place, park, court, and cottage, Northanger turned up an abbey, and she was to be its inhabitant. Its long, damp passages, its narrow cells and ruined chapel, were to be within her daily reach, and she could not entirely subdue the hope of some traditional legends, some awful memorials of an injured and ill- fated nun' (Austen, p. 117). Not only are the speculations grounded in the fiction she has read (for example, Radcliffe), but the speculations foreground the reader for the possibility of a Gothic betrayal. That is, like Walpole's *The Castle of Otranto* (1764) Catherine's focus is on 'the castle or great house as a field of force for its usurping tyrant, and as simultaneously a harbourer and revealer of secrets' (Radcliffe, *Sicilian*, p. ix); however, the reader has already been put on notice that whatever is deemed to be Gothic is merely Catherine's fiction and Austen's metafiction. Northanger Abbey becomes, as the 'critical space' a mantissa in that it is and has been supplemental, almost ancillary, to the diegetic pose that Austen has presented.

To underscore the difference in poetic structure between Austen and Radcliffe, we can use a 'classic' of Gothic scenery from *The Mysteries of Udolpho*:

> On the other side of the valley, immediately opposite to the spot where the travellers rested, a rocky pass opened towards Gascony. Here no sign of cultivation appeared. The rocks of granite, that screened the glen, rose abruptly from their base, and

stretched their barren points to the clouds, unvaried with woods, and uncheered even by a hunter's cabin. Sometimes, indeed, a gigantic larch threw its long shade over the precipice, and here and there a cliff reared on its brow a monumental cross, to tell the traveller the fate of him who had ventured thither before. This spot seemed the very haunt of the banditti; and Emily, as she looked down upon it, almost expected to see them stealing out from some hollow cave to look for their prey. Soon after an object not less terrific struck her, – a gibbet standing on a point of rock near the entrance of the pass, and immediately over one of the crosses she had before observed. These were the hieroglyphics that told a plain and dreadful story.

[Radcliffe, *Udolpho*, p. 54]

Radcliffe's work is notable for its exceptional use of picturesque description, the type of description that will be advanced by Balzac and Turgenev. Her scenes are 'painted with care because Radcliffe wants us to see it and to understand it with her. The understanding, however, is more complicated than it might at first seem. This is a sublime setting, one that is meant to inspire a mood of awe. The adjectives are selected to establish mood rather than describe in any specific way – they depict the scene less than they create a response to it ... The language is gauged much more for effect than for meaning' (Haggerty, p. 23). But here, too, Austen attempts to achieve a kind of Radcliffean enterprise only to deny it. As Catherine approaches Northanger Abbey, Austen purposefully begins with a kind of gothic discourse relative to scene only to counterwrite it. Not only that, but in two sentences she links the expectation with the realization; the gothic discourse with the parodic gothic discourse.

One can also contrast this presentation of 'the critical space' with either Radcliffe's *The Mysteries of Udolpho* or her *A Sicilian Romance* in which the critical space of the chateau of Monsieur St Aubert and that of the Mazzini castle are mentioned on the first page and the narrative about them is taken up immediately. But in *Northanger Abbey*, not only is the critical space mentioned after half the novel, but it is as quickly dispatched since Austen says nothing about it again for another three chapters. So while the reader may be expecting the abbey to take over as the focus of the fictional discourse, Austen once again returns to describing the pedestrian activities of her mundane characters.

It is not until Chapter XX when Austen finally pairs Catherine with Tilney during the journey to the abbey that Tilney says, ' "You have formed a very favourable idea of the abbey". "To be sure I have. Is not it a fine old place, just like what one reads about?" ' (Austen, p. 130). Which allows Tilney to play off on the whole notion of reading and reader's expectations by saying, ' "And are you prepared to encounter all the horrors that a building such as 'what one reads about' may produce? – Have you a stout heart? – Nerves fit for sliding pannels and tapestry?" ' (Austen, p. 130) and which prompts Tilney to continue for several pages in a discourse that is not unlike the form of Gothic discourse, but written in the active present:

> 'No we shall not have to explore our way into a hall dimly lighted by the expiring embers of a wood fire – nor be obliged to spread our beds on the floor of a room without windows, doors, or furniture. But you must be aware that when a young lady is (by whatever means) introduced into a dwelling of this kind, she is always lodged apart from the rest of the family. While they snugly repair to their own end of the house, she is formally conducted by Dorothy the ancient housekeeper up a different staircase, and along many gloomy passages, into an apartment never used since some cousin or kin died in it about twenty years before. Can you stand such a ceremony as this? Will not your mind misgive you, when you find yourself in this gloomy chamber – too lofty and extensive for you, with only the feeble rays of a single lamp to take in its size – its walls hung with tapestry exhibiting figures as large as life, and the bed, of dark green stuff or purple velvet, presenting a funeral appearance. Will not your heart sink within you?'.   (Austen, p. 131)

Tilney's Gothic discourse continues until they reach the outskirts of the abbey at which point Austen writes:

> and every bend in the road was expected with solemn awe to afford a glimpse of its massy walls of grey stone, rising amidst a grove of ancient oaks, with the last beams of the sun playing in beautiful splendour on its high Gothic windows. But so low did the building stand, that she found herself passing through the great gates of the lodge into the very grounds of Northanger, without having discerned even an antique chimney.   (Austen, p. 133)

Expectation denied once again, Catherine is led to her chamber where we read:

> An abbey! – yes, it was delightful to be really in an abbey! – but she doubted, as she looked around the room, whether anything within her observation, would have given her the consciousness. The furniture was in all the profusion and elegance of modern taste. The fire-place, where she had expected the ample width and ponderous carving of former times, was contracted to Rumford, with slabs of plain though handsome marble, and ornaments over it of the prettiest English china. The windows, to which she looked with peculiar dependence, from having heard the General talk of his preserving them in their Gothic form with reverential care, were yet less what her fancy had portrayed . . . To an imagination which had hoped for the smallest divisions, and the heaviest stone-work, for painted glass, dirt and cobwebs, the difference was distressing.   (Austen, p. 134)

Distressing indeed for Catherine, but this is truly a marvellous chapter because it works so effectively in creating and maintaining the notions of expectation denied. As it augments the parody of the Gothic convention it simultaneously brings Catherine more into the world of experience. This notion is reemphasized at the beginning of chapter XXI with 'A moment's glance was enough to satisfy Catherine that her apartment was very unlike the one which Henry had endeavored to alarm her by the description of' (Austen, p. 135). Alas, this apartment confounds expectations. It contained neither tapestry nor velvet; the walls were papered, the floor was carpeted; the windows were neither less perfect nor more dim than those of the drawing-room below; the furniture was handsome and comfortable and the air of the room altogether far from uncheerful (Austen, p. 135). In short, the abbey was too pleasant for one's expectations and with that pleasantness came a denial of mood and mood is what one expects most of in Gothic novels.

But the genuine tremor one feels upon reading a Gothic novel is found in the manipulation of tension and terror. In two very similar situations we have Radcliffe and Austen working at point and counterpoint.

> A return of the noise again disturbed her; it seemed to come from that part of the room, which communicated with the private

staircase, and she instantly remembered the odd circumstance of the door having been fastened, during the preceding night, by some unknown hand. Her late alarming suspicion, concerning its communication, also occurred to her. Her heart became faint with terror. Half raising herself from the bed, and gently drawing aside the curtain, she looked towards the door of the stair-case, but the lamp, that burnt on the hearth, spread so feeble a light through the apartment, that the remote parts of it were lost in shadow. The noise, however, which, she was convinced, came from the door, continued. It seemed like that made by the undrawing of rusty bolts, and often ceased, and was then renewed more gently, as if the hand, that occasioned it, was restrained by fear of discovery. While Emily kept her eyes fixed on the spot, she saw the door move, and then slowly open, and perceived something enter the room, but the extreme duskiness prevented her distinguishing what it was. Almost fainting from terror, she had yet sufficient command over herself, to check the shriek, that was escaping from her lips, and, letting the curtain drop from her hand, continued to observe in silence the motions of the mysterious form she saw.   (Radcliffe, *Udolpho* p. 261)

Radcliffe attempts to maintain a kind of static tension throughout the piece, adding layer upon layer until, finally, Emily sees Count Morano. Expectation is not denied here. There is a kind of 'Gothic payoff' in that what she sees does, in fact, exist. That is, there is a person in her room and it is, in fact, Morano who expresses his love for her albeit in a rather perverse way.

Austen counters by writing: 'The night was stormy; the wind had been rising at intervals the whole afternoon; and by the time the party broke up, it blew and rained violently. Catherine, as she crossed the hall, listened to the tempest with sensations of awe...' (Austen, pp. 138–9). Once Catherine is securely ensconced in her room, Austen begins in earnest, to undermine the Gothic method, but with a resoluteness of wry humour.

The window curtains seemed in motion. It could be nothing but the violence of the wind penetrating through the divisions of the shutters; and she stepped boldly forward, carelessly humming a tune, to assure herself of its being so, peeped courageously behind each curtain, saw nothing on either low window seat to scare her, and on placing a hand against the shutter, felt the strongest conviction of the wind's force. A glance at the old chest, as she turned away from this examination, was not without its use; she scorned the causeless fears of an idle fancy, and began with a most happy indifference to prepare herself for bed... Catherine, having spent the better part of an hour in her arrangements, was beginning to think of stepping into bed, when, on giving a parting glance around the room, she was struck by the appearance of a high, old-fashioned black cabinet, which, though in a situation conspicuous enough, had never caught her notice before...The key was in the door, and she had a strange fancy to look into it...She paused a moment in breathless wonder. The wind roared down the chimney, the rain beat in torrents against the windows, and everything seemed to speak the awfulness of her situation...Again, therefore she applied herself to the key, and after moving it in every possible way for some instants with the determined celerity of hope's last effort, the door suddenly yielded to her hand: her heart leaped with exultation at such a victory, and having thrown open each folding door, the second being secured only by bolts of less wonderful construction than the lock, though in that her eye could not discern anything unusual, a double range of small drawers appeared in view, with some larger drawers above and below them; and in the centre, a small door, closed also with a lock and key, secured in all probability a cavity of importance. Catherine's heart beat quick, but her courage did not fail her. With a cheek flushed by hope, and an eye straining with curiosity, her fingers grasped the handle of a drawer and drew it forth. It was entirely empty. With less alarm and greater eagerness she seized a second, a third, a fourth; each was equally empty. Not one was left unsearched, and in not one was anything found. (Austen, pp. 140–1).

Austen balances the prose with an exactness of tension worthy of the best exponents of the genre. In a way, the text is a challenge for Austen to see if she can mimic the Gothic method and she does so quite handily. She also prepares the reader for an expectation worth fulfilling. There must be a payoff. And there is, but the payoff is not an expected payoff. The payoff yields nothing. But Austen doesn't repair to idle narrative at that point. Satisfied that she has alarmed the reader's interest only to disarm the reader's interest she repeats the process.

Her quick eyes directly fell on a roll of paper pushed back into the further part of the cavity, apparently for concealment, and her feelings at that moment were indescribable. Her heart fluttered, her knees trembled, and her cheeks grew pale. She seized, with an unsteady hand, the precious manuscript, for half a glance sufficed to ascertain written characters; and while she acknowledge the awful sensations this striking exemplification of what Henry had foretold, resolved instantly to peruse every line before she attempted to rest. The dimness of the light her candle emitted made her turn to it with alarm; but there was no danger of its sudden extinction; it had yet some hours to burn; and that she might not have any greater difficulty in distinguishing the writing than what its ancient date might occasion, she hastily snuffed it. Alas! It was snuffed and extinguished in one. A lamp could not have expired with more awful effect. Catherine, for a few moments, was motionless with horror. It was done completely; not a remnant of light in the wick could give hope to the rekindling breath. Darkness impenetrable and immovable filled the room. A violent gust of wind, rising with sudden fury, added fresh horror to the moment. Catherine trembled from head to foot. In the pause which succeeded, a sound like receding footsteps and the closing of a distant door struck on her affrighted ear. Human nature could support no more. A cold sweat stood on her forehead, the manuscript fell from her hand, and groping her way to bed, she jumped hastily in, and sought with some suspension of agony by creeping far underneath the clothes ... The storm still raged, and various were the noises, more terrific even than the wind, which struck at intervals on her startled ear. The very curtains of her bed seemed at one moment in motion, and at another the lock of her door was agitated, as if by the attempt of somebody to enter. Hollow murmurs seemed to creep along the gallery, and more than once her blood was chilled by the sound of distant moans. Hour after hour passed away, and the wearied Catherine had heard three proclaimed by all the clocks in the house before the tempest subsided or she unknowingly fell asleep.   (Austen, pp. 141–2)

So ends Chapter XXI with Catherine in the throes of unnamable horrors. But there has been no Gothic payoff here since the reader is delayed from discovering what, in fact, is contained in the manuscript. With the exactness of a serial writer (if not the calculation of a Hitchcock) Austen delays the payoff. Early in Chapter XXII we discover what the manuscript actually contains: 'An inventory of linen, in coarse and modern characters. She seized another sheet, and saw the same articles with little variation; a third, a fourth, and fifth presented nothing new. Shirts, stockings, cravats, and waistcoats faced her in each. Two others, penned by the same hand, marked an expenditure scarcely more interesting, in letters, hairpowder, shoe-string, and breeches-ball' (Austen, p. 143). So not only is the expectation denied in terms of the Gothic payoff, but when there is a payoff the realization is not worth the price of the expectation in the first place.

One might 'expect' that Austen has had enough of the process of dissimulation, but she hasn't. In Chapter XXIII she sets up yet another scene to be misperceived. Catherine is treated to a tour of the house by Eleanor Tilney and 'believed herself at last within the reach of something worth her notice; and felt, as she unwillingly paced back to the gallery, that she would rather be allowed to examine that end of the house than see all the finery of all the rest. The general's evident desire of preventing such an examination was an additional stimulant. Something was certainly to be concealed...' (Austen, p. 155). Eleanor plans to take Catherine to see the room of her dead mother, 'a room in all probability never entered by him [the general] since the dreadful scene had passed, which released his suffering wife, and left him to the stings of conscience' (Austen, p. 155).

To Catherine's question, ' "You were with her, I suppose, to the last?" ' Eleanor Tilney responds that she died before she came home. 'Catherine's blood ran cold with the horrid suggestions which naturally sprang from these words. Could it be possible? Could Henry's father—? And yet how many were the examples to justify even the blackest suspicions! And, when she saw him in the evening, while she worked with her friend, slowly pacing the drawing-room for an hour together in silent thoughtfulness, with downcast eyes and contracted brow, she felt secure from all possibility of wronging him. It was the air and attitude of Montoni! What could more plainly speak the gloomy workings of a mind not wholly dead to every sense of humanity, in its fearful review of past scenes of guilt?' (Austen, p. 156) All of these examples play into that pioneering work of the Gothic, Walpole's *The Castle Otranto*, in which are woven 'most of the main elements of this form of fiction, notably the supposedly Gothic castle, with its subterranean passages, the supernatural events, the lonely heroine and the elderly aristocratic villain, heartlessly domineering' (Radcliffe, *Udolpho*, p. viii). Each of these items has been systematically defused by Austen. The Gothic castle is neither Gothic nor a castle; there are no subterranean passages; the supernatural events are all porously explainable; and the lonely heroine isn't lonely which leaves the elderly aristocratic villain, in the person of General Tilney, as Catherine's last recourse to salvage her neo-Gothic cause in this most uneventful anti-Gothic novel.

With the family early to bed, Catherine supposes that something nefarious is planned.

> There must be some deeper cause: something was to be done which could be done only while the household slept; and the probability that Mrs. Tilney yet lived, shut up for causes unknown, and receiving from the pitiless hands of her husband a nightly supply of coarse food, was the conclusion which necessarily followed. Shocking as was the idea, it was at least better than a death unfairly hastened, as, in the natural course of things she must ere long be released. The suddenness of her reputed illness, the absence of her daughter, and probably of her other children, at the time – all favoured the supposition of her imprisonment. Its origin – jealousy perhaps, or wanton cruelty – was yet to be unraveled.   (Austen 157)

Austen sets up the reader for what is to follow in Chapter XXIV though as the chapter opens we read that, 'The next day afforded no opportunity for the proposed examination of the mysterious apartments' (Austen, p. 168). This tactic is merely meant to defer expectations not deny them, the denial is yet to come for many things transpire in Catherine's head since 'Catherine had read too much not to be perfectly aware of the ease with which a waxen figure might be introduced, and a suppositious funeral carried on' (Austen, p. 159). She finally finds herself alone in the gallery and clandestinely secures her way into Mrs Tilney's apartments.

> She beheld what fixed her to the spot and agitated every feature. She saw a large, well-proportioned apartment, an handsome dimity bed, arranged as unoccupied with an housemaid's care, a bright Bath stove, mahogany wardrobes, and neatly painted chairs, on which the warm beams of a western sun gaily poured

through two sash windows! . . . She could not be mistaken as to the room; but how grossly mistaken in everything else! – in Miss Tilney's meaning, in her own calculation! This apartment, to which she had given a date so ancient, a position so awful, proved to be one end of what the general's father had built.

(Austen, pp. 161–2)

Austen constantly alludes to Catherine's being 'well read', but the fact is all of her clever speculations based upon her prior readings have resulted in false allegations. Not only is the entire *oeuvre* of her speculations patently incorrect, but to compound the problem she is discovered by no one other than Henry Tilney while snooping in Mrs Tilney's apartment. 'At that instant a door underneath was hastily opened; someone seemed with swift steps to ascent the stairs, by the head of which she had yet to pass before she could gain the gallery. She had no power to move. With a feeling of terror not very definable, she fixed her eyes on the staircase, and in a few moments it gave Henry to her view' (Austen, p. 162). At that point, Catherine compounds the false assumptions with the embarrassment of telling Tilney what she is doing there and why. Her motives merely make her appear even more naive than Tilney had imagined her to be and provoke a panoply of guilt-ridden anxieties which for Catherine could only result in the end of the romance. Chapter XXV begins: 'The visions of romance were over. Catherine was completely awakened. Henry's address, short as it had been, had more thoroughly opened her eyes to the extravagance of her late fancies than all their several disappointments had done. Most grievously was she humbled. Most bitterly did she cry' (Austen, pp. 165–6).

At this point in the novel, there is a critical fictional bifurcation in that the anti-Gothic story ends and the conclusion of the *Bildungsroman* commences. In other words, throughout the entire novel Catherine has been on a quest and within the quest the reader has been witness to Austen's parody of the Gothic. But with her discovery by Tilney and her revelations about the abbey come a new understanding of herself. What has been shattered in Catherine's ethos is her innocence and the naïveté with which she had been directed. 'The painful remembrance of the folly it had helped to nourish and perfect was the only emotion which could spring from a consideration of the building. What a revolution in her ideas! She, who had so longed to be in an abbey!' (Austen, p. 177).

Catherine is unceremoniously discharged from the abbey because of yet another false speculation, but this time on the part of General Tilney who mistakenly believes Catherine's financial situation is more fluid than it actually is: an economic expectation denied. After the general abruptly and rudely dismisses Catherine from the abbey, one recognizes that she is on her way home. But where is she going and where has she been? One can see this 'journey' from Fullerton to Bath to Northanger Abbey to Fullerton as Catherine's quest. In uniquely Campbellian terms there is a clear separation, initiation and return, yet the return is very unlike her initial separation. The journey begins with major expectations and ends with a clear realization of the quotes Austen presented at the outset of the novel. For in Chapter XXIX we read:

> Catherine was too wretched to be fearful. The journey in itself had no terrors for her; and she began it without either dreading its length or feeling its solitariness... Unfortunately, the road she now travelled was the same which only ten days ago she had so happily passed along in going to and from Woodston; and, for fourteen miles, every bitter feeling was rendered more severe by the review of objects on which she had first looked under impressions so different. Every mile, as it brought her nearer Woodston, added to her sufferings, and when within the distance of five, she passed the turning which led to it, and thought of Henry, so near, yet so unconscious, her grief and agitation were excessive.
>
> (Austen, pp. 192–3)

So the road travelled *from* the abbey is not the same road she traveled *to* the abbey. The notion of travel and of roads is a very curious one in that many of the roads, though the same roads, become different roads. The road to the abbey was, of course, a road less travelled for Catherine; the road back, has become a road endured. But even in writing a *Bildungsroman*, Austen cannot avoid a self-reflexive pose which is entirely in keeping with the consistency of voice begun at the outset of the novel. Austen writes:

> A heroine returning, at the close of her career, to her native village, in all the triumph of recovered reputation, and all the dignity of a countess, with a long train of noble relations in their several phaetons, and three waiting-maids in a travelling chaise and four, behind her, is an event on which the pen of the contriver may

well delight to dwell; it gives credit to every conclusion, and the author must share in the glory she so liberally bestows. But my affair is widely different; I bring back my heroine to her home in solitude and disgrace; and no sweet elation of spirits can lead me into minuteness. A heroine in a hack post-chaise is such a blow upon sentiment, as no attempt at grandeur or pathos can withstand. Swiftly therefore shall her post-boy drive through the village amid the gaze of Sunday groups, and speedy shall be her descent from it. (Austen, pp. 194–5).

Which clearly clarifies the posture of the quest and of Catherine's becoming something other than she was when she left. Her quest takes her from the rarefied atmosphere of romantic expectations, of mysterious speculations and Gothic intrigue to the more mundane atmosphere of the road of realization for 'it was not three months ago since, wild with joyful expectation, she had there run backwards, and forwards some ten times a day, with an heart light, gay, and independent; looking forward to pleasures untasted and unalloyed, and free from the apprehension of evil as from the knowledge of it. Three months ago had seen her all this; and now, how altered a being did she return!' (Austen, p. 199).

Austen ties up the 'loose ends' of the novel as neatly as she can by directly appealing to her readers as the self-reflexive narrator then, in a self-deprecating manner, appeals to her readers with: 'The anxiety, which in this state of their attachment must be the portion of Henry and Catherine, and of all who loved either, as to its final event, can hardly extend, I fear, to the bosom of my readers who will see in the tell-tale compression of the pages before them, that we are all hastening together to perfect felicity' (Austen, p. 210).

Then in an innovative way which not only comments on the 'act of novel writing', but on the diegetic level she concludes the novel by following up on probably the greatest of all mysteries in the novel: whose laundry list was it? 'Concerning the one in question, therefore, I have only to add – aware that the rules of composition forbid the introduction of a character not connected with my fable – that this was the very gentleman whose negligent servant left behind him the collection of washing-bills, resulting from a long visit at Northanger, by which my heroine was involved in one of her most alarming adventures' (Austen, p. 210).

So Austen has thus taken the reader on a kind of 'magical mystery tour' in terms of plot and poetics in that she has directed the reader to take the same kind of manipulated directions as she has done with Catherine. She has, in fact, been playing a game with the reader and 'Most literary games rest on the strength of human curiosity – the mind's avid desire for knowledge of outcome, for resolution of problems, in short, for "truth". A concern for pattern and harmony seems firmly related to this fundamental urge. Further, just as nature abhors a vacuum, so too does the reader abhor what might be termed a thematic or sense 'void', or in fact any degree of thematic uncertainty' (Hutchinson, p. 21). To that end, Austen has mastered the technique and with that mastery puts to rest any notion of *Northanger Abbey* as being something less than a poetic achievement, something less than a mature work of art.

3

The Poetics of Climate in Brontë's *Wuthering Heights*

The title of the novel *Wuthering Heights* has often held a kind of mystique about it. The immediate assumption one might make, and an erroneous one at that, would be to think it a synonym for 'withering' which is much different than 'whithering'. Perhaps that was what Brontë 'intended' to bring to mind for the reader, but the word 'wuther' is a variation of the word 'wither' which, related to the Old Norse, deals with the sound the wind makes, (i.e. blustery, raging, violent) and as such would indeed be related to 'wheather' so a phrase like 'wuthering heights' holds multiple allusions to the wind, to the weather and, ultimately, to nature. As such it would be natural to deal with the novel as a novel whose poetics are fundamentally orchestrated around the weather. Brontë writes as much in Chapter I when she says: 'Wuthering Heights is the name of Mr. Heathcliff's dwelling. "Wuthering" being a significant provincial adjective, descriptive of the atmospheric tumult to which its station is exposed in stormy weather. Pure, bracing ventilation they must have up there, at all times, indeed: one may guess the power of the north wind, blowing over the edge, by the excessive slant of a few stunted firs at the end of the house; and by a range of gaunt thorns all stretching their limbs one way, as if craving alms of the sun' (Brontë, pp. 25–6). Even in the description of the word itself, Brontë preconditions the reader for what is to follow in terms of juxtaposing the weather with the prevailing conditions at Wuthering Heights. For example, she emphasizes that there are *few* and *stunted* firs, and there are *gaunt* thorns which stretch their limbs *as if craving* alms of the sun for if, indeed, limbs crave alms of the sun then there are few to have at all; and this approach seems to be Brontë's poetic method of choice which comprises most of the 34 chapters in the novel.

Much has been made of the chronology of *Wuthering Heights* and it would be useful to use it as a kind of blueprint for the poetics of weather to follow.

Table 1. *Wuthering Heights*: Chronology

Chapter			
	1757	before September	Hindley Earnshaw born
	1762	''	Edgar Linton born
	1764	''	Heathcliff born
	1765	summer	Catherine Earnshaw born
	''	late	Isabella Linton born
IV.	1771	summer, beginning of harvest	Heathcliff brought to Wuthering Heights
	1773	spring or early summer	Mrs Earnshaw dies
V.	1774	October	Hindley sent to college
	1777		Hindley marries
	''		Mr Earnshaw dies
VI.	''		Hindley returns with wife
III.	''	October or November	Scene described by Catherine
VI.	''	November, third week Sunday	Catherine and Heathcliff at Thrushcross Grange
VII.	''	Christmas Eve	Catherine returns to WH
	''	Christmas Day	The Lintons visit WH
VIII	1778	June	Hareton Earnshaw born
	''	late	Frances Earnshaw dies
	1780	summer	Edgar Linton calls at WH and proposes to Catherine
IV.	''	''	Hindley returns drunk
	''	''	Catherine tells Ellen about Edgar
	''	''	Heathcliff goes off
IV.	1780	summer	Catherine gets wet through and catches fever
	''	autumn	Catherine, convalescent goes to Thrushcross Grange Mr and Mrs Linton catch fever and die
	1783	April	Edgar marries Catherine
X.	''	September	Heathcliff returns and sees Catherine
	''	autumn	Isabella falls in love with Heathcliff, who visits Thrushcross Grange
XI.	1783	December	Ellen Dean sees Hareton Heathcliff kisses Isabella
	1784	January 6	Violent scene at Thrushcross Grange. Heathcliff is turned out and Catherine goes on hunger strike
XII.	''	January 10	Catherine delirious
	''	January 10, 2am	Isabella elopes with Heathcliff

Chapter

XIII.	''	March 13	Heathcliff's return to WH
XIV.	''	March 15	Ellen Dean goes to WH
XV.	''	March 19	Heathcliff sees Catherine; violent scene
XVI.	''	March 19 midnight	Catherine Linton born
	''	March 20 2am	Catherine the elder dies
	''	March 21	Heathcliff puts a lock of hair in Catherine's locket
	''	March 24	Catherine's funeral
XVII.	''	March 24, midnight	Heathcliff nearly kills Hindley who tried to kill him
	''	March 25	Isabella runs off
XVII.	1784	September	Linton Heathcliff born
''		Sept or Oct.	Hindley Earnshaw dies; all his property is mortgaged to Heathcliff
XVIII.	1797	early June	Catherine goes to Penistone Crags and meets Hareton
XIX.	''	June	Isabella dies; Edgar brings back Linton Heathcliff
XX.	''	''	Linton is take to live at WH
XXI.	1800	March 20	Catherine and Ellen meet Hareton and go to WH where they see Linton
	''	Mar or April	Catherine and Linton write
XXII.	''	late Oct or Nov	Catherine sees Heathcliff, who says that Linton is ill
XXIII.	''	late Oct or Nov	Catherine and Ellen go to see Linton; Ellen catches cold and is ill for three weeks
XXIV.	''	November	During Ellen's illness Catherine visits Linton secretly
XXV.	1801	March 20	Edgar too ill to visit his wife's grave
	''	June	Edgar declining
XXVI.	''	August	Ellen and Catherine meet Linton
	''	August, week later	They are kidnapped
	''	Monday	Catherine and Linton marry
XXVIII.	''	Aug or Sept	Ellen is let out
	''	following Tues	Edgar is dying; he sends for Mr Green, the lawyer, who does not come
XXVIII.	1801	Wed, 3am Harvest moon	Catherine escapes and comes to Thrushcross Grange
XXIX.	''	Sept, after funeral	Heathcliff comes to WH and takes off Catherine

Chapter

XXX.	''	October	Linton Heathcliff dies; Hareton tries to please Catherine
I.	''	late November	Lockwood calls at WH
II	''	next day	He calls again and has to stay the night. He finds Catherine's diary and sees Heathcliff's outburst
	''	next day	Leaves at eight; catches cold
IV.	''	next day	Ellen Dean begins her story
X.	''	3 weeks later	Heathcliff sends grouse
	''	1 week later	Heathcliff calls
XV.	1802	January, week later	Lockwood continues his account
XXXI.	''	January, 2nd week	Lockwood calls at WH
XXXII.	''	beginning of Feb	Ellen goes to live at WH
	''	March	Hareton has an accident
	''	Easter Monday	Catherine is nice to Hareton
XXXIII.	''	Easter Tuesday	Scene about altering garden
	''	after March 18	Heathcliff getting old
XXXIV.	''	April	Heathcliff goes on hunger strike
	''	May	Heathcliff dies
	''	September	Lockwood visits Thrushcross Grange and WH
XXXIV	1803	January 1	Catherine and Hareton marry

Source: Vogler, 1968, pp. 25–27

From that chronology of events, two lists can be created: one, with the results of the months both *directly named* or *alluded to* and one with only those months *mentioned directly*.

List (A), a combination of direct and indirect, yields the following results:

Month	*Number of mentions*	*Total*
January	6	
February	1	
March	15	22
April	2	
May	2	
June	7	11

July	5	
August	8	
September	9	22
October	5	
November	8	
December	3	16

List (B), with only those months directly cited, yields the following results:

Month	Number of mentions	Total
December	3	
January	5	
February	1	
March	7 on or before 21/3	16
March	3 after 21/3	
April	2	
May	1	
June	5	11
July	0	
August	3	
September	4	7
October	2	
November	9	11

In order of the number of times a month is either mentioned or alluded to there is a kind of seasonal hierarchy: (1) January–March; (2) July–September; (3) October–December; (4) April–June with January–March and July–September each garnering the most allusions. The emphasis here is clearly on as combination of the *winter–spring* and *summer–autumn* months with the autumn months and the spring months alone lagging behind. Within those categories there are a number of days that are privileged days; the most important events being: in January, New Year's Day; in March, the onset of Spring; in September, the onset of Autumn; in October, the harvest; in December, Christmas is privileged more than is the onset of summer. Of those months, Brontë tends to privilege the months of August–November and January–March as the most

narratologically weatherly. Of all the events that garner meteorolo-
gical import, Brontë cites the months between August and November 13 times, January–March 8 times, and April–June 4 times and
the narratological presence of those scenes is significant since the
relationship between dying, death and rebirth is precisely what
Brontë is creating with the utilization of those scenes. It is with
that climatic arrangement in mind that one can approach the text
with a kind of poetics of *weather*ing or *wuther*ing.

What has been said of much of Turgenev's work could also be
said of *Wuthering Heights*, that 'nature in Turgenev's novels is both
the natural scene that so often supplies the backcloth and human
nature that occupies the foreground. The natural scene both reflects
and contrasts with the human emotions of the heroes and heroines
in the foreground: it reflects their moods and their hopes and their
feelings and it sets in relief their tragedies...It is in Turgenev's
poetic ability to understand and evoke the natural scene that his
artistic mastery, which might be tempted so easily into the bathetic
and meretricious, is astonishing for its delicacy of proportion and
subtlety of feeling' (Freeborn, p. 50). The fact that there is less than
a decade between the publication of *Rudin* (1856) and *Wuthering
Heights* (1847) is significant in that there is a common approach not
only to the poetics of climate and nature, but to how the description
of such relates to the novel as a whole and to the individual
narratological incidents. 'There is nothing vague about this novel
[*Wuthering Heights*]; the mists in it are the mists of the Yorkshire
moors; if we speak of it as having an elemental quality it is because
the very elements, the great forces of nature are evoked, which
change so slowly that in the span of human life they seem unchan-
ging...we seem to smell the kitchen of Wuthering Heights, to feel
the force of the wind across the moors, to sense the very change of
the seasons. Such concreteness is achieved not by mistiness but by
precision' (Vogler, p. 28). What Brontë seems to initiate in *Wuthering Heights*, Turgenev seems to master and the precision one finds
in her novel is deeply associated with how and at what times
Brontë utilizes nature and the weather as a function of narratological description.

In *Rudin* the narratological measure is clear as in the famous
scene in Chapter 9 at which point Natalia decides to end her
relationship with Rudin:

Avdiukin Pond, where Natalia had asked Rudin to meet her, had
long ceased to be a pond. It had overflowed its banks about thirty

years earlier, and had been empty ever since. Only the smooth, flat surface of a hollow, once covered with slimy mud, and traces of the banks enabled one to guess that it had ever been a pond. A farmhouse had stood near it at one time, but had also disappeared long ago. Two huge pine trees preserved its memory; the wind eternally whispered and sullenly moaned their tall, stark, green tops. Mysterious rumours circulated among the local people about a horrible crime allegedly committed at the pines' very roots. They also said that neither of these trees would fall without bringing death to someone, and that a third had formerly stood there, which had fallen during a storm, crushing a young girl. The entire area around the old pond was supposed to be haunted. It was barren, dark, and drearier due to the proximity of an ancient forest of dead, withered oak trees. A few of those huge trees reared their gray shapes above the low undergrowth of bushes like weary ghosts. They were a sinister sight – it seemed as though wicked old men had gathered in order to plot some evil deed. A narrow, almost indiscernible path wound alongside the banks. No one went near Avdiukhin Pond without some special reason. Natalia had intentionally chosen this solitary place, which was less than half a verst from Daria Mikhailovna's house. 　　　　(Turgenev, pp. 260–1)

Clearly, the presentation of the setting underscores the purposeful intent of the scene to follow. To gain a clearer understanding of what Brontë is attempting in *Wuthering Heights* in relation to the notion of narratological description, one can examine Mieke Bal's itemization of different types of description. Between theme and sub-theme, Bal distinguishes six types of description only two of which seem somewhat pertinent to Brontë's style, yet neither adequately portray the description in a truly Brontëan manner.

1　The Referential, Encyclopaedic Description in which the 'selection of components is based upon the contiguity of the elements of the contents. This means that the presence of some elements implies the absence of others. The missing detail can be filled in by the reader.'

2　The Referential Rhetorical Description which is 'the tourist guidebook rather than the encyclopaedia [and] is the model for this second type of description. The units are now combined on the basis of both the contiguity of the components and their thematic function'. 　　　　(Bal, p. 133)

These two approaches seem to be amalgamated into what Brontë is attempting to do with the utilization of descriptive components in *Wuthering Heights*, though neither one adequately deals with the poetic element; however, what one finds in the novel is that particular events are more privileged than others and the events relating to death are seemingly not as important as the events relating to life. But the one thing that tends to stand out in her descriptions is the metonymic quality, a kind of metonymic narratology that constantly comments on the action of an individual episode.

In Chapter 2, Lockwood calls at Wuthering Heights, but must stay the night. 'The business of eating being concluded, and no one uttering a word of sociable conversation, I approached a window to examine the weather. A sorrowful sight I saw; dark night coming down prematurely, and sky and hills mingled in one bitter whirl of wind and suffocating snow' (Brontë, p. 34). The weather as such preconditions the remainder of the narrative since what transpires in Chapter 3 is Lockwood's first-hand experience of Heathcliff's wrath. 'The spectre showed a spectre's ordinary caprice; it gave no sign of being; but the snow and wind whirled wildly through, even reaching my station, and blowing out the light' (Brontë, p. 45). The anguish precipitated by the previous evening's weather is then linked with the beginning of Chapter 4 as Lockwood begins 'What vaia weather-cocks we are! I, who had determined to hold myself independent of all social intercourse, and thanked my stars that, at length, I had lighted on a spot where it was next to impracticable. I, weak wretch, after maintaining till dusk a struggle with low spirits, and solitude, was finally compelled to strike my colours...' (Brontë, p. 48).

One can contrast scenes such as this one with scenes of death in which one would presume Brontë would precondition the text with a weatherly scene coterminous with the condition of the episode, but she does not. When Mrs Earnshaw dies in Chapter 4 there is barely a mention of the weather; but when Mr Earnshaw dies an October death in Chapter 5 the weather does precondition the death with: 'A high wind blustered around the house, and roared in the chimney; it sounded wild and stormy, yet it was not cold, and we were all together...' (Brontë, p. 56) as if there was something 'in the air' and that something was inevitably to be Earnshaw's demise.

But though there are eleven death scenes none of them is ever pre-conditioned to the extent that the non-death scenes are pre-conditioned. In Chapter 9 there is an excessively narrated pre-condition weather scene which comes subsequent to Catherine's admission that she has no 'business' to marry Edgar, that she loves Heathcliff and that she is concerned that because Heathcliff has left that, perhaps, he was 'vexed at my bad humour'. Joseph leaves to find Heathcliff and returns to an irate Catherine who says, 'Have you found Heathcliff, you ass?' interrupted Catherine. 'Have you been looking for him, as I ordered?' (Brontë, p. 89). What follows is the passage that not only comments on Catherine's behaviour, but on what may follow:

It *was* a very dark evening for summer: the clouds appeared inclined to thunder, and I said we had better all sit down; the approaching rain would be certain to bring him home without further trouble.

However, Catherine would not be persuaded into tranquility. She kept wandering to and fro, from the gate to the door, in a state of agitation which permitted no repose: and, at length, took up a permanent position on one side of the wall, near the road; where, heedless of my expostulations, and the growling thunder, and the great drops that began to plash around her, she remained calling, at intervals, and then listening, and then crying outright. She beat Hareton, or any child, at a good, passionate fit of crying. About midnight, while we still sat up, the storm came rattling over the Heights in full fury. There was a violent wind, as well as thunder, and either one or the other split a tree off at the corner of the building; a huge bough fell across the roof, and knocked down a portion of the east chimney- stack, sending a clatter of stones and soot into the kitchen fire.   (Brontë, p. 89)

The entire scene relates to Heathcliff's departure. As in *Rudin* so too with *Wuthering Heights* that whenever there is a traumatic situation, Brontë establishes a kind of parallel description that comments on the action. In other words, the scene becomes a major character in the poetic development of the plot. She could, of course, merely explain Heathcliff's disappearance without the use of scene, but the scenic representation blends into the poetic development of the narrative. Certainly the 'full fury' of the storm parallels the action of both Heathcliff's departure and the kind of emotional maelstrom that Catherine is experiencing. The storm has cleansed the evening and by daybreak, 'Neither of us wished to mention Heathcliff's absence, as long as we could conceal it; so, I replied, I didn't know how she took it into her head to sit up; and she said nothing. The morning was fresh and cool; I threw back the lattice, and presently the room filled with sweet scents from the garden.' (Brontë, p. 91). Just as the initial scene establishes the apparent turmoil within the house, the subsequent scene alludes to a 'new dawn'.

Apparently it is in the nature of Brontë's prose to privilege the living situations over the dead ones. It is within the conflict of the living characters in which the poetic quality of the scenic description is most vividly rendered. For example, she writes scantily about the Lintons' demise with 'she, and her husband, both took the fever, and died within a few days of each other' (Brontë, p. 92). There is nothing in the way of scenic description, of 'weatherly' description to parallel the death. The Lintons, like the Earnshaws, are merely supporting characters in the novel and as such demand little in the way of private arousal.

By Chapter X Lockwood speaks: 'A charming introduction to a hermit's life! Four weeks' torture, tossing and sickness! Oh, these bleak winds, and bitter, northern skies, and impassable roads, and dilatory country surgeons! And oh, this dearth of the human physiognomy, and worse, than all, the terrible intimation of Kenneth that I need not expect to be out of doors till spring!' (Brontë, p. 94). This weatherly September scene is followed by the line that 'Mr. Heathcliff has just honoured me with a call' (Brontë, p. 94). Though there is a shift in time in that it is Lockwood who is narrating the story and not Nelly, there is the concomitant metonymic relationship between Heathcliff and the augured weather. The choice of weather is not serendipitous. There is the clear indication that certain situations or certain characters merit certain types of weatherly scenes. 'On a mellow evening in September, I was coming from the garden with a heavy basket of apples that I had been gathering. It had got dusk, and the moon looked over the high wall of the court, causing undefined shadows to lurk in the corners of the numerous projecting portions of the building. I set my burden on the house steps by the kitchen door, and lingered to rest, and drew in a few more breaths of the soft, sweet air; my eyes were on the moon, and my back to the entrance, when I heard a voice behind me say – "Nelly, is that you?" ' (Brontë, p. 95). Of course, the type of night presages the type of figure to appear. Clearly the phrase 'undefined shadows to lurk' does not presage something vital and that she 'distinguished a tall man dressed in dark clothes, with dark face and hair' can only presage the return of Heathcliff, 'a ray [of the moon] fell on his features; the cheeks were sallow, and half covered with black whiskers; the brows lowering, the eyes deep set and singular' (Brontë, p. 96). It is only by the light of the moon, not the sun, (Brontë is careful not to have Heathcliff return in sunlight) that Nelly makes out the darkest of the darkest of shadows. It could be no other way.

Catherine's January delirium (Chapter XII) is not presaged by any weatherly scenes, but the weather acts in a manner coterminous with the narratological description: 'She could not bear the notion which I had put into her head of Mr. Linton's philosophical resignation. Tossing about, she increased her feverish bewilderment to madness, and tore the pillow with her teeth, then raising herself up all burning, desired that I would open the window. We were in the middle of winter, the wind blew strong from the northeast, I objected' (Brontë, p. 118). As in Flaubert's *Madame Bovary*, a work already in progress, the *blowing wind* presages the initiation of new events, something that will, in fact, advance the storyline. 'To pacify her, I held the casement ajar, a few seconds. A cold blast rushed through; I closed it, and returned to my post' (Brontë, p. 120). The constant tension between Catherine's delirium and the elements continues until 'I entreated, and finally attempted to force her to retire. But I soon found her delirious strength much surpassed mine (she *was* delirious, I became convinced by her subsequent actions and ravings). There was no moon, and everything beneath lay in misty darkness; not a light gleamed from any house, far or near; all had been extinguished long ago; and those at Wuthering Heights were never visible... still she asserted she caught their shining' (Brontë, p. 122). This scene is followed by: 'The first time she left her chamber, was at the commencement of the following March. Mr. Linton had put on her pillow, in the morning, handful of golden crocuses...' '"These are the earliest flowers at the Heights!'' she exclaimed. ''they remind me of *soft thaw winds* [my emphasis], and warm sunshine, and nearly melted snow – Edgar, is there not a *south wind*, and is not the snow almost gone?''

' ''The snow is quite gone down here, darling!'' replied her husband, ''and I only see two white spots on the whole range of the moors – The sky is blue, and the larks are singing, and the becks and brooks are all brim full. Catherine, last spring at this time, I was longing to have you under this roof – now, I wish you were a mile or two up those hills; the air blows so sweetly, I feel that it would cure you'' ' (Brontë, p. 128). The parallel here is with the onset of spring. Just as the commencement of March is also the prelude to spring Nelly records: 'We knew she was really better, and therefore, decided that long confinement to a single place produced much of this despondency, and it might be partially removed by a change of scene' (my emphasis) (Brontë, p. 128).

Not only are there allusions to a change of scene, but there are allusions to style as well. The opening of Chapter XV reads: 'Another week over – and I am so many days nearer health, and spring! I have now heard all my neighbour's history, at different sittings, as the housekeeper could spare time from more important occupations. I'll continue it in her own words, only a little condensed. She is, on the whole, a very fair narrator and I don't think I could improve her style' (Brontë, p. 144). Of course, Brontë's voices do not have any dialogic quality to them relative to Bakhtin's notion of dialogy and Lockwood's voice is not much different than Nelly's voice which is not much different than any of the other voices, but in Nelly's voice (mediated by Lockwood) she says: 'but on that occasion, the *w*eather *w*as so *w*arm and pleasant that I set them *w*ide open; and to fulfil my engagement, as I knew *w*ho *w*ould be coming, I told my companion that the mistress *w*ished very much for oranges...' (Brontë, p. 145). And again: 'It was a sweet substitute for the yet absent murmur of the summer foliage, which drowned that music about the Grange, when the trees were in leaf. At Wuthering Heights it always sounded on quiet days, following a great thaw, or a season of steady rain...' (Brontë, p. 146). The movements presage Heathcliff's return and a presumed transformed Heathcliff. Not only does the alliteration tend to mollify the description, but the poetic passage of 'a sweet substitute for the yet absent murmur of the summer foliage' and the allusion to a 'great thaw' as opposed to a 'minor thaw' presages Heathcliff's appearance one page later.

March continues in Chapter XVI, but in a way consistent with what she'd done in the past, Brontë does not privilege death in any substantial way. 'About twelve o'clock, that night, was born the Catherine you saw at Wuthering Heights, a puny, seven months' child; and two hours after the mother died, having never recovered sufficient consciousness to miss Heathcliff, or to know Edgar' (Brontë, p. 151). And that's the end of it. Subsequent to Catherine's death one reads: 'Next morning – bright and cheerful out of doors – stole softened in through the blinds of the silent room, and suffused the couch and its occupant with a mellow, tender glow' (Brontë, p. 151) a passage which poetically parallels Catherine's deathly features which were of 'perfect peace' as opposed to Heathcliff's of 'exhausted anguish'. Nelly continues: 'Her brow smooth, her lids closed, her lips wearing the expression of a smile. No angel in heaven could be more beautiful than she appeared; and I partook of the infinite calm in which she lay. My mind was never in a holier frame than while I gazed on that untroubled image of Divine rest' (Brontë, p. 151). Soon after, Nelly steals out to 'the pure, refreshing air' where Heathcliff awaits. 'He was there – at least a few yards further in the park; leant against an old ash tree, his hat off, and his hair soaked with the dew that had gathered on the budded branches, and fell pattering around him. He had been standing a long time in that position, for I saw a pair of ousels passing and repassing, scarcely three feet from him, busy in building their nest, and regarding his proximity no more than that of a piece of timber' (Brontë, p. 152). It is curious that Heathcliff is leaning against an old 'ash tree' as the cult of the ash is reflected in Norse mythology and especially in the *Edda* it is said 'that the immortal gods hold their court beneath an ash tree whose branches cover the entire surface of the world. The highest point of the tree touches Heaven, and its roots pierce through as far as Hell. From those two roots two fountains issue. In one of them wisdom is hidden; in the other is concealed all our knowledge of the future. This majestic conception, entirely supporting the symbolism of grandeur in the ash, had inevitably to be diminished by the downbeat philosophy of the pessimists:

The Ash, aspiring, upwards, rears its head,
As if still higher from its native bed
It sought to grow until it reach the sky;
Yet 'tis so tied to earth that it will die
If but some roots be bared of soil, and cease
To draw supplies which make the tree increase;
Thus man to grandeur raised and high estate
By public favour, will, if that abate,
Sink down again, and then his name shall ne'er
Be heard with aught of love, or hate, or fear
                                        '(Powell 35–37)

By Chapter 17 the whimsicality of March takes over and the introduction of the chapter clearly presages what is to come. Brontë writes:

'That Friday, made the last of our fine days, for a month. In the evening, the weather broke; the wind shifted from the south to the north-east, and brought rain first, and then sleet, and snow. On the morrow one could hardly imagine that there had been three weeks of summer: the primroses and crocuses were hidden under wintry drifts: the larks were silent, the young leaves of the early trees smitten and blackened – And dreary, and chill, and dismal that morrow did creep over!' (Brontë, p. 155). And dreary, and chill, and dismal that morrow did creep over, creep over to the extent that the chapter deals with Hindley's impotent attempts at killing Heathcliff, who almost kills Hindley, and with Isabella's departure. There is the mention of Hindley Earnshaw's death, but, as with most of the other deaths, it is treated with less attention than with the rudiments of the plot: 'The end of Earnshaw was what might have been expected: if followed fast on his sister's, there was scarcely six months between them' (Brontë, p. 167). Better less said the better said.

There is little in the way of acclimatized action in what follows until Chapter XX, June, which focuses on Linton's removal to Wuthering Heights: 'The pure heather-scented air, and the bright sunshine, and the gentle canter of Minny relieved his despondency after a while. He began to put questions concerning his new home, and its inhabitants, with greater interest and liveliness.

''Is Wuthering Heights as pleasant a place as Thrushcross Grange?' he inquired, turning to take a last glance into the valley, whence a light mist mounted, and formed fleecy clouds, on the skirts of the blue'' (Brontë, p. 183).

The apparent cheerfulness of the ride is in stark juxtaposition with the arrival and Brontë's description before the farm-house garden gate does not belie what will inevitably happen beyond the threshold: 'He surveyed the carved front and low-bowed lattices, the straggling gooseberry bushes and crooked firs, with solemn intentness, and then shook his head: his private feelings entirely disapproved of the exterior of his new abode; but he had a sense to postpone complaining – there might be compensation within' (Brontë, p. 184).

Little in the way of natural phenomena presaging narrative action until Chapter XXII and as:

Summer drew to an end, and early Autumn – it was past Michaelmas, but the harvest was late that year, and a few of our fields were still uncleared.

Mr. Linton and his daughter would frequently walk out among the reapers: at the carrying of the last sheaves, they stayed till dusk, and the evening happening to be chill and damp, my master caught a bad cold, that settling obstinately on his lungs, confined him indoors through the whole of the winter, nearly without intermission. (Brontë, p. 201).

Of course the cold has been predetermined by the textual apparatus. The death of spring (summer), the death of summer (autumn) presages a kind of funeral weather report and with the master catching a cold, the narrative moves into a more descriptive kind of atmosphere that presages things to come:

'On an afternoon in October, or the beginning of November, a fresh watery afternoon, when the turf and paths were rustling with moist, withered leaves, and the cold, blue sky was half hidden by clouds, dark grey streamers, rapidly mounting from the west, and boding abundant rain; I requested my young lady to forego her ramble because I was certain of showers' (Brontë, p. 201). This description is followed by the onset of a 'chill wind' to follow. The description clearly reports that sad and melancholy measures are anticipatory. 'She [Cathy] went sadly on; there was no running or bounding now, though the chill wind might well have tempted her to race' (Brontë, p. 201).

'I [Nelly] gazed round for a means of diverting her thoughts. On one side of the road rose a high, rough bank, where hazels and stunted oaks, with their roots half exposed, held uncertain tenure: the soil was too loose for the latter; and strong winds had blown some nearly horizontal' (Brontë, p. 202).

' "No," she repeated, and continued sauntering on, pausing, at intervals, to muse over a bit of moss, or a tuft of balanched grass, or fungus spreading its bright orange among the heaps of brown foliage; and, ever and anon, her hand was lifted to her averted face' (Brontë, p. 202).

The allusions to hazels and oaks is, once again, not serendipitous. Mercury gave Apollo a tortoise-shell from which he made a lyre, and received in exchange a hazel rod which had the power to inspire with a love of virtue and to reconcile heart divided by hatred and envy. The hazel wand is till the symbol of healing to bring peace and reconciliation. Juxtaposed with a thriving oak, the measure of hospitality, and the combination would be a fecund one; but Brontë is clear to state that the oaks were 'stunted' their roots 'half exposed' and they held 'uncertain tenure' which renders any notion of hospitality a frail one. It is soon after this that there are not only allusions to death, but, as the reader has been informed, they are on the road to visit Heathcliff.

'As we talked, we neared a door that opened on the road: and my young lady, lightening into sunshine again, climbed up, and seated herself on the top of the wall, reaching over to gather some hips that bloomed scarlet on the summit branches of the wild rose trees, shadowing the highway side: the lower fruit had disappeared, but only birds could touch the upper, except from Cathy's present station' (Brontë, p. 203).

Cathy drops her hat, 'But the return was no such easy matter; the stones were smooth and neatly cemented, and the rosebushes and the blackberry stragglers could yield no assistance in re-ascending' (Brontë, p. 203). But roses have thorns and blackberries have stragglers.

Cathy needs the key to escape and at that moment Heathcliff arrives with the news that Linton is dying. The intercourse is brief and 'I [Nelly] closed the door, and rolled a stone to assist the loosened lock in holding it; and spreading my umbrella, I drew my charge underneath, for the rain began to drive through the moaning branches of the trees, and warned us to avoid delay' (Brontë, p. 205). They return home.

By Chapter XXIII one detects the relative scheme that Brontë has been using throughout the novel as she writes on that October–November night: 'The rainy night had ushered in a misty morning – half frost, half drizzle – and temporary brooks crossed our path, gurgling from the uplands. My feet were thoroughly wetted; I was cross and low, exactly the humour for making the most of these disagreeable things' (Brontë, p. 206) and exactly the kind of weather to contribute to Linton's illness which happens in that chapter. The opening of the November Chapter XXIV alludes to a coldness that is verified by the focus of the chapter: 'The moon shone bright; a sprinkling of snow covered the ground, and I reflected that she might, possibly, have taken it into her head to walk about the garden, for refreshment' (Brontë, p. 214). This passage is followed by yet another passage in which Nelly recalls a particular July day with Linton:

One time, however, we were near quarelling. He said the pleasantest manner of spending a hot July day was lying from morning

till evening on a bank of heath in the middle of the moors, with the bees humming dreamily about among the bloom, and the larks singing high up over head, and the blue sky and bright sun shining steadily and cloudlessly. That was his most perfect idea of heaven's happiness – mine was rocking in a rustling green tree with a west wind blowing, and bright, white clouds flitting rapidly above; and not only larks, but throstles, and blackbirds, and linnets, and cuckoos pouring out music on every side, and the moors seen at a distance, broken into cool dusky dells; but close by great swells of long grass undulating into waves to the breeze; and woods and sounding water, and the whole world awake and wild with joy. He wanted all to lie in an ecstacy of peace; I wanted all to sparkle, and dance in a glorious jubilee.
(Brontë, p. 215).

Certainly the latter paragraph alludes to a more joyous time, but the paragraph is not coterminous with the season, but is an allusion to another season, a season when the balance of nature was equivalent to the balance of character events. The July paragraph is imbedded in the November chapter and in the November chapter the focus is predominately on Linton's health and Brontë closes it with: 'In vain she wept and writhed against the interdict, and implored her father to have pity on Linton: all she got to comfort her was a promise that he would write, and give him leave to come to the Grange when he pleased; but explaining that he must no longer expect to see Catherine at Wuthering Heights. Perhaps, had he been aware of his nephew's disposition and state of health, he would have seen fit to withhold even that slight consolation' (Brontë, p. 221).

Chapter XXV finds a new point of departure as Nelly recounts what transpired the winter before: 'Edgar sighed; and, walking to the window, looked out towards Gimmerton Kirk. It was a misty afternoon, but the February sun shone dimly, and we could just distinguish the two fir trees in the yard, and the sparely scattered gravestones' (Brontë, p. 222). The juxtaposition of Edgar, the mist, fir trees and gravestones is an interesting one in that firs are associated with 'elevation' since normal firs range between twenty to one-hundred feet in height, but some have been recorded to grow as high as four-hundred feet. The combination of Edgar and mist, of elevation and death clearly presages Edgar's dying. By Chapter XXVI, Nelly informs the reader that 'Summer was already past its prime, when Edgar reluctantly yielded his assent to their entreaties, and Catherine and I set out on our first ride to join her cousin.

It was a close, sultry day; devoid of sunshine, but with a sky too dappled and hazy to threaten rain; and our place of meeting had been fixed at the guide-stone, by the cross-roads' (Brontë, p. 225). Though nothing of great significance happens in the chapter, the weather does presage the rather murky meeting of Ellen, Catherine and Linton which leads into the rather formidable Chapter XXVII which is distinguished by two major events: the kidnapping and the marriage. The chapter alludes early to the weather as Nelly confirms:

'We deferred our excursion till the afternoon; a golden afternoon of August – every breath from the hills so full of life, that it seemed whoever respired it, though dying, might revive.

Catherine's face was just like the landscape – shadows and sunshine flitting over it, in rapid succession; but the shadows rested longer and the sunshine was more transient, and her poor little heart reproached itself for even that passing forgetfulness of its cares' (Brontë, p. 229).

It's clear by the weatherly prose that the allusion to someone dying yet by breathing the 'breath of the hills' and reviving is meant for Linton, but the notion of 'breathing' carries with it the notion of scent, of odour, and that could presage the appearance of something other than a revivifying life force. That 'Catherine's face was just like the landscape' with shadows and sunshine with the shadows predominating certainly presages something foreboding for in Brontë's climate nature, weather and narrative action are all coalesced into a structural whole. 'When hearing a rustle among the ling, I looked up, and saw Mr. Heathcliff almost close upon us, descending the Heights' (Brontë, p. 230) the appearance of whom lies in close proximity to the 'breath' that was so revivifying. His appearance certainly works in tandem with both the 'shadowy' forces Brontë has constructed with the prevailing weather and the resulting 'kidnapping' to the Heights itself. The 'marriage' could only be a marriage in name and not signature since there is nothing in the weather that would indicate a climate of joyful celebration and what was presaged by the weather in Chapter XXVII manifests in Chapter XXVIII with the simple line 'He [Linton] died blissfully' (Brontë, p. 243) only casually presaged by the phrase 'The harvest moon shone clear outside' (Brontë, p. 242) as the only bell-weather of a kind of leaden laden eternity.

Chapter XXIX begins with: 'The evening after the funeral, my young lady and I were seated in the library; now musing mournfully, one of us desparingly, on our loss; now venturing conjectures as to the gloomy future' (Brontë, p. 244) and the 'gloomy future' relates to the paragraph that begins: 'It was the same room into which he had been ushered, as a guest, eighteen years before: the same moon shone through the window; and the same autumn landscape lay outside' (Brontë, p. 244). The 'same moon' and the 'same autumn landscape' alluding to the climatic fact that as the weather ushered in the arrival of Heathcliff it also presaged the eventual horrors of Heathcliff which have now been manifest.

In a dialogue between Heathcliff and Nelly, Heathcliff talks about the exhumation of Catherine's body in a way that clearly registers necrophilia. Heathcliff then recalls: 'The day she was buried there came a fall of snow. In the evening I went to the churchyard. It blew bleak as winter – all round was solitary: I didn't fear her fool of a husband would wander up the glen so late – and no one else had business to bring them there.

'Being alone, and conscious two yards of loose earth was the sole barrier between us, I said to myself—

"I'll have her in my arms again! If she be cold, I'll think it is this north wind that chills *me*; and if she be motionless it is sleep"' (Brontë, p. 247).

That Catherine died in the spring, but that her burial is accompanied by snow which 'blew bleak as winter' is a clear demonstration of how Brontë manipulates the weather to comment on action. From Heathcliff's point of view, Catherine's burial could not, under any fictional circumstances, be accompanied by anything as celebratory as 'good weather' since good weather would presage something that would totally antagonistic in relation to Heathcliff's character.

The worst seemingly over Chapter XXXI begins with Lockwood's account that: 'Yesterday was bright, calm, and frosty. I went to the Heights as I proposed; my housekeeper entreated me to bear a little note from her to her young lady, and I did not refuse, for the worthy woman was not conscious of anything odd in her request' (Brontë, p. 254). The weather presages very little and very little happens. It's not until Chapter XXXII that the weather again comments on the action. It's September, 1802 and Lockwood is on his way 'to devastate the moors of a friend', but detours to his own Gimmerton as he comments on the day: 'The grey church looked greyer, and the lonely churchyard lonelier. I distinguished a moor sheep cropping the short turf on the graves. It was sweet, warm weather – too warm for travelling; but the heat did not hinder me from enjoying the delightful scenery above and below; had I seen it nearer August, I'm sure it would have tempted me to waste a month among its solitudes. In winter, nothing more dreary, in summer, nothing more divine, than those glens shut in by hills, and those bluff, bold swells of heath' (Brontë, p. 259). But it's neither summer nor winter, it is autumn and the implication is that he is somewhere in between the dreary and the divine both in juxtaposition with the greyness of death and the sweetness of warm weather which presages the inevitable.

After a brief stop at Gimmerton: 'I turned away and made my exit, rambling leisurely along with the glow of a sinking sun behind, and the mild glory of a rising moon in front; one fading, and the other brightening, as I quitted the park, and climbed the stony by-road branching off to Mr. Heathcliff's dwelling. Before I arrived in sight of it, all that remained of the day was a beamless, amber light along the west; but I could see every pebble on the path, and every blade of grass, by that splendid moon' (Brontë, p. 260). The 'sinking sun', the 'mild glory of a rising moon', the 'beamless, amber light' are all equivalents of a beautiful, albeit inevitable, death and it is soon thereafter that upon arriving at the Heights he is met with Mrs Dean's information that Heathcliff is dead and at that point she takes up the story of Heathcliff's demise which climaxes in Chapter XXXIV.

'We were in April then, the weather was sweet and warm, the grass as green as showers and sun could make it, and the two dwarf apple trees, near the southern wall, in full bloom...I was comfortably revelling in the spring fragrance around, and the beautiful soft blue overhead, when my young lady, who had run down near the gate to procure some primrose roots for a border, returned only half laden, and informed us that Mr. Heathcliff was coming in' (Brontë, p. 276). The paragraph seemingly presages 'pleasant events' and if Heathcliff's death be a pleasant event then the passage is prophetic since only two pages later one reads: 'He was leaning against the ledge of an open lattice, but not looking out; his face was turned to the interior gloom. The fire had smouldered to ashes; the room was filled with the damp, mild air of the cloudy evening, and so still, that not only the murmur of the beck down Gimmerton was distinguishable, but its ripples and its gurgling over the pebbles, or through the large stones which it could not cover' (Brontë, p. 278) the smouldering, damp, cloudiness of which could only presage the following passage; 'The light flashed on his features, as I spoke. Oh, Mr. Lockwood, I cannot express what a terrible start I got, by the momentary view! Those deep black eyes! That smile, and ghastly paleness! It appeared to me, not Mr. Heathcliff, but a goblin; and, in my terror, I let the candle bend towards the wall, and it left me in darkness' (Brontë, p. 278). Heathcliff's appearance is only mediated by a 'ghastly paleness' since before and after the passage what remains the same is his smile and the darkness of his eyes; it's the smouldering, damp, cloudiness that presages his goblin-like appearance which, in a kind of deductive narratological fashion, leads to: 'The following evening was very wet; indeed it poured down, till day-dawn; and, as I took my morning walk around the house, I observed the master's window swinging open, and the rain driving straight in' (Brontë, p. 283) which leads to: 'Yet that old man by the kitchen fire affirms he has seen two on 'em looking out of his chamber window, on every rainy night since his death . . .' (Brontë, p. 284) which leads ultimately to:

> My walk home was lengthened by a diversion in the direction of the kirk. When beneath its walls, I perceived decay had made progress, even in seven months – many a window showed black gaps deprived of glass; and slates jutted off, here and there, beyond the right line of the roof, to be gradually worked off in coming autumn storms. I sought, and soon discovered, the three head-stones on the slope next the moor – the middle one grey, and half buried in heath – Edgar Linton's only harmonised by the turf, and moss creeping up its foot – Heathcliff's still bare. I lingered round them, under that benign sky; watched the moths fluttering among the heath, and hare-bells; listened to the soft wind breathing through the grass; and wondered how anyone could ever imagine unquiet slumbers for the sleepers in that quiet earth. (Brontë, p. 285)

This final paragraph is of interest in that it closes the novel with the fact that 'decay had made progress', but that there is too a 'benign sky' and a 'soft wind breathing through the grass' as a kind of climatic homage to the bodies of those buried and a kind of implied notion of a 'sweet hereafter' in the line 'and wondered how anyone could ever imagine unquiet slumbers for the sleepers in that quiet earth'. The sibilants work in a kind of harmony with the frame of 'unquiet-quiet' and paragraph is laden with a kind of solitude that is paralleled in the notion of the heath itself which in flower lore signifies 'solitude'. It would seem that in death alone could Heathcliff find the solitude he sought in life and Brontë's novel itself climatically follows a kind of path established by her sister in *Jane Eyre* in which Charlotte Brontë 'seeks in the natural world, not order, but a reflection of the turbulent, fluctuating inner life of her heroine' (Lodge, p. 121).

4

The Poetics of Irony in Flaubert's *Madame Bovary*

Life in Croisset was neither a catalfaque in the Far East nor a café on the boulevard Montparnasse. Perhaps that was the humour of Croisset. What else could one do there suffering with the foibles of the bourgeois, but to write *Madame Bovary*? And the *Madame Bovary* Flaubert envisioned and wrote is a novel whose artistic resonance, whose poetics, is decidedly comedic and ironic. Of course there are elements of the pathetic, but those do not supersede the bathetic and it is not coincidental that not long after he began writing *Madame Bovary* (September, 1851) he also began renewing the idea of the *Dictionary of Accepted Opinions (Dictionnaire des Idées Reçues)* (December, 1852). Flaubert writes: 'Meanwhile an old idea has come back to me – that of my *Dictionary of Accepted Opinions* (do you know what it is?) The preface, especially, greatly excites me, and in the way I conceive it (it would be a book in itself) no law could touch me although I would attack everything... I would declare that this apologia for human vulgarity in all its aspects – and it would be raucous and ironic from beginning to end, full of quotations, proofs (which would prove the opposite), frightening texts (easily found) – was aimed at doing away, once and for all, with all eccentricities, whatever they might be' (Flaubert, *Letters* 175–6).

Flaubert's *Dictionary* was a work in progress, yet its vestiges are rife with the things Flaubert deplored most: the fatuity of the bourgeois, their homage to the cliché and what Jacques Barzun called their ignorance of ignorance. So not quite a year after beginning *Madame Bovary*, Flaubert, who had been both enfatuated and debilitated by the provinces, considers initiating the *Dictionary* again. But what Flaubert envisioned in the *Dictionary* is, in a way, what he executed in the fiction. The comedic element is replete in *Madame Bovary*, a comedic element that, in its own poetic construction, tends to satirize the bourgeois and their petty predilections – constituents which were totally ignored in the cinematic adaptation by Chabrol. The rudiments of this comedic element can be seen as early as the first page of the novel when Flaubert writes:

> Nous étions à l'Etude, quand le Proviseur entra, suivi d'un *nouveau* habillé en bourgeois et d'un garçon de classe qui portait un grand pupitre. Ceux qui dormaient se réveillèrent, et chacun se leva comme surpris dans son travail.
>
> Le Proviseur nous fit signe de nous rasseoir; puis, se tournant vers le maître d'études:
>
> 'Monsieur Roger, lui dit-il à demi-voix, voici un élève que je vous recommande, il entre en cinquième. Si son travail et sa conduite sont méritoires, il passera *dans les grands*, où l'appelle son âge'.   (Flaubert, p. 23)

> We were in class when the headmaster entered, followed by a new boy not wearing the school uniform and a school servant carrying a large desk. Those who had been asleep woke up, and every one rose as if just surprised at his work.
>
> The headmaster made a sign to us to sit down. Then, turning to the teacher he said to him in a low voice:
>
> 'Monsieur Roger here is a pupil whom I recommend to your care; he'll be in the second. If his work and conduct are satisfactory, he will go into one of the upper classes, as becomes his age'
>   (Flaubert, Norton, p. 1).

Clearly, it appears that the narrator is someone who is and has been privy to the life and times of Charles Bovary, but who also recounts the episode in first person plural. That separation tends to disassociate the narrator (and the writer) with the work and that distance gives it a semblance of fragile credibility. In other words, the narrator does not speak of the episode as witnessed by an 'I', but a 'we' and such a posture allows him the 'flexibility' to make errors of memory and insights of omniscience as he subtly shifts from first person plural to third person singular. But beyond the relative reliability of the narrator lies the foundation of the humour to follow for the *layering* (Nabokov's term) of character has already begun; not only is Charles in the last year of the lower school, but he is in a class of pupils who are his junior. But even being in a class of pupils who are younger than he, Charles is still out of place and nothing accents his marginality than the description of his clothes and, specificially, his cap.

Resté dans l'angle, derrière la porte, si bien qu'on l'apercevait à peine, le nouveau était un gars de la campagne, d'une quinzaine d'années environ, et plus haut de taille qu'aucun de nous tous. Il avait les cheveux coupés droit sur le front, comme un chantre de village, l'air raisonnable et fort embarrassé. Quoiqu'il ne fût pas large de épaules, son habit-veste de drap vert à boutons noirs devait le gêner aux entournures el laissait voir, par la fente des parements, des poignets rouges habitués à être nus. Ses jambes, en bas bleus, sortaient d'un pantalon jaunâtre très tiré par les bretelles. Il était chaussé de souliers forts, mal cirés, garnis de clous (Flaubert, p. 23).

The new boy, standing in the corner behind the door so that he could hardly be seen, was a country lad of about fifteen, and taller than any of us. His hair was cut squre on his forehead like a village choir boy; he looked reliable, but very ill at ease. Although he was not broad-shouldered, his short jacket of green cloth with black buttons must have been tight around the armholes, and showed at the opening of the cuffs red wrists accustomed to being bare. His legs, in blue stockings, looked out from beneath yellowish trousers, drawn tight by suspenders. He wore stout, ill-cleaned, hobnailed boots

(Flaubert, Norton, p. 2).

This accumulation of elements in relation to character suggests certain comedic elements in terms of Charles's appearance: tight clothes, yellowish pants with suspenders, blue stockings and hobnailed shoes whose appearance is accented by being badly shined. Each one of those elements contributes to the relative comic absurdity of the wardrobe. But Flaubert saves the best description, the most comedic description for Charles's cap.

C'était une de ces coiffures d'ordre composite, où l'on retrouve les éléments du bonnet à poil, du chapska, du chapeau rond, de la casquette de loutre et du bonnet de coton, une de ces pauvres choses, enfin, dont la laideur muette a des profondeurs d'expression comme le visage d'un imbécile. Ovoïde et renflée de baleines, elle commençait par trois boudins circulaires; puis s'alternaient, séparés par un bande rouge, des losanges de velours et de poils de lapin; venait ensuite une façon de sac qui se terminait par un polygone cartonné, couvert d'une broderie en

soutache compliquée, et d'où pendait, au bout d'un long cordon
trop mince, un petit croisillon de fils d'or, en manière de gland.
Elle était neuve; la visière brillait   (Flaubert, p. 24).

It was one of those headgears of composite order, in which we
can find traces of the bear and coonskin, the shako, the bowler,
and the cotton nightcap; one of those poor things, in fine, whose
dumb ugliness has depths of expression, like an imbecile's face.
Ovoid and stiffened with whalebone, it began with three circular
strips; then came a succession of lozenges of velvet and rabbit fur
separated by a red band; after that a sort of band that ended in a
cardboard polygon covered with complicated braiding, from
which hung, at the end of a long thin cord, small twisted gold
threads in the manner of a tassel. [The cap was new; its peak
shone]   (Flaubert, Norton, p. 2).

In and of itself the description may lack any comedic elements at
all. That is, at first reading one may have difficulty visualizing the
hat or even paying attention to the description, but when one
actually views a picture of the cap (which was based on a drawing
appearing in the paper *Charivari*, 21 June 1833) not only is the
comedic element of the hat clear, but its absurdity apparent. (See
Figure 1.)

One would be hard-pressed to believe that anyone would wear a
hat like that and the fact that Madame Bovary, the mother, purchased such an article for Charles to wear only accents the relative
absurdity of his character and the authority of the mother. As if the
hat were not ridiculous enough in its own absurdity, Flaubert adds
the line: the cap was new; the peak shiny; a line which implicitly
states to the reader that the hat was newly purchased just for
the occasion of returning to school. But beyond the accumulative
technique, the addition of the 'narrative codicil' at the end of
the description is something Flaubert often uses and the codicil
tends to augment (always in an ironic way) the article or
situation previously described as in [The cap was new; its peak
shone]. Without the use of the codicil, the hat is still clearly
an article of absurd proportions and absurd fabrication which
characterizes Charles's personality, but the inclusion of the codicil
only accents Charles's pathetic nature and lays the foundation for
other codicils to follow which will clearly act in the same poetic
manner.

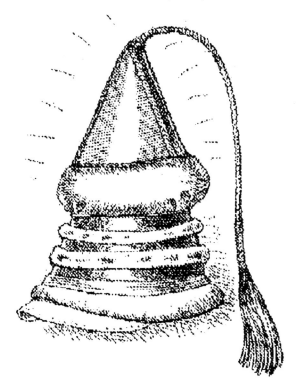

Figure 1. Charles Bovary's cap

The description of Charles's cap is merely the foundation upon which Flaubert drapes Charles's entire character. Given the purposefully created manner in which Flaubert sets out to describe the hat, any subsequent allusion to or description of Charles's character would, doubtless, contain the same brand of ludic intent. One can read that ludic intent in the way Flaubert addresses Charles's study of medicine, a profession chosen, of course, by his mother.

Il prit l'habitude du cabaret, avec la passion des dominos. S'enfermer chaque soir dans un sale appartement public, pour y taper sur des tables de marbre de petits os de mouton marqués de points noirs, lui semblait un acte précieux de sa liberté, qui le rehaussait d'estime vis-à-vis de lui-même. C'etait comme l'initiation du monde, l'accès des plaisirs défendus; et, en entrant, il

posait la main sur le bouton de la porte avec une joie presque
sensuelle. Alors, beaucoup de choses comprimées en lui, se dila-
tèrent; il apprit par coeur des couplets qu'il chantait aux bienve-
nues, s'enthousiasma pour Béranger, sut faire du punch et
connut enfin lámour.

Grâce à ces travaux préparatoires, il echoua complètement à son
examen d'officier de santé. On l'attendait le soir même à la
maison pour fêter son succès!   (Flaubert, p. 32)

He got into the habit of going to the cafés, and had a passion for
dominoes. To shut himself up every evening in the dirty public
room, to push about on marble tables the small sheep-bones with
black dots, seemed to him fine proof of his freedom, which raised
him in his own esteem. It was beginning to see life, the sweetness
of stolen pleasures; and when he entered, he put his hand on the
door-handle with a joy almost sensual. Then many things com-
pressed within him expanded; he learned by heart student songs
and sang them at gatherings, became enthusiastic about Béranger, learnt how to make punch, and, finally how to make love.

Thanks to these preparatory labors, he failed completely in his
examination for his degree of *officier de santé*. [He was expected
home the same night to celebrate his success]
                                         (Flaubert, Norton, p. 8).

Clearly, the method Flaubert uses is to present, albeit ironically,
Charles's world. He raises Charles's hedonistic interests (at least
hedonistic for Charles) to an almost sanctified level as if the things
in which Charles were engaging were somehow crucial to the
product of his life: playing dominoes, singing songs, making
punch, losing his virginity. Flaubert writes as much when the
narrator states the ironic line 'thanks to these preparatory labors'
which relates to the rather inocuous things in which Charles occupied himself; and thanks to those labours he failed his degree on
the same night he was to celebrate his success. Once again Flaubert
employs the codicil at the end of a passage which accents the
previous passage and augments the relative absurdity of Charles's
character. The humour lies in the way Flaubert sets up the passage
about Charles's education, deploys, in ironic ways, the method of
Charles's study, then substantiates it with the codicil.

The relationship between the erotic and humorous is clear in Flaubert's work and the method he uses to advance the plot is carefully choreographed. One reads in Part I, Chapter III:

> Selon la mode de la campagne, elle lui proposa de boire quelque chose. Il refusa, elle insista, et enfin lui offrit, en riant, de prendre un verre de liqueur avec elle. Elle alla donc chercher dans l'armoire une bouteille de curaçao, atteignit deux petits verres, emplit l'un jusqu'au bord, versa à peine dans l'autre, et, après avoir trinqué, le porta à sa bouche. Comme il était presque vide, elle se renversait pour boire; et, la tête en arrière, les lèvres avancées, le cou tendu, elle riait de ne rien sentir, tandis que le bout de la langue, passant entre ses dents fines, léchait à petits coups le fond du verre   (Flaubert, p. 47).

> After the fashion of the country folks she asked him to have something to drink. He said no; she insisted, and at least laughingly offered to have a glass of liqueur with him. So she went to fetch a bottle of curacoa from the cupboard, reached down two small glasses, filled one to the brim, poured scarcely anything into the other, and, after having clinked glasses, carried hers to her mouth. As it was almost empty she bent back to drink, her head thrown back, her lips pouting, her neck straining. She laughed at getting none, while with the tip of her tongue passing between her small teeth [she licked drop by drop the bottom of her glass]   (Flaubert, Norton, p. 16).

Needless to say, Charles was seduced and the seduction not only results in Charles's proposal of marriage, but offers Emma a way to get off the farm. But rather than move the novel along by summarizing the situation after the seduction scene (through the voice of the officious narrator), and take the reader up to the honeymoon, Flaubert once again relies on the layering method to characterize the relationship between Charles and Emma as a reflection of the 'article'. Just as he did with Charles's cap, Flaubert continues with the wedding feast.

In Part I, Chapter IV Flaubert first establishes the layout of the table which includes: four roasts of beef, six chicken fricassées, stewed veal, three legs of mutton, a roast suckling pig, four pork sausages with sorrel, decanters of brandy, sweet bottled cider, and dishes of yellow cream. Flaubert then imbeds the wedding cake within the circumference of the table, but, as with the cap, attempts to draw no attention to the cake whatsoever. As the confectioner brings out the cake, Flaubert writes:

> A la base, d'abord, c'était un carré de carton bleu figurant un temple avec portiques, colonnades et statuettes de stuc tout autour, dans des niches constellées d'étoiles en papier doré; puis se tenait au second étage un donjon en gâteau de Savoie, entouré de menues fortifications en angélique, amandes, raisins sec, quartiers d'oranges; en enfin, sur la plate-forme supérieure, qui était une prairie verte où il y avait des rochers avec des lacs de confitures et des bateaux en écales de noisettes, on voyait un petite Amour, se balançant à une esparpolette de chocolat, dont les deux poteaux étaient terminés par deux boutons de rose naturels, en guise de boules, au sommet   (Flaubert, p. 55).

> At its base there was a square of blue cardboard, representing a temple with porticoes, colonnades and stucco statuettes all round, and in the niches constellations of gilt paper stars; then on the second level there was a dungeon of Savoy cake, surrounded by many fortifications in candied angelica, almonds, raisins and quarters of oranges; and finally, on the upper platform a green field with rocks set in lakes of jam, nutshell boats, and a small Cupid balancing himself in a chocolate swing whose [two uprights ended in real roses for balls at the top]   (Flaubert, Norton, p. 20).

The question that should come to mind after reading this description is: Why does Flaubert write it at all? A wedding cake in and of itself is no cause for description, certainly lengthy description, unless the description is a marked feature in the poetics of the novel. And that is certainly the case with *Madame Bovary*. Once again one needs to visualize this cake and then make some speculations on why it is decorated that way. (See Figure 2.)

By dissecting the cake layer by layer one discovers the following:

Base: Layer 1
A square of blue cardboard (i.e. a cardboard base)
representing:

 a) a temple with porticos and colonnades
 b) adorned on all sides with stucco (a fine plaster) statuettes
 c) standing in niches spangled with gold-paper stars

Figure 2. Charles and Emma Bovary's wedding cake

Second tier: Layer 2
A medieval castle:

    a) in gateau de Savoie
    b) surrounded by miniature fortifications of angelica (aromatic
       plant used in making confections), almonds, raisins and
       orange sections

Third Tier: Layer 3
A green meadow with:

    a) rocks
    b) jelly lakes and
    c) boats made of hazelnut shells

Fourth tier: Layer 4
Cupid sitting in a chocolate swing with:

  a) the tips of the two uprights, the highest points of the whole, made of two real rosebuds

Decomposing what Flaubert has written one can then come up with his statement (objective?) on the wedding between Charles and Emma and the future of their marriage. The base of the cake, the foundation, is cardboard fashioned with arches and columns, stucco statuettes and gold stars. This foundation itself gives the impression of something rather flimsy, certainly not substantial, and at the same time registers something classical, noble, regal. But the irony lies in the fact that this 'classical' motif is merely paper. A foundation of paper fashioned to *appear* as if it were something sturdy and classical which certainly plays into Emma's notions of the romantic.

On the second level there is a medieval castle fashioned out of sponge cake and made with 'fortifications' of fruit and nuts. Not only are the condiments curious ones for a wedding cake (perhaps not for a rustic one) the implications of medievalism with its notions of a romantic, chivalric time with knights and damsels, is obvious. Notions of 'camelot[e]' are everywhere apparent, but Flaubert also has recourse to use words such as 'dungeon' and 'fortification' which lends credibility to one's notions of 'imprisonment' and 'battle' both imminent objects of the marriage's destiny if not Emma's.

The third layer is made up of lakes ('Have a woman with you when you sail on it')[1] of jam and boats of hazelnut shells set in a green meadow. The implications of that level, as in the others, is the allusion to the romantic, but the romantic in a treacly-like condensation. No doubt there is some allusion here to 'romantic' poets such as Lamartine and, possibly, Musset, whom Flaubert held in a certain amount of contempt.

At the very top, the fourth layer, Cupid sits in a chocolate swing. It is not stated of what substance Cupid is made, but that his swing is composed of chocolate and at the very top of the cake are two real rosebuds essentially puts 'the icing on the cake'. One, if the rose buds are real, they are already dead; and two, as rosebuds they are not yet roses. So the implication is that even though they have the appearance of being roses, they are not roses. And even though they have the appearance of being alive, they are, in fact, dead. When one takes all of these things into consideration the wedding cake is clearly an arbiter of things to come. Not only does the cake acknowledge the flimsy, romantic and absurd state of their marriage, but the appearance of the cake *qua* cake signifies the comic absurdity of their entire relationship.

But Flaubert has not finished with the couple yet and Charles in particular. There does not seem to be any apparent end to what Flaubert wants to do with Charles in terms of characterization. The description of Charles's home is yet another example of how Flaubert characterizes the mode. Rather than summarize the scene, Flaubert goes into great detail to augment something about Charles as a person *vis-à- vis* his home. He writes:

> et sur l'étroit chambranle de la cheminée resplendissait une pendule à tête d'Hippocrate, entre deux flambeaux d'argent plaqué, sous des globes de forme ovale. De l'autre côté du corridor était le cabinet de Charles, petite pièce de six pas de large environ, avec une table, trois chaises et un fauteuil de bureau. Les tomes du *Dictionnaire des sciences médicales*, non coupés, mais dont la brochure avait souffert dans toutes les ventes successives par où ils avaient passé, garnissaient presque à eux seuls les six rayons d'une bibliothèque en bois de sapin. L'odeur des roux pénétrait à travers la muraille, pendant les consultations, de même que l'on entendait, de la cuisine, les malades tousser dans le cabinet et débiter toute leur histoire   (Flaubert, p. 59)

> and on the narrow mantelpiece a clock with the head of Hippocrates shone resplendent between two plate candlesticks under oval shades. On the other side of the passage was Charles's consulting room, a little room about six paces wide, with a table, three chairs, and an office-chair. Volumes of the *Dictionary of Medical Sciences*, uncut, but the binding rather the worse for the successive sales through which they had gone, occupied almost alone the six shelves of a pinewood book-case. The smell of sauces penetrated through the walls when he saw patients, just as in the kitchen one could hear the people coughing in the consulting room and recounting their whole histories   (Flaubert, Norton, p. 23)

The humour, of course, lies in the manner in which Flaubert 'cinematizes' the prose and in the language he uses. He moves in a deductive fashion, not unlike Balzac's method of deductive description, moving from the general (i.e. the outside of the house) to the specific (i.e. the items inside the house). Once inside, he methodically approaches each item that, in effect, makes a comment on Charles's character. The absurd items Charles possesses (e.g. the clock with the head of Hippocrates which is a bit of *kitsch* that would only invigorate someone like Charles) illustrate to what lengths Flaubert goes in order to substantiate fully the character. The fact the *Dictionary of Medical Sciences* is uncut not only augments the type of character Charles is, but lays the foundation for the equally absurd operation of Hippolyte's club-foot. As a matter of fact, on a number of occasions Flaubert alludes to the imminent operation which both invigorates the absurdity of Charles's character and augments the comedic moment. This is seen at the end of Part I, Chapter VII where one reads about the Marquis d'Andervilliers' delicate medical condition:

> Il avait eu, lors des grandes chaleurs, un abcès dans la bouche, dont Charles l'avait soulagé comme par miracle, en y donnant à point un coup de lancette.   (Flaubert, p. 77)

> During the height of the Summer heat he had suffered from an abcess in his mouth, which Charles had cured as if by miracle by giving a timely little touch with the lancet.
> (Flaubert, Norton, pp. 32–3)

The 'nick in time' not only establishes Charles's medical superficiality and, hence, his incompetence, but sets up his inevitable failure in the Hippolyte scene by utilizing the same ludicrous method.

On 15 January 1853, as he was about to begin Part II, Flaubert wrote to Louise Colet: 'Last week I spent five days writing one page, and I dropped everything else for it – my Greek, my English; I gave myself up to it entirely... It is an uniterrupted portrayal of a bourgeois existence and of a love that remains inactive – a love all the more difficult to depict because it is both timid and deep, but alas! lacking in inner turbulence, because my gentleman is of a sober temperament. I had something similar in the first part: the husband loves his wife somewhat after the same fashion as her lover [Léon]. Here are two mediocrities in the same milieu, and I must differentiate between them' (Flaubert, *Letters*, p. 178)

Everything, says Flaubert, is a matter of style, or more exactly of the particular turn and aspect one gives to things. His letters are clear on that subject. What his letters do not pronounce is the degree of perfection he achieves in writing about romantic moments in ironic ways. A clear example of this is the afternoon walk that Emma takes with Léon in Part II, Chapter III:

Pour arriver chez la nourrice, il fallait, après la rue, tourner à gauche, comme pour gagner le cimetière, et suivre entre des maisonnettes et des cours un petit sentier que bordaient des troènes. Ils étaient en fleur et les véroniques aussi, les églantiers, le orties et les ronces légères qui s'élançaient des buissons. Par le trou des haies, on apercevait, dans les *masures*, quelque pourceau sur un fumier, ou des vaches embricolées, frottant leurs cornes contre le tronc des arbres. Tous les deux, côte à côte, il march-aient doucement, elle s'appuyant sur lui et lui retenant son pas qu'il mesurait sur les siens; devant eux, un essaim de mouches voltigeait, en bourdonnant dans l'air chaud.   (Flaubert, p. 134)

To get to the nurse's it was necessary to turn to the left on leaving the street, as if heading for the cemetery, and to follow between the little houses and yards a small path bordered with privet hedges. They were in bloom, and so were the speedwells, eglan-tines, thistles, and the sweetbriar that sprang up from the thick-ets. Through openings in the hedges one could see into the huts, some pig on a dung-heap, or tethered cows rubbing their horns against the trunk of trees. The two, side by side, walked slowly, she leaning upon him, and he restraining his pace, which he regulated by hers; in front of them flies were buzzing in the warm air.   (Flaubert, Norton, p. 65)

The walk is meant to be romantic, but with obvious ironic edges. Not only does Flaubert have them walk in the direction of the cemetery (a walk towards death – metaphoric or otherwise), but the entire passage is written in such a manner as to undermine anything romantic. Not only does the pig wallowing in a manure pile or the flies buzzing in the warm air dispel notions of the romantic, but the selection of plants Flaubert uses clearly does the same thing. Each of the flowers has a uniqueness which comments on the scene in progress: the 'budding' relationship between Emma and Léon. Eglantines and sweetbriar are the same plant both of

which have pink flowers, but *prickly* stems; speedwells are either
blue, white or red arranged in axillary or terminal spikes, but
whose main use is as a *diuretic*; thistles are either white, purple,
pink or yellow, but which also have *prickly* leaves. These plants are
all confined within the privet hedges, the main purpose of which is
chiefly to screen, and all of the plants spring from the thickets, or
coarse underbrush. Each of the plants that line the path are aesthe-
tically pleasing, but also have an 'edge' to them that renders them
both beautiful and potentially harmful. No where does Flaubert
record the reason he uses particular flowers in particular scenes,
but the use of these plants recalls the same technique used by
Balzac in works like *Le Père Goriot*. In addition to the botanical
aspects of these flowers there is also the 'secret meaning' of the
flowers *vis-à-vis* Greek mythology. For example, the speedwell
'means' *female fidelity* while the sweetbriar, *simplicity* (Powell, p.
154); the choice of these flowers may appear to be serendipitous,
but clearly the manner in which Flaubert worked would lend
credence to the suggestion that he had studied something about
the flowers he uses in order to make a comment upon the scene
and/or character at hand.

Flaubert often uses a combination of techniques at one time. He
uses layering in combination with the allusion to 'the wind' in
order to announce changes in the progress of the plot. The finest
example of that in the entire novel comes in Part II, Chapter VIII,
the agricultural fair.

One has already read of Rodolphe in a previous chapter so his
imminent appearance at the fair has already been set up. Emma
meets Rodolophe and Flaubert writes:

> Ainsi, sa chemise de batiste à manchettes plissées bouffait au
> hasard du vent, dans l'ouverture de son gilet, qui était de coutil
> gris, et son pantalon à larges raies découvrait aux chevilles ses
> bottines de nankin, claquées de cuir verni. Elles étaient si vernies,
> que l'herbe s'y reflétait. Il foulait avec elles les crottins de cheval,
> une main dans la poche de sa veste et son chapeau, de paille mis
> de côté.   (Flaubert, p. 190).

The wind, blowing up his batiste shirt with pleated cuffs revealed
a waistcoat of grey linen, and his broad-striped trousers disclosed
at the ankle nankeen boots with patent leather gaiters. These
were so polished that they reflected the grass. He trampled on

horse's dung, one hand in the pocket of his jacket and his straw
hat tilted on one side.   (Flaubert, Norton, p. 99)

Apparently this description is enough for Emma who, by now, has
become truly smitten by the debonair Rodolphe regardless of the
faecal matter on his boots. The scatalogical element is never far from
Flaubert and whenever he can make a scatalogical statement to comment on either the plot or the character he takes full advantage of it.

Throughout this meeting between Rodolphe and Emma, Flaubert
has, as a counterpoint, situated the speeches of the dignitaries in
attendance, the most famous, and most comedic, of which comes at
the end of Part II, Chapter VIII:

'Ainsi, nous', disait-il, 'pourquoi nous sommes-nous connus?
quel hasard l'a voulu? C'est qu'à travers l'éloignement, sans
doute, comme deux fleuves qui coulent pour se rejoindre, nos
pentes particulières nous avaient poussés l'un vers l'autre.'

Et il saisit sa main; elle ne la retira pas.
'Ensemble de bonnes cultures!' cria le président.
'– Tantôt, par example, quand je suis venu chez vous...'
'A M. Bizet, de Quincampoix.'
'– Savais-je que je vous accompagnerais?'
'Soixante et dix francs!'
'–Cent fois même j'ai voulu partir, et je vous ai suivie, je suis
resté.'
'Fumiers.'
'–Comme je resterais ce soir, demain, les autres jours, toute ma
vie!'
'A M. Caron, d'Argueil, une médaille d'or!'
'–Car jamais je n'ai trouvé dans la société de personne un charme
aussi complet.'
'A M. Bain, de Givry-Saint-Martin!'
'–Aussi, moi, j'emporterai votre souvenir.'
'Pour un bélier mérinos...'
'– Mais vous m'oublierez, j'aurai passé comme une ombre.
'A M. Belot, de Notre-Dame...'
'–Oh! non, n'est-ce pas, je serai quelque chose dans votre pensée,
dans votre vie?'
'Race porcine, prix *ex oequo*: à MM. Lehérissé et Cullembourg;
soixante francs!'   (Flaubert, pp. 202–3)

'Take us, for instance,' he said, 'how did we happen to meet?
What chance willed it? It was because across infinite distances,
like two streams uniting, our particular inclinations pushed us
toward one another.'
And he seized her hand; she did not withdraw it.
'First prize for general farming!' announced the president.
'– Just now, for example, when I went to your home...'
'To Mr. Bizet of Quincampoix.'
'– Did I know I would accompany you?'
'Seventy francs!'
'– A hundred times I tried to leave; yet I followed you and
stayed...'
'For manures!'
'–As I would stay to-night, to-morrow, all other days, all my life!'
'To Monsieur Caron of Argueil, a gold medal!'
'– For I have never enjoyed anyone's company so much.'
'To Monsieur Bain of Givry-Saint-Martin.'
'–And I will never forget you.'
'For a merino ram...'
'–Whereas you will forget me; I'll pass through your life as a
mere shadow...'
'To Monsieur Belot of Notre Dame.'
'–But no, tell me there can be a place for me in your thoughts, in
your life, can't there?'
'Hog! first prize equally divided between Messrs Lehérissé and
Cullembourg, sixty francs!'.   (Flaubert, Norton, p. 107)

What Flaubert attempts (and which was extraordinary original) is
the use of ironic *cross-cutting* which not only augments the comedic
moment, but continues to comment on the notion of love in general
and especially on the bourgeois notion of it: '– A hundred times I
tried to leave; yet I followed you and stayed...For manures!' The
technique, of course, predates its cinematic use by over a half-
century which is what makes its use so original and yet in the
Chabrol adaptation of the novel, the film ignores the scheme and
by so doing undermines the overall effect Flaubert had certainly
intended. Flaubert was clear about his intentions in this scene as he
writes in the 15 July 1853 letter to Louise Colet: 'Tonight I have just
sketched my entire big scene of the Agricultural Show. It will be
enormous – thirty pages at least. Against the background of this
rustico-municipal celebration, with all its details (my secondary will

be shown talking and in action), there must be continuous dialogue between a gentleman and the lady he is 'warming up'.... Once this is behind me, I shall soon reach my fornication in the autumn woods, with the lovers' horse cropping the leaves beside them...' (Flaubert, *Letters*, p. 194).

So the agricultural scene sets up the less famous fornication scene between Emma and Rodolphe in the forest, Part II, Chapter IX, where Flaubert writes:

> Il l'entraîna plus loin, autour d'un petit étang, où des lentilles d'eau faisaient une verdure sur les ondes. Des nénuphars flétris se tenaient immobliles entre les joncs. Au bruit de leurs pas dans l'herbe, des grenouilles sautaient pour se cacher.
> – 'J'ai tort, j'ai tort,' disait-elle. 'Je suis folle de vous entendre.'
> – 'Porquoi?...Emma! Emma!'
> – 'Oh! Rodolphe!...fit lentement la jeune femme en se penchant sur son épaule.
> Le drap de sa robe s'accrochait au velours de l'habit. Elle renversa son cou blanc, qui se gonflait d'un soupir et, défaillante, tout en pleurs, avec un long frémissement et se cachant la figure, elle s'abandonna   (Flaubert, p. 217)

> He drew her father on to a small pool where duckweeds made a greenness on the water. Faded waterlilies lay motionless between the reeds. At the noise of their steps in the grass, frogs jumped away to hide themselves.
> 'I shouldn't, I shouldn't!' she said. 'I am out of my mind listening to you!'
> 'Why?...Emma! Emma!'
> 'Oh, Rodolphe!...' she said slowly and she pressed against his shoulder.
> The cloth of her dress clung to the velvet of his coat. She threw back her white neck which swelled in a sigh, and, faltering, weeping, and hiding her face in her hands, with one long shudder, she abandoned herself to him.   (Flaubert, Norton, p. 116)

The duckweeds act as a green carpet (allusions to the green meadows of the wedding cake) and act as a counterpoint to the 'faded' waterlilies hidden in the reeds. After the 'fornication' scene, as she is feeling the 'blood course through her flresh like a river of milk', Rodolphe, cigar between lips, mends a broken bridle on the horse.

But, for Emma, the experience, leads her to exclaim, 'I have a lover! a lover!' and the narrator talks about the words 'passion, ecstasy, and delirium' which acts as a refrain from Emma in Part I, Chapter V.

But Flaubert often makes Emma work extremely hard to garner the fruits of her adultery and the obstacles he puts in her way are both ironic and comedic. Later in Part II, Chapter IX he writes:

> Mais, quand la planche aux vaches était levée, il fallait suivre les murs qui longeaient la rivière; la berge était glissante; elle s'accrochait de la main, pour ne pas tomber, aux bouquets de ravenelles flétries. Puis elle prenait à travers des champs en labour, où elle s'enfonçait, trébuchait et empêtrait ses bottines minces. Son foulard, noué sa tête, s'agitait au vent dans les herbages; elle avait peur des boeufs, elle se mettait à courir; elle arrivait essoufflée, les joues roses, et exhalant de toute sa personne un frais parfum de sève, de verdure et de grand air. Rodolphe, à cette heure-là, dormait encore. C'était comme une matinée de printemps, qui entrait dans sa chambre.   (Flaubert, p. 220)

> But when the cow plank was taken up, she had to follow the walls alongside the river; the bank was slippery; to keep from falling, she had to catch hold of the tufts of faded wall-flowers. Then she went across the ploughed fields, stumbling, her thin shoes sinking in the mud. Her scarf, knotted round her head, fluttered to the wind in the meadows. She was afraid of the oxen; she began to run; she arrived out of breath, with rosy cheeks, and breathing out from her whole person a fresh perfume of sap, of verdure, of the open air. At this hour Rodolphe was still asleep. It was like a spring morning bursting into his room.
>   (Flaubert, Norton, p. 118)

This particular course from the conjugal bed to the adulterous one is mediated by the 'rigours of the swamp'. Flaubert is careful not to make the journey too easy. He shods Emma with thin-soled shoes and has her endure the hardships of traipsing in the mud, avoiding oxen, gingerly traversing walls of faded-wall flowers, stumbling through ploughed fields. The victory, hers exclusively, since Rodolphe is asleep, is not unlike what Hardy does to Tess in her 'swampy' meeting with Angel Claire.

But chief among the comedic and ironic elements in the novel comes in Chapter XI. The sequence of the chapter is actually broken up into six movements:

1. the manipulation
2. the preparation
3. the operation
4. the adulation
5. the complication
6. the failure

In each of these movements, Flaubert attempts to link the ironic and the comedic with the result that the ethos of the bourgeoisie is manifestly presented.

In the *manipulation* Homais has recently 'read a paper praising a new method for curing club-foot, and since he was a partisan of progress, he conceived the patriotic idea that Yonville should show its pioneering spirit by having some club- foot operations performed there' (Flaubert, Norton, p. 125). He convinces Emma of the operation and the two of them coerce Charles into agreeing to execute it which leads to the *preparation* in which Charles sends to Rouen for Dr. Duval's volume (only one) in order to 'study' it. 'While he struggled with the equinus, varus and valgus – that is to say, *katastrephopody, endostrephopody,* and *exostrephopody,* or in other words, the various deviations of the foot, to the inside, outside, or downwards, as well as with *hypostrephopody* and *anastrephopody* or torsion below and contraction above, – Monsieur Homais was trying out all possible arguments on the stable boy in order to persuade him to submit to the operation' (Flaubert, Norton, p. 125). All of the information Charles reads is very technical and it works as a counterpoint to the fact that Charles has never read. His study habits, as well as his reading habits, have already been established in Part I and so Flaubert has laid the groundwork for the inevitable conclusion to the black comedy to follow.

The *operation* is set up with the fact that the Achilles tendon has to be cut first and that 'Neither Ambroise Paré, applying a ligature to an artery, for the first time since Celsus did it fifteen centures before; nor Dupuytren, cutting open abscesses through a thick layer of brain; nor Gensoul on first removing the superior maxilla, had hearts that trembled, hands that shook, minds that strained as

Monseiur Bovary's when he approached Hippolyte, his tenotomy knife between his fingers...Charles pierces the skin; a dry crackling was heard. The tendon was cut, the operation over. Hippolyte could not believe his eyes; he bent over Bovary's hands to cover them in kisses' (Flaubert, Norton, p. 127). The operation itself takes up less of the text than anything else surrounding the operation and Flaubert is careful to include Charles's anxieties as coterminous with the great men of modern medicine as he approaches the delicate task of snipping the tendon.

The *adulation* follows and here one sees Homais come to the fore. Homais is very careful to take as much credit for the apparent success of the operation as possible since by announcing it he has somehow included himself in the operation. He even writes that: 'The operation, moreover, was performed as if by magic, and barely a few drops of blood appeared on the skin, as though to say the rebellious tendon had at last given way under the efforts of the medical arts' (Flaubert, Norton, 1998, 128). The actual snip of the tendon 'as if by magic' acts as a refrain from Part I in which Charles lances the abscess of the Marquis and, miraculously, cures it. Studying aside, it appears that Charles is skilled only in the physical act of 'snipping' whatever appears to be snipped and Flaubert is careful to create that.

Five days later the *complication* sets in. The operation has resulted in gangrene and Dr Canivet is brought in three days later. So over a week has passed for infection to spread leading Canivet to exclaim "Straighten club-feet! As if one could straighten club-feet indeed! It is as if one wished to make a hunchback straight!" (Flaubert, Norton, p. 131). Which inevitably leads to the thigh amputation and to the subsequent *failure*. 'There was a sound of footsteps on the pavement. Charles looked up and through the lowered blinds he saw Dr Canivet standing in broad sunshine at the corner of the market, wiping his brow with his handkerchief. Homais, behind him, was carrying a large red bag in his hand, and both were going towards the pharmacy.

Then with a feeling of sudden tenderness and discouragement Charles turned to his wife and said:

'Oh, kiss me, my dear!'

'Don't touch me!' she cried, flushed with anger.

'What is it? what is it?' he repeated in utter bewilderment. 'Don't be upset! calm down! You know that I love you...come!...'

'Stop it!' she cried with a terrible look.

And rushing from the room, Emma closed the door so violently that the barometer fell from the wall and smashed on the floor (Flaubert, Norton, 1967, 134).

The entire sequence of scenes re-emphasizes Charles's incompetence and Homais's strength at manipulation as well as his overwhelming desire for recognition.

As with so much of Flaubert, his use of irony is directed in a myraid of ways from *direct layering* (as in the cap and the cake) to an indirect kind of layering. One excellent example of *indirect layering*, in which he uses both description and dialogue to convey the ironic mode, is in Part III, Chapter I.

With Rodolphe absent, the scene is set up with the rearrival of Léon who is impatiently waiting for Emma at the church; she finally shows up and they are about to leave the cathedral when the verger comes up to them.

At this point there is the juxtaposition of the verger's historical account of the church with Léon's apparent randyness. This particular scene recalls the agricultural scene with Rodolphe, but while Rodolphe was telling Emma how much he cared for her accompanied by cross-cuts of agricultural talk, here we have Léon not at all interested in even the pretense of telling Emma his interest, cross-cut with historical information about the church. His desire for her is expressed in his lustful anxiety with Flaubert writing:

> Léon fuyait; car il lui semblait que son amour, qui, depuis deux heures bientôt, s'était immobilisé dans l'église comme les pierres, allait maintenant s'évaporer telle qu'une fumée, par cette espèce de tuyau tronqué, de cage oblongue, de cheminée à jour, qui se hasarde si grotesquement sur la cathédrale, comme la tentative extravagante de quelque chaudronnier fantaisiste.   (Flaubert, p. 315)

> Léon fleeing, for it seemed to him that his love, that for nearly two hours, had been frozen in the church like the stones, would now vanish like a vapor through that sort of truncated funnel, rectangular cage or open chimney that rises so grotesquely from the cathedral like the extravagant brainchild of some fantastic roofer   (Flaubert, Norton, pp. 175–6)

The key phase here is 'que son amour...s'était immobilisé dans l'église comme les pierres' for it is clear that his 'love' is merely a metaphor for his 'erection' and to quote Flaubert 'Life! Life! To have erections! That is everything, the only thing that counts' (Flaubert, *Letters*, p. 193). Certainly if Léon did not abandon the church his 'love' (if not Flaubert's) would, metaphorically, 'go up in smoke'.

The movement of the scene goes from inside the church, where there is a veiled religiosity on Emma's part, to where Léon, desperately needing to flee, calls the verger a fool, he then has a cab hailed to which Emma says:

–'Ah! Léon!... Vraiment... je ne pais... si je dois!...'
Elle minaudait. Puis, d'un air sérieux:
–'C'est très inconvenant, savez-vous?'
–'En quoi?' répliqua le clerc. 'Cela se fait à Paris!'
Et cette parole, comme un irrésistible argument, la détermina.
                                                        (Flaubert p. 315)
'Oh Léon! Truly... I don't know... if I should...'
She simpered. Then, in a serious tone:
'It's very improper, you know, it isn't done.'
'Everybody does it in Paris!' replied the clerk.
This, like a decisive argument, entirely convinced her. She had made up her mind.   (Flaubert, Norton, p. 315).

Regardless of what Flaubert himself has written: 'An author in his book must be like God in the universe, present everywhere and visible nowhere' (Flaubert, *Letters*, p. 173), Flaubert *is* present everywhere and his presence is not opaque, but transparent. Léon knows Emma's weaknesses. Anything that has to do with Paris must be okay. After all, it is Paris. So her statement not only comments on Emma's follishness, but the narrator's interjection of Léon's statement being a clinching argument clearly plays into the role that Flaubert himself has presented for himself and which leads into one of the most comedic moments in the novel. This sequence, like the operation, is actually broken down into eight rather distinct *movements*, accompanied with *transitions*, all of which have been choreographed in a unique way. The sequence of movements actually begins with the driver asking: 'Où Monsieur va-t-il?' and Léon answers 'Où vous voudrez!' dit Léon poussant Emma dans la voiture. Et la lourde machine se mit en route (Flaubert, p. 316). What follows are the external movements the carriage takes *en route* to nowhere in particular and the internal movements the lovers make inside the cab.

Movement I–
Elle descendit la rue Grand-Pont, traversa la place des Arts le quai Napoléon, le pont Neuf et s'arrêta court devant la statue de Pierre Corneille. (Flaubert, p. 316)

It went down the rue Grant-Port, crossed the Place des Arts, the Quai Napoléon, the Pont Neuf, and stopped short before the statue of Pierre Corneille.   (Flaubert, Norton, p. 176)

Transition–
–'Continuez!' fit une voix qui sortait de l'intérieur.
                                        (Flaubert, p. 316)

'Go on' cried a voice that came from within.
                                        (Flaubert, Norton, p. 176)

Movement II–
La voiture repartit, et, se laissant, dès le carrefour LaFayette, emporter par la descente, elle entra au grand galop dans la gare du chemin de fer.   (Flaubert, p. 316)

The cab went on again, and as soon as it reached the Carrefour Lafayette, set off down-hill, and entered the railroad station at a gallop.   (Flaubert, Norton, p. 176)

Transition–
– 'Non, tout droit!' cria la même voix.   (Flaubert, p. 316).
   'No, straight on!' cried the same voice.
                                        (Flaubert, Norton, p. 176)

Movement III–
Le fiacre sortit les grilles, et, bientôt arrivé sur le Cours, trotta doucement, au milieu des grand ormes. Le cocher s'essuya le front, mit son chapeau de cuir entre ses jambes et poussa la voiture en dehors des contre-allées, au bord de l'eau, près du gazon.
   Elle alla de long de la rivière, sur le chemin de halage, pavé de cailloux secs, et longtemps, du côté d'Oyssel, au-delà des îles.
   Mais, tout à coup, elle s'élança d'un bond à travers Quatre-Mares, Sotteville, la Grande-Chaussée, la rue d'Elbeuf, et fit sa troisième halte devant le Jardin des plantes.   (Flaubert, p. 316)

The cab came out by the gate, and soon having reached the Mall, trotted quietly beneath the elm trees. The coachman wiped his brow, put his leather hat between his knees, and drove his carriage beyond the side alley by the meadow to the margin of the waters.

It went along by the river, along the towing-path paved with sharp pebbles, and for a long while in the direction of Oyssel, beyond the islands.

But suddenly it turned sideways across Quatremares, Sotte-ville, Le Grande-Chaussée, the Rue d'Elbeuf, and made its third halt in front of the Jardin de Plantes.

(Flaubert, Norton, pp. 176–7).

Transition–
–'Marchez donc!' s'écria la voix plus furieusement.

(Flaubert, p. 316)

'Get on, will you?' cried the voice more furiously.

(Flaubert, Norton, p. 177)

Movement IV–
Et assitôt, reprenant sa course, elle passa par Sainte-Sever, par le quai des Curandiers, par le quai aux Meules, encore une fois par le pont, par la place du Champ-du-Mars et derrière les jardins de l'hôpital, où des vieillards en veste noire se promènent au soleil, le long d'une terrassetoute verdie par des lierres. Elle remonta le boulevard Bouvreuil, parcourut le boulevard Cauchoise, puis tout le Mont-Riboudet jusqu'à la côte de Deville.

(Flaubert, pp. 316–17)

And at once resuming its course, it passed by Saint Sever, by the Quai de Curandiers, the Quai aux Meules, once more over the bridge, by the Place du Champ de Mars, and behind the hospital gardens where old men in black coats were walking in the sun along the ivy-covered terraces. It went up the Boulevard Bouvreuil, along the Boulevard Cauchoise, then the whole of Mont- Riboudet to the Deville hills.   (Flaubert, Norton, p. 177)

Movement V–
Elle revint; et alors, sans parti pris ni direction, au hasard, elle vagabonda. On la vit à Saint-Pol, à Lescure, au mont Gargan, à la Rouge-Mare, et place du Gaillardbois; rue Maladrerie, rue Dinanderie, devant Saint-Romain, Saint-Vivien, Saint-Maclou,

Saint-Nicaise, – devant la Douane, – à la basse Vieille-Tour, aux Trois-Pipes et au Cimetière monumental. De temps à autre, le cocher sur son siège jetait aux cabarets des regards désespérés. Il ne comprenait pas quelle fureur de la locomotion poussait ces indivdus à ne vouloir point s'arrêter. (Flaubert, p. 317)

It came back; and the, without any fixed plan or direction, wandered about at random. The cab was seen at Saint-Pol, at Lescure, at Mont Gargan, at La Rougue-Marc [sic] and Place du Gaillardbois; in the Rue Maladrerie, Rue Dinanderie, before Saint-Romain, Saint-Vivien, Saint-Maclou, Saint-Nicaise – in front of the Customs, at the Basse-Vieille-Tour, the 'Trois Pipes', and the Cimetière monumental. From time to time the coachman on his seat cast despairing glances at the passing cafés. He could not understand what furious locomotive urge prevented these people from ever coming to a stop. (Flaubert, Norton, p. 177)

Transition–
Il essayait quelquefois, et aussitôt il entendait derrière lui partir des exclamations de colère. Alors il cinglait de plus belle ses deux rosses tout en sueur, mais sans prendre garde aux cahots, accrochant par-ci, par-là, ne s'en souciant, démoralisé, et presque pleurant de soif, de fatigue et de tristesse. (Flaubert, p. 317)

Time and again he would try, but exclamations of anger would at once burst forth behind him. Then he would whip his two sweating nags, but he no longer bothered dodging bumps in the road; the cab would hook onto things on all sides but he couldn't have cared less, demoralised as he was, almost weeping with thirst, fatigue and despair. (Flaubert, Norton, p. 177)

Movement VI–
Et sur le port, au milieu des camions et des barriques, et dans les rues, au coin des bornes, le bourgeois ouvraient de grands yeux ébahis devant cette chose si extraordinaire en province, une voiture à stores tendus, et qui apparaissait ainsi continuellement, plus close qu'un tombeau et ballottée comme un navire. (Flaubert, p. 317)

Near the harbor, among the trucks and barrels, and along the street corners and the sidewalks, bourgeois stared in wonder at

this thing unheard of in the provinces: a cab with all blinds drawn
that reappeared incessantly, more tightly sealed than a tomb and
tosed around like a ship on the waves.

(Flaubert, Norton, p. 177)

Movement VII–

Une fois, au milieu du jour, en pleine campagne, au moment
où le soleil dardait le plus fort contre les vieilles lanternes argen-
tées, une main nue passa sous les petits rideaux de toile jaune et
jeta des déchirures de papier qui se dispersèrent au vent et
s'abattirent plus loin, comme de papillons blancs, sur un
champ de trèfles tout en fleur.   (Flaubert, p. 317)

One time, around noon, in the open country, just as the sun
beat most fiercely against the old plated lanterns, a bare hand
appeared under the yellow canvass curtain, and threw out some
scraps of paper that scattered in the wind, alighting further off
like white butterflies on a field of red clover all in bloom.

(Flaubert, Norton, p. 177)

Movement VIII–

Puis, vers six heures, la voiture s'arrêta dans une ruelle du
quartier Beauvoisine, et une femme en descendit qui marchait
le voile baissé, sans détourner la tête.   (Flaubert, p. 318)

Then, at about six o'clock, the carriage stopped in a back street
of the Beauvoisine Quarter, and a woman got out, walking with
her veil down and without looking back.

(Flaubert, Norton, p. 177)

At this point, one must take exception with Barthes's statement that
Flaubert's text[s] 'never succumbs to the good conscience (and bad
faith) of parody (of castrating laughter, of "the comical that makes
us laugh")' (Barthes, p. 9). To the contrary. The laughter may not be
castrating, but it does indeed make one laugh. The number of
movements the carriage makes mimic the sexual actions inside the
carriage and the feeling the driver has is, at times, if not a projection
of the two lovers, then, perhaps, of Léon. The balance and rythmn
of each paragraph parallels the sexual balance and rythmn of what
is happening inside the cab: at one time slow, at another rapid, at
still another, langorous. Depending on how one reads the text

(Flaubert makes a rare error in time), the two lovers have been fornicating for almost six hours a testament not only to their endurance and recovery, but to Flaubert's as well as he was prone to screaming aloud during his writing sessions.

Flaubert takes the reader from the fornication in the carriage to the fornication in the hotel. As he describes the bed in which Emma and Léon are to make love there are allusions to past and future beds.

> Le lit était un grand *lit d'acajou* [my emphasis] en forme de nacelle. Les rideaux de levantine rouge, qui descendaient du plafond, se cintraient trop bas près du chevet évasé...
> (Flaubert, p. 341)

> The bed was a large one, made of *mahogany* and shaped like a boat. The red silk curtains which hung from the ceiling, were gathered together too low, close to the lyre-shaped head-boards...   (Flaubert, Norton, p. 191)

This description is paired with that in Part I, Chapter V:

> Emma monta dans les chambres. La première n'était point meu-blée; mais la seconde, qui était la chambre conjugale, avait un *lit d'acajou* dans une alcôve à draperie rouge.   (Flaubert, p. 60)

> Emma went upstairs. the first room was not furnished, but in the second, the conjugal bedroom, was a *mahogany bedstead* in an alcove with red drapery.   (Flaubert, Norton, p. 23)

These are two of the three beds that are important: the conjugal bed, the adulterous bed and, finally, the death bed. The two beds are made of mahogany and the second, in the shape of a dinghy, presupposes a trip, a journey, and that is satisfied by her death.

The entire Emma–Lheureux episode that has been layered throughout the novel reaches its climax with Emma's return to Rodolphe to seek financial aid. With Rodolphe's rejection, the dis-course shifts once again. Amidst the scattered leaves and the hover-ing crows, Emma makes the conscious decision to commit suicide. Subsequent to swallowing the arsenic, as she is in her final agonies, one hears the beggar's refrain from the previous chapter, plus the additional stanzas. It is the blind beggar who is singing the song, a song that reveals who Emma is better than she can reveal it to

herself. And it is the refrain of the wind, sung by the beggar that
makes all the other references to the wind so significant since it
predisposes Emma to the inevitability of her fate and in a way the
wind, arbitrary, impossible to predict, an element that can be
soothing or chaotic, does the same thing with everyone's life. For
Emma, each time the wind blows it becomes less of an ally and
more of enemy.

But even at Emma's imminent death, Flaubert weaves the comedic element in among the pathos of her violent demise. As the
esteemed Dr Larivière arrives to see what can be done for
the dying Emma, Homais, always the opportunist, seizes the
chance to ingratiate himself with the learned doctor and asks him
to come to lunch.

On envoya bien vite prendre des pigeons au *Lion d'or*, tout ce
qu'il y avait de côtelettes à la boucherie, de la crème chez
Tuvache, des oeufs chez Lestiboudois, et l'apothicaire aidait lui-
même aux préparatifs, tandis que Mme Homais disait, en tirant
les cordons de sa camisole:
— 'Vous ferez excuse, monsieur; car dans notre malheureux pays,
du moment qu'on n'est pas prévenu la vielle...'
— 'Les verres à patte!!!' souffla Homais.
— 'Au moins, si nous étions à la ville, nous aurions la ressource des
pieds farcis.'
— 'Tais-toi!...A table, docteur!'
— Il jugea bon, après les premiers morceaux, de fournir quelques,
détails sur la catastrophe:
— 'Nous avons eu d'abord un sentiment de siccité au pharynx, puis
des douleurs intolérables à l'épigastre, superpuration, coma.'
— 'Comment s'est-ell donc empoisonnée?'
— 'Je l'ignore, docteur, et même je ne sais pas trop où elle a pu se
procurer cet acide arsénieux.'
    Justin, qui apportait alors une pile d'assiettes, fut saisi d'un
    tremblement.
— 'Qu'as-tu?' dit le pharmacien.
    Le jeune homme, à cette question, laissa tout tomber par terre,
avec un grand fracas.
— 'Imbécile!' s'ecria Homais, 'maladroit! lourdaud! fichu âne!'
    Mais, soudain, se maîtrisant:
— 'J'ai voulu, docteur, tenter une analyse, et *primo*, j'ai délicatement
introduit dans un tube...'

– 'Il aurait mieux valu, dit le chirugien, lui introduire vos doigts
  dans la gorge.   (Flaubert, pp. 407–8)

He sent quickly to the 'Lion d'Or' for some pigeons; to the
butcher's for all the cutlets that could be found; to Tuvache for
cream; and to Lestiboudois for eggs; and Homais himself aided
in the preparations, while Madame Homais was saying as she
tighened her apron strings;
   'I hope you'll forgive us, sir, for in this village, if one is caught
unawares...'
   'Stemmed glasses!' whispered Homais.
   'If only we were in the city, I'd be able to find stuffed pig's
feet...'
   'Be quiet... Please, doctor, à table!'
   He thought fit, after the first few mouthfuls, to supply some
details about the catastrophe.
   'We first had a feeling of siccity in the pharynx, the intolerable
pains at the epigastrum, super-purgation, coma.'
   'But how did she poison herself?'
   'I don't know, doctor, and I don't even know where she can
have procured the arsenious acid.'
   Justin, who was just bringing in a pile of plates, began to
tremble.
   'What's the matter?' said the pharmacist.
   At this question the young man dropped the whole lot on the
floor with a dreadful crash.
   'Imbecile!' cried Homais, 'clumsy lout! blockhead! confounded
ass!'
   But suddenly controlling himself:
   'I wished, doctor, to make an analysis, and *primo* I delicately
introduced a tube...'
   'You would have done better,' said the physician, 'to introduce
your fingers into her throat'.   (Flaubert, Norton, pp. 234–5)

But Homais, oblivious to the doctor's sarcasm, then proceeds to
have all his children checked out by the doctor and as Larivière is
about to leave, Madame Homais asks him if Homais is making his
blood too thick by sleeping after dinner to which Larivière
responds:

– 'Oh! ce n'est pas le *sens* qui le gêne.'

Et, souriant un peu de ce calembour inaperçu, le docteur ouvrit la porte. Mais la pharmacie regorgeait de monde; et il eut grand-peine à pouvoir se débarrasser du sieur Tuvache, qui redoutait pour son épouse une fluxion de poitrine, parce qu'elle avait coutume de cracher dans les cendres; puis de M. Binet, qui éprouvait parfois des fringales; et de Mme Caron, qui avait des picotements; de Lheureux, qui avait des vertiges; de Lestiboudois, qui avait un rhumatisme; de Mme Lefrançois, qui avait des aigreurs. Enfin les troi chevaux détalèrent, et l'on trouva généralement qu'il n'avait point montré de complaisance.

(Flaubert, p. 409)

'Oh, it isn't his blood I'd call too thick,' said the physician.

And, smiling a little at his unnoticed joke, the doctor opened the door. But the shop was full of people; he had the greatest difficulty in getting rid of Monsieur Tuvache, who feared his wife would get pneumonia because she was in the habit of spitting on the ashes; then of Monsieur Binet, who sometimes experienced sudden attacks of great hunger; and of Madame Caron, who suffered from pricking sensations; of Lheureux, who had dizzy spells; of Lestiboudois, who had rheumatism; and of Madame Lefrançois, who had heartburn. At last the three horses started; and it was the general opinion that he had not shown himself at all obliging.   (Flaubert, Norton, p. 236)

Imbedded between Emma's poisoning and her death throes, Flaubert has continued to use the comedic moment not only to draw attention to Homais's unmitigated slavishness, but to the unmitigated selfishness of the bourgeoisie to which Larivière is keenly aware.

At the conclusion of Emma's funeral one returns to Charles as he and his mother talk about the past while at the same time one reads alternating summary views of what happened to the significant male characters: what Rodolphe did, what Léon did and, finally, what Justin did.

All of this leads, of course, to the final chapter. One might have thought that Flaubert would have taken some pity on Charles, but life is not like that. Life is much like 'the wind'. Money issues survive even the death of a loved one. In a sense, there is no final peace until the accountant has been paid. And, like vultures, everyone is picking at whatever can be taken from Charles. His condition slowly deteriorates. So even in death, Emma is taking advantage of Charles's love. In Part III, Chapter XI, Charles discovers Léon's letters and as he goes to sell his last resource – his horse – he meets Rodolphe which leads to the penultimate irony. They engage in conversation.

L'autre continuait à parler culture, bestiaux, engrais, bouchant avec des phrases banales tous les interstices où pouvait se glisser une allusion. Charles ne l'écoutait pas; Rodolphe s'en apercevait, et il suivait sur la mobilité de sa figure le passage des souvenirs. Elle s'empourprait peu à peu, les narines battaient vite, les lèvres frémissaient; il y eut même un instant où Charles, plein d'une fureur sombre, fixa ses yeux contre Rodolphe qui, dans une sorte d'effroi, s'interrompit. Mais bientôt la même lassitude funèbre réapparut sur son visage.   (Flaubert, pp. 439–440)

The other went on talking of agriculture, cattle and fertilizers, filling with banalities all the gaps where an allusion might slip in. Charles was not listening to him; Rodolphe noticed it, and he could follow the sequence of memories that crossed his face. This face gradually reddened; Charles's nostrils fluttered, his lips quivered. For a moment, Charles stared at him in somber fury and Rodolphe, startled and terrified, stopped talking. But soon the same look of mournful weariness returned to his face.
        (Flaubert, Norton, p. 254)

The conversation, of course, is an ironic refraction of the agricultural meeting between Rodolphe and Emma. The allusions are paradigmatic and clear. The context has changed, but the substance of the context has not. What awaits Charles is a kind of death that is mingled with sexual irony.

Le lendemain, Charles alla s'asseoir sur le banc, dans la tonnelle. Des jours passaient par le treillis; les feuilles de vigne dessinaient leurs ombres sur le sable, le jasmin embaumait, le ciel était bleu, des cantharides bourdonnaient autour des lis en fleur, et Charles suffoquait comme un adolescent sous les vagues effluves amoureux qui gonflaient son coeur chagrin.   (Flaubert, p. 440)

The next day Charles sat down on the garden seat under the arbor. Rays of light were straying through the trellis, the vine leaves threw their shadows on the sand, jasmines perfumed the blue air, Spanish flies buzzed round the lilies in bloom, and Charles was panting like an adolescent under the vague desires of love that filled his aching heart.   (Flaubert, Norton, p. 255)

Certainly the venue Flaubert selected for Charles's death was not chosen serendipitously as it is the venue of Emma's assignations. But the key phrase here is 'des cantharides bourdonnaient autour des lis en fleur' which works on the levels of both sexuality and purity. The Spanish flies and the cantharides, those genitourinary stimulants that are synthesized from them, are juxtaposed with the majesty and purity of the lily. The 'panting' (as Flaubert was doubtlessly aware) is clearly the difficulty Charles has in breathing as he suffers a heart attack. And then he is dead. Yet the story does not end there. The novel continues in the directions of consummation of death and money; the appropriation of power by Homais; and, finally, the grandest of ironies, Homais's awarding of the Legion of Honor.

These three items point out to one of the key themes in *Madame Bovary* Flaubert seems to relate a philistinian philosophy of mankind. Philistinian in this sense is equated with the life style of the bourgeoisie. He depicts the small bourgeois rural life for all its pettiness, ugliness, and vulgarity, while concentrating on man's weakness and stupidity (e.g. Charles operation on Hippolyte). To Flaubert, everyone is either stupid or mean or void of the capacity for generosity, love, friendship (except for the marginal characters such as Justin); his characters seem without affection or empathy (e.g. Rodolphe's farewell letter to Emma). Apart from her adulterous exploits, Emma was compassionless for her own child. She is frustrated with the loneliness of home and so is Charles; frustrated with Charles and the mediocrity of marriage she falls in love with Léon; frustrated by Léon's leaving she attaches to Rodolphe; frustrated by his betrayal she returns to Léon. Emma becomes over and over the victim of her own self-deception. Yet within the context of the pathos one may feel for Emma, Flaubert has recourse to using both the poetics of irony and comedy to create a work that, upon scrutiny, elevates them both. As Baudelaire has written: 'I repeat that I should have found it easy to show that Gustave Flaubert has deliberately veiled in *Madame Bovary* the brilliant lyrical and ironic gifts so freely displayed in the *Tentation*...' (Baudelaire, p. 255).

5

The Poetics of Sacrifice in Hardy's *Tess of the D'Urbervilles*

By the middle of the nineteenth century England had overcome an unsettling financial period between 1815 to 1842 and had begun an economic recovery. 'The Bank of England, after the discouragements of the years down to 1842, was prepared to provide loans at a low rate of interest...Brickworks, mines, machine making, iron production, all boomed; the wages of heavy labourers rose; a general stimulus followed. Traders felt the same exhilaration, both in the West and East' (Checkland, p. 36). The industrial and commercial classes that verily controlled economic conditions and dominated English society and culture were both aggressive and mercenary when it came to exploiting the lower orders. In terms of working conditions, the *Ten Hours Act* was not effected until 1833 and the act was not extended to women and children until the *Ten Hours Act for Women and Young Persons* (1847). 'The Act, strengthened by further legislation in 1850 and 1853, provided a ten and a half hour day, from 6 am to 6 pm with one and a half hours for meals' (Checkland, pp. 248–9), but there were rearguard reactions to these laws and in some cases even courts ruled against the law showing it to be 'ambiguous' (Checkland, p. 249). Even though those laws were designed to mitigate the working conditions for children and women, women did not have any inherent voting rights until 1884, were not extended the full right to vote until 1918 and a woman's suffrage movement was not even founded until 1897 only six years after the publication of *Tess*.

With the growth in the industrial state came the growth of capital and competition. In that sense, perhaps to a greater extent than before, every group without a negotiable power base was exploited: hence women and children were most appealing and both were appropriated as commodities to be used in the quest for capital gain. This 'economic slavery', of course, could only result in the perception that women were property. As such, one discovers that Tess (Greek, *she who reaps*) is a viable commercial 'property' not only in terms of her use-value, but in terms of her innocent beauty a combination which could only result in a novel predicated on the exploitation of innocence and, as we shall see, the implementation of sacrifice.

PHASE THE FIRST: THE MAIDEN

Tess, of course, is thick with 'potential meaning' (secular and sacred) and a poetics of the entire novel is not within the scope of this book; however, there are some very significant items which manifest in the first 'phase' of the novel which lay the poetic foundation for the entire novel. Key among those devices is that Hardy does not use the word 'chapter' in the novel (sections of the novel indicated by Roman numerals), but, rather, uses the word 'phase' and the notion of a phase rather than a chapter is a distinguishing feature of the novel. What one knows of a phase is that it can be a discernible part in a stage or process. Though the titles of the phases are not of Hardy's doing, they focus on the Predominant feature of each phase. And so the clear implication of the title of 'Phase the First, The Maiden', yields to all things that imply maidenhood: namely, virginity, innocence, trustworthiness. If one can talk about stages or developments, one can also include in that process the notion of 'discovery', an action of uncovering, whose origins are closely related to those of 'revelation', the disclosure of something often by a divine or supernatural agency. It is not coincidental, then, that the entire novel hinges on one unique revelation: that is, the Durbeyfield family is related to the D'Urbervilles.

On the first page of 'Phase the First: The Maiden', we meet the parson as he encounters John Derbyfield on the road and calls him 'Sir John' to the bemusement of the latter. 'The parson rode a step or two nearer. "It was only my whim," he said; and, after a moment's hesitation: "It was on account of a discovery I made some little time ago, whilst I was hunting up pedigrees for the new county history. I am Parson Tringham, the antiquary, of Stagfoot Lane. Do not you really know, Durbeyfield, that you are the lineal representative of the ancient and knightly family of the d'Urbervilles, who derive their descent from Sir Pagan d'Urberville, that renowned knight who came from Normandy with William the Conqueror, as appears by Battle Abbey Roll?"' (Hardy, p. 1). From that moment on, the plot line of the entire novel is contingent on revelations, on disclosures, on discoveries that virtually propel Tess on a 'journey' which, ultimately, becomes her final sacrifice.

The motivating device in Tess's journey to 'Fulfilment' (the final phase of her journey) is the death of the family horse, Prince. Because her father is incapable of delivering the beehives to the retailers in Casterbridge, Tess, as the eldest child, volunteers thus replacing 'Sir John' and becoming the primary marker of sacrifice. In certain 'primitive' royal societies when sacrifice became an immanent issue for community welfare, 'An alternative procedure was for either a member of the royal family (e.g. the son of the king)...to be put to death instead of the reigning monarch. If the victim was a blood relative of the real king this had the advantage that to some extent he was already in possession of the royal soul-substance which gave him the right status for the office...' (James, p. 69) In essence, then, Tess is that 'royal' replacement whose body and soul (*The Body and Soul of Sue*, being an earlier title of the novel) is subject to appropriation and metaphorical, if not actual, immolation. Hardy subsequently initiates the beginning of her end with: 'The rickety little waggon was already laden, and the girl led out the horse Prince, only a degree less rickety than the vehicle. The poor creature looked wonderingly round at the night, at the lantern, at their two figures, as if he could not believe that at that hour, when every living thing was intended to be in shelter and at rest, he was called upon to go out and labour' (Hardy, p. 20). As Tess continues the journey she enters into a discussion with her brother, Abraham, during which she tells him that they live on a blighted planet. Tess's comment comes after the revelation of the D'Urberville name and that Tess could help out the family economically if she sought employment with their D'Urberville relatives. It is curious that Tess comments that the difference between a *splendid planet* and a *blighted one* deals entirely with the appropriation of capital for were this a splendid planet and not a blighted one she would already be a 'rich lady ready-made, and not have had to be made rich by marrying a gentleman' (Hardy, p. 21).

Hardy has clearly formulated the events of the tale to unfold in a manner which will inevitably destroy Tess. By describing Prince's condition and establishing the fact that should *anything* happen to Prince the family would be in a more desperate state of privation than they already are, Hardy has done two things: 1) situated Tess

in a position of irrecoverable destiny and 2) manipulated events so
that a salvation in the future is lost. We read that when Hardy
writes:

> Then examining the mesh of events in her own life, she seemed
> to see the vanity of her father's pride; the gentlemanly suitor
> awaiting herself in her mother's fancy; to see him as a grimacing
> personage, laughing at her poverty, and her shrouded knightly
> ancestry. Everything grew more and more extravagant, and she
> no longer knew how time passed. A sudden jerk shook her in her
> seat, and Tess awoke from the sleep into which she, too, had
> fallen... A hollow groan, unlike anything she had ever heard in
> her life, came from the front, followed by a shout of 'Hoi,
> there!'... The pointed shaft of the cart had entered the breast of
> the unhappy Prince like a sword; and from the wound his life's
> blood was spouting in a stream, and falling with a hiss into the
> road.   (Hardy, p. 22).

That revelation prompts Abraham to reiterate the blightedness of
the planet when he says: ' "Tis because we be in a blighted star, and
not a sound one is not it, Tess?' murmured Abraham through this
tears' (Hardy, p. 23). But it also points out one of the main themes
of the novel which the apparent arbitrary absurdity of the human
condition.

Prince's death and the revelation of the Durbeyfield connection to
the D'Urberville ancestral name acts as a coupling mechanism; that
is, the revelation that they are D'Urbervilles plus the realization that
Prince is dead establishes a premise for Tess *to be used* in order to
sustain the economic viability of the family. In that sense, sending
her away (that is, banishing) for the good of the family becomes
tantamount to using her as a 'sacrifice' on both metaphorical and,
ultimately, physical levels. In its broadest sense 'sacrifice' (from the
Latin sacrificium; sacer, "holy" and facere, "to make") involves the
destruction of a victim for the purpose of maintaining or restoring a
right relationship of man to the sacred order' (James, p. 13). It also 'is
a substitute for all the members of the community, offered up by the
members themselves. The sacrifice serves to protect the entire community from its own violence; it prompts the entire community to
choose victims outside of itself. The elements of dissension scattered
throughout the community are drawn to the person of the sacrificial
victim and eliminated, at least temporarily, by its sacrifice'

(Girard, p. 8). Since Tess feels guilty because of Prince's death (a contributing factor, though Prince should have known better) it is easier to establish her primarily as a 'scapegoat' for 'killing Prince' and, consequently, as a sacrifice, since Tess must assume personal responsibility for the family's welfare.

> The haggling business, which had mainly depended on the horse, became disorganized forthwith. Distress, if not penury, loomed in the distance... Tess, meanwhile, as the one who had dragged her parents into this quagmire, was silently wondering what she could do to help them out of it: and then her mother broached her scheme. 'We must take the ups wi'the downs, Tess,' said she; 'and never could yor high blood have been found out a more called-for moment. You must try your friends. Do ye know that there is a very rich Mrs d'Urberville living on the outskirts o'The Chase, who must be our relation? You must go to her and claim kin, and ask for some help in our trouble'. (Hardy, p. 24)

In a sense, Tess becomes the victim of her own scapegoating due, in fact, to her own volunteering. Her guilt forces her to volunteer herself in whatever capacity for the welfare of the family and Hardy sustains that poetics of sacrifice throughout. The relationship between scapegoating and sacrifice is better understood in its relation to its Biblical origins. 'When the English Bible was undertaken after 1538 it was based essentially upon [William] Tyndale's translation... Tyndale's reading of Leviticus, chapter 16 verse 10, is as follows: But the goat, on which the lot fell to be scapegoat, shall be presented alone before the Lord, to make an atonement with him and to let him go for a scapegoat into the wilderness' (Douglas, pp. 6–7). What Tyndale was essentially trying to convey 'was a significant difference between the process of sacrifice, which was the fate of the Lord's goat, and that of the ritual transfer of evil. In the second process, death might be the ultimate outcome as far as the scapegoat was concerned' (Douglas, p. 8). And here is the link between the scapegoat and the *piacular sacrifice* 'which was expiatory in character and design, brought about by the need to expiate some offence or avert some potential evil or disaster... It is into this type of sacrifice that the scapegoat appears to fit in the sense that the offender(s) is basically the sacrifice, having forfeited his or her life to atone for some sins' (Douglas, pp. 20–1). This scapegoating prompts Tess into an initial, but not terminal, meeting

with the D'Urberville family. It is only subsequent to that meeting
that her sacrifice ensues.

Yet on her initial visit to the family D'Urbervilles what one discovers is that they are *Stoke-D'Urberville's*; that is to say, they are
Stoke's, *not* D'Urbervilles since one reads that Mr Simon Stoke:
'Conning for an hour in the British Museum the pages of works
devoted to extinct, half-extinct, obscured, and ruined families
appertaining to the quarter of England in which he proposed to
settle he considered that *d'Urberville* looked and sounded as well as
any of them: and d'Urberville accordingly was annexed to his own
name for himself and his heirs eternally' (Hardy, p. 27) so there is
an implied deception to begin with. Alec (Alexander – *Greek pro-
tector of men*) is described by Hardy as having:

> an almost swarthy complexion, with full lips, badly moulded,
> though red and smooth, above which was a well-groomed black
> moustache with curled points, though his age could not be more
> than three or four-and-twenty. Despite the touches of barbarism
> in his contours there was a singular force in the gentleman's face,
> and in his bold rolling eye.   (Hardy, p. 28)

Clearly Alec is described as the 'devil's surrogate' in more ways
than one and the description is aptly applied as it alludes to how
Alec will appear in a subsequent phase of the novel. Alec is also
counterpointed with Angel whom Hardy introduces *au passant* as
the youngest of three brothers who are observing the country girls:
'the appearance of the third and youngest would hardly have been
sufficient to characterize him; there was an uncribbed, uncabined
aspect in his eyes and attire, implying that he had hardy as yet
found the entrance to his professional groove. That he was a
desultory, tentative student of something and everything might
only have been predicated of him' (Hardy, p. 8). This is all we
hear about Angel at the outset, but it is enough to recognize that
whatever he is he is, presumably, unlike Alec.

It is also at this point that the refrain of Tess's lips appears and
will, of course, like a 'labial leitmotif', appear again. The allusion
appears early in the novel with:

> Tess Durbeyfield at this timeof her life was a mere vessel of
> emotion untinctured by experience. The dialect was on her ton-
> gue to some extent, despite the village school...The pouted-up

deep red mouth to which this syllable was native had hardly as yet settled into its definite shape, and her lower lip had a way of thrusting the middle of her top one upward, when they closed together after a word. Phases of her childhood lurked in her aspect still. As she walked along today, for all her bouncing handsome womanliness, you could sometimes see her twelfth year in her cheeks, or her ninth sparkling from her eyes; and even her fifth would flit over the curve of her mouth now and then. (Hardy, p. 8)

This time it comes within the context of the strawberries the ' "British Queen" variety he stood up and held it by the stem to her mouth. "No, no!" she said quickly, putting her fingers between his hand and her lips. "I would rather take it in my own hand." "Nonsense," he insisted; and in a slight distress she parted her lips and took it in' (Hardy, p. 29). One can overlook the rather apparent oral sexual connotations of Alec's insistence and Tess's reluctance, but this particular interest in Tess's mouth is not the overture of an anxious pedophile since Angel Clare has an equal, if not greater, obsession to it.

But Hardy has already doomed Tess from the outset and he writes as much when one reads:

Thus the thing began. Had she perceived this meeting's import she might have asked why she was doomed to be seen and coveted that day by the wrong man, and not by some other man, the right and desired one in all respects – as nearly as humanity can supply the right and desired; yet to him who amongst her acquaintance might have approximated to this kind, she was but a transient impression half-forgotten.

(Hardy, p. 31)

Hardy follows that line with the aphorism: 'In the ill-judged execution of the well-judged plan of things the call seldom produces the comer, the man to love rarely coincides with the hour for loving' (Hardy, p. 31). The choice of words is select and the word 'execution', renders Tess choiceless in her journey. These lines all prefigure Tess pricking her chin on the rose: 'Then she fell to reflecting again, and in looking downwards a thorn of the rose remaining in her breast accidentally pricked her chin' (Hardy, p. 31). Presumably she bled, though Hardy fails to be so intrusive here, but the act does prefigure significant events; namely, the seduction and her rape. The deception continues as Alec writes the letter for her employment and the entire ritual of the sacrifice is then established. 'She had hoped to be a teacher at the school, but the fates seemed to decide otherwise' (Hardy, p. 35). But what is of interest here is how the notion of sacrifice relates to Tess's journey.

Hubert and Mauss establish that a sacrifice is usually connected with any religious act which, through the consecration of a victim, modifies the condition of the moral person who accomplishes it or that of certain objects with which s/he is concerned. And in the 'scheme of a sacrifice' as they outline it there are a number of conditions that must be met. Though Hubert and Mauss use a Vedic Hindu scheme, it is a scheme that has its parallels in the journey that Tess takes. For, 'in general, before the ceremony neither sacrifier nor sacrifier, nor place, instruments, or victim, possess the characteristic to a suitable degree. The first phase of the sacrifice is intended to impart it to them. They are profane; their condition must be changed' (Hubert and Mauss, pp. 19–20). The fact that both Hubert and Mauss and Hardy use the word 'phase' here is propitious. In relation to the family, the victim, or sacrifice, whose sacrificial act will alter the condition of the *status quo*, must be apparent. Her sacrifice will be made purely for materialistic gain and will maintain or positively modify the economic condition of the family. In the victim, *the act of destruction* is essential in the action of the sacrifice since the victim must be separated from the profane world and become sanctified.

Likewise, there must be a sacrfier, the person(s) whom will benefit from the sacrifice and it is incumbent upon the sacrfier to dress the sacrifice, which must be *pure* [my emphasis], for the sacred act and Tess, according to Hardy, is 'a pure woman'. This portion of the scheme is acknowledged when Hardy writes:

> On the morning appointed for her departure Tess was awake before dawn...She remained upstairs packing till breakfast, and then came down in her ordinary weekday clothes, her Sunday apparel being carefully folded in her box. Her mother expostulated. 'You will never set out to see your folks withut dressing up more the dand than that?'...And to please her parent the girl put herself quite in Joan's hands, saying serenely, 'Do what you like with me, mother.' Mrs. Durbeyfield was only too delighted at this tractability. First she fetched a great basin, and washed Tess's

hair with such thoroughness that when dried and brushed it looked twice as much as at other times. She tied it with a broader pink ribbon than usual. Then she put upon her the white frock that Tess had worn at the club-walking, the airy fulness of which, supplementing her enlarged coiffure, imparted to her developing figure an amplitude which belied her age, and might cause her to be estimated as a woman when she was not much more than a child. (Hardy, p. 35)

The sacrificer, of course, is generally an intermediary, usually a member of the clergy, but at any rate, a visible agent of consecration in the sacrifice who stands between the sacred and the profane. Clearly, Parson Tringham stands as that intermediary who not only initiated the entire event, but who stands between profane and sacred space.

At this point Tess stands ready to 'be delivered' from one space to another. And Hardy is clear about this movement within the phase:

However, as the moment for the girl's setting out drew nigh, when the first excitement of the dressing had passed off, a slight misgiving found place in Joan Durbeyfield's mind. It prompted the matron to say that she would walk a little way – as far as to the point where the acclivity from the valley began its first steep ascent to the outer world. At the top Tess was going to be met with the spring-cart sent by the Stoke- D'Urbervilles, and her box had already been wheeled ahead towards this summit by a lad with trucks, to be in readiness. (Hardy, p. 36)

In the so called *Gift Theory* 'when such offerings are made sacrifi- cially they are normally immolated, as the destruction of the victim is an integral element in any holocaust...but usually the life of the victim is required, actually or by symbolic ritual representation. The gift then is the offering of the inherent vital principle, the death or destruction of the victim being incidental to the process of the liberation of its life by the pouring out of its blood' (James, p. 26). Tess is the embodiment (in more ways than one) of the sacrifice. Having been washed, cleaned, combed and dressed she is, in effect, set out on her own to be exploited by the 'family'. 'The purpose of the sacrifice is to restore harmony to the commu- nity, to reinforce the social fabric. Everything else derives from that' (Girard, p. 8).

This particular ritual movement is not unlike the ritual movement we find in Joseph Campbell's quest motifs found in *The Hero of a Thousand Faces*, where the hero moves from the ordinary world into the unusual world. In other words, there is a separation, an initiation and a return. In Tess's case, the instrument of her sacrifice is simply Alec's 'sexual instrument' and as a result of Alec's use (or mis-use) of his 'sexual instrument' the Derbyfield family will be satisfied. Though these movements are all associated with the change from a profane world to a sacred world, we are also dealing with terms of economic survival. Certainly, if Tess could accomplish the task of marrying money it would be a 'blessing from God'. So the relationship between economic survival and religion is not entirely disassociative.

Tess's sacrifice is pre-determined from the outset of Phase One and is determined by the end of the phase which is accomplished with Alec's discovery of Tess:

> There was no answer. The obscurity was now so great that he [Alec] could see absolutely nothing but a pale nebulousness at his feet, which represented the white muslin figure he had left upon the dead leaves. Everything else was blackness alike. D'Urberville stooped; and heard a gentle regular breathing. He knelt, and bent lower, till her breath warmed his face, and in a moment his cheek was in contact with hers. She was sleeping, soundly, and upon her eyelashes there lingered tears...But might some say, where was Tess's guardian angel? where was the Providence of her simple faith? Perhaps, like that other god of whom the ironical Tishbite spoke, he was talking, or he was pursuing, or he was in a journey, or he was sleeping and not be awaked. (Hardy, p. 57)

The biblical allusion here is to Kings 18:27 'Elijah mocked them, and said, Cry aloud: for he is a god; either he is talking, or he is in a journey, or peradventure he sleepeth, and must be awaked' which neatly coincides with the entire notion of the sacrifice and, presently, with the imminent rape of Tess. But this rape is somewhat different than one might read in Lawrence, for example. In *Women in Love* Gerald's rape of Gudrun is an acknowledged 'vindication'; in *The Virgin and the Gypsy*, the gypsy's rape of Yvette is all done in the course of a 'rescue'. But Hardy could have titled the section as 'the seduction *and* rape'; seduction being *the act of leading aside* and has even been defined as *the enticement of a female to unlawful intercourse without the use of force.* Alec's rape of Tess is anything but forceless enticement; it is a clear case of possession and 'the meaning of possession without the consolations of privacy, romance, or social regulation (law, marriage). The power of men over women – including the power of men to possess women in the fuck – is endangered by a social reality of impersonal possession' (Dworkin, p. 78).

> Why it was that upon this beautiful feminine tissue, sensitive as gossamer, and practically blank as snow as yet, there should have been traced such a coarse pattern as it was doomed to receive; why so often the coarse appropriates the finer thus, the wrong man the woman, the wrong woman the man, many thousand years of analytical philosophy have failed to explain to our sense of order. (Hardy, p. 57)

The fact that Alec has 'appropriated' her body lends additional credence to the notion of woman as chattel. Hardy makes no attempt to disguise or mitigate Alec's intentions and in Section XI we read where Alec feels completely within his rights of appropriation. 'Good God,' he burst out, 'what am I. to be repulsed so by a mere chit like you? For near three mortal months have you trifled with my feelings, eluded me and snubbed me; and I won't stand it!' (Hardy, p. 54). These are the words of a twenty-three year old man to a sixteen-year old girl. As Alec uses the word 'chit' (a pejorative word at best) Tess is a pert or impudent girl or child which is exactly what Alec would expect because she does not willingly bend to his demands. Since Alec has already bought off the family (a new cob for Tess's father; new toys for the siblings) Tess somehow feels beholden to Alec for his affected kindness. His apparent 'randyness' and inability to accept Tess's refusal of him conclude in yet another of his deceptions since had ridden in a desultory fashion 'for over an hour, taking any turning that came to hand in order to prolong companionship with her, and giving far more attention to Tess's moonlit person than to any wayside object. A little rest for the jaded animal being desirable he did not hasten his search for landmarks' (Hardy, pp. 56–7). Tess is simply 'grist for Alec's mill' so for Irving Howe to claim that: 'Hardy manages the seduction scene with a tact not always characteristic of his novels. With so much tact, indeed, that readers have often supposed Tess to be a victim of rape...' (Hardy, p. 412) is patently false. Supposed? Alec's behaviour is simply one of sexual pursuit and conquest and when that has been accomplished Alec reflects indifference. To Tess's remonstration ' "If I had gone for love o'you, if I had ever sincerely loved you, if I loved you still, I should not so loathe and hate myself for my weakness as I do now! . . . My eyes were dazed by you for little, and that was all." He shrugged his shoulders' (Hardy, p. 59).

As the first phase ends, the formative stages of the sacrifice have been established and the family, as a community, has protected itself from the possibility of its own violence by choosing a victim, Tess, thus projecting the element of dissension upon the the sacrificial victim, and thereby eliminating that dissension, at least temporarily, by her sacrifice (Girard, p. 8). What follows is a continuation of that poetics of sacrifice Hardy has established.

PHASE THE SECOND: MAIDEN NO MORE

'Phase the Second, Maiden no More' begins with Tess returning to her family after several months at Trantridge. We read: 'The incline was the same down which d'Urberville had driven with her so wildly on that day in June . . . It was always beautiful from here; it was terribly beautiful to Tess today, since her eyes last fell upon it she had learnt that the serpent hisses where the sweet birds sing, and her views of life had been totally changed for her by the lesson' (Hardy, pp. 58–9). The 'lesson' (that is, serpents and sweet singing birds inhabit the same quarters where rape takes place) seems a rather curious word to use, but then again the lesson is part of Tess's quest, part of her initiation, for the road she travels now *from* Trantridge is not the same she traveled *to* Trantridge. Like Catherine Morland before her, Tess returns home on the same, but different, road and though Alec freely admits that what he did was bad, it appears to be a genetic, Zolaesque quality: 'I suppose I am a bad fellow – a damn bad fellow. I was born bad, and I have lived bad, and I shall die bad, in all probability' (Hardy, p. 60).

As Tess finally leaves Alec, denying him her mouth and the kiss of equal emotion, the allusion to Angel Clare appears again like some apparition with the acknowledgement of his father Mr Clare of Emminster. But the focus of this phase is not so much on the the disquisition of her relationship with Alec as it is a reformation of Tess's return home and what effect her return has on the family since the family is not at all happy to see her:

It would have been something like a story to come back with, if you had [married]! continued Mrs Durbeyfield, ready to burst into tears of vexation. 'After all the talk about yo and him which has reached us here, who would have expected it to end like this! Why didn't ye think of dong some good for your family instead o'thinking only of yourself? See how I've got to teave and slave, and your poor weak father with his heart clogged like a dripping-pan. I did hope for something to come out o'this!'

(Hardy, p. 63)

Her return diminishes the chances for the family's economic survival. 'You ought to have been more careful, if you didn't mean to get him to make you his wife!' (Hardy, p. 64) says Joan Durbeyfield which not only implants the fact that it is Tess's fault, but alternates the role of 'victim' projecting it onto the family as a collective unit rather than on Tess. The whole notion of 'victim' is crucial here because the word itself has Latinate origins at *victima*, an animal used as a sacrifice, a victim. And so this all becomes palpably clear: the animal in question, the sacrifice, is Tess who is victimized not only by Alec, but by her family both before she leaves and after she returns. For Tess, the return breeds nothing but a future of ennui: 'In place of the excitement of her return and the interest it had inspired, she saw before her a long and stony highway which she had to tread, without aid, and with little sympathy. Her depression was then terrible, and she could have hidden herself in a tomb' (Hardy, p. 65) and 'she looked at herself as a figure of Guilt intruding into the haunts of Innocence' (Hardy, p. 67). Clearly her reappearance is not cause for celebration since it unjustifiably brings hardship to the family.

Hardy then calculates what a woman in that position should require as an equitable punishment. Vexatious, presumably solipsistic, self-centered, the only pure punishment would be for her to lose the child she created. In the absence of her parents, in the absence of clergy, but in the presence of her siblings, she baptizes her dying child, SORROW, and we hear the echoes of Hardy as he writes: 'So passed away Sorrow the Undesired – that intrusive creature, that bastard gift of shameless Nature who respects not the social law; a waif to whom eternal Time had been a matter of days merely; who knew not that such things as years and centuries ever were; to whom the cottage interior was the universe, the week's weather climate, new-born babyhood human existence, an the instinct to suck human knowledge' (Hardy, p. 75).

The hypocrisy of the Church is beautifully exposed on the levels of both the sacred and the profane. On one level, that of the unsanctioned Baptism, the profane approach, done *without* the mediation of the church, the Vicar accepted; but the burial of the child was unacceptable, and though he said it would be 'just the same' in fact it wasn't by virtue of where and how the infant is buried. 'So the baby was carried in a small deal box, under an ancient woman's shawl, to the churchyard that night, and buried by lantern-light, at the cost of a shilling and a pint of beer to the sexton, in that shabby coner of God's allotment where He lets the nettles grow, and where all unbaptised infants, notorious drunkards, suicides, and others of the conjecturally damned are laid' (Hardy, p. 76).

The fact that Tess has suffered doubly (the rape, the death of her baby) only intensifies the Hardian notion of the absurdity of the human condition. In Hardy, we find the victimizer is not only, Alec, not only the family, but also the Church and, by extension, the system that exploits those on the margins.

'By experience,' says Roger Ascham, 'we find out a short way by a long wandering' (Hardy, p. 76). So does Hardy begin the end of the second phase. In short, Tess is on the road again. 'She had held so aloof of late that her trouble, never generally known was nearly forgotten in Marlott. But it became evident to her that she could never be really comfortable again in a place which had seen the collapse of her family's attempt to "claim kin" – and through her, even closer union – with the rich d'Urbervilles' (Hardy, pp. 77–8). It is time again for a 'new departure' and so her journey continues.

PHASE THE THIRD: THE RALLY

Tess's departure for the second time finally introduces her to Angel (Greek – *a messenger*) Clare (clear) whose description, of course, is totally different than Alec's. He is described in much gentler terms than Alec and he plays a harp (what Angel wouldn't) which is clearly ironic. Hardy describes him as:

Angel Clare rises out of the past not altogether as a distinct figure, but as an appreciative voice, a long regard of fixed, abstracted eyes, and mobility of mouth, somewhat too small and delicately lined for a man's, though with an unexpectedly firm close of the lower lip now and then; enough to do away with any inference of indecision. Nevertheless, something nebulous, pre-occupied, vague, in his bearing and regard, marked him as one who probably had no definite aim or concern about his material future. Yet as a lad people had said of him that he was one who might do anything if he tried. (Hardy, p. 89)

Two distinct items manifest themselves in this description: 1) the allusion to Lavater's essays on physiognomy and 2) the binary and proleptic visions of both Alec and Angel. In terms of the former, one reads in Hardy almost a preoccupation with the *lips* and *mouth* of his characters. Not only do we find Hardy spending a lot of time writing about Tess's lips and mouth, but he describes both Alec's and Angel's as well. Concerning Angel, Hardy's line '*mobility of mouth*, somewhat too small and delicately lined for a man's, though with an *unexpectedly firm close of the lower lip* now and then; *enough to do away with any inference of indecision*' seems a clear demonstration of what Lavater had set out in his essays. For example, from Lavater we read: 'When the under lip, with the teeth, projects horizontally, the half of the breadth of the mouth seen in profile, expect, allowing for other gradations, one of the four following qualities, or all the four, Stupidity, Rudeness, Malignity, Avarice' (Lavater, p. 474). If one recalls Hardy's depiction of Alec 'with full lips, *badly moulded*, though red and smooth' Lavater writes: 'All disproportion between the upper and under lip, is a sign of folly or wickedness' (Lavater, p. 475); and though Lavater writes practically nothing about the lips of women one can recall how Hardy describes Tess with a '*pouted-up deep red mouth* to which this syllable was native had hardly as yet settled into its definite shape, and *her lower lip had a way of thrusting the middle of her top one upward*, when they closed together after a word. Lavater issues no warrant for women with these lips, but he does write: 'If the manner of walking of a woman be disgust-ing, decidedly disgusting, not only disagreeable, but impetuous, without dignity, contemptible, verging sideways – let neither her beauty allure thee to her, nor her understanding deceive thee, nor the confidence she may seem to repose in thee, betray thee – her mouth will be like her gait; and her conduct harsh and false like her mouth' (Lavater, p. 482). Though Angel does not comment on Tess's gait, he does mention that 'He was surprised to find this young woman – who though but a milkmaid had just that touch of rarity about her which might make her the envied of the housemates – shaping such sad imaginings' (Hardy, p. 98). The description also sets up the rather obvious dichotomy with Alec, *the dark one*, set off against Angel, *the light one*, with Tess in the middle as the two of them apparently struggle for Tess's 'body and soul' and Hardy is not one to choose the most valuable to win.

Both Angel and Tess are, of course, smitten by each other and Hardy sets up a meeting between them in the following fashion:

> The outskirt of the garden Tess found herself had been left uncultivated for some years, and was now damp and rank with juicy grass which sent up mists of pollen at a touch, and with tall blooming weeds emitting offensive smells – weeds whose red and yellow and purple hues formed a polychrome as dazzling as that of cultivated flowers. She went stealthily as a cat through this profusion of growth, gathring cukoo-spittle on her skirts, cracking snails that were underfoot, staining her hands with thistle-milk and slug-slime, and rubbing off upon her naked arms sticky blights which, though snow-white on the appletree-trunks, made madder stains on her skin; thus she drew quite near to Clare, still unobserved of him.   (Hardy, p. 98)

No passage in *Tess* is more relevant than this one in terms of Hardy's poetics of sacrifice. For not only does Hardy 'play his hand' in a very self-reflexive non-self-reflexive way (as does Flaubert), but the passage underscores Tess as both victim *and* sacrifice. The passage itself could have been taken wholesale from Turgenev's *Rudin* in which two 'star-crossed lovers' meet at place of her choosing (a place descriptively laden with death and decay) for her to end the relationship. The difference here is the place has been created by Hardy and he has sacrificed Tess to make the journey to Angel as Angel is unaware of Tess's approach. The choice of words is not serendipitous: '*uncultivated*', '*damp*', '*rank*', '*weeds*', '*offensive smells*', '*cuckoo-spittle*', '*cracking snails*', '*stain[ed] her hands*', '*slug-slime*', '*sticky blights*', '*madder stains*'; this is the rather tortuous 'journey' Tess must make to reach Angel on the other side which he, in a sacred state of repose, strumming his harp, awaits her arrival. For Tess to reach Angel she must, of course, pass across yet another threshold. She is the active agent in this journey; Angel, the passive.

> He concluded his plaintive melody, a very simple performance, demanding no great skill; and she waited, thinking another might be begun. But, tired of playing, he had desultorily come round the fence, and was rambling up behind her. Tess, her cheeks on fire, moved away furtively as if hardly moving at all. Angel however saw her light summer gown; and he spoke, his low tones reaching her though he was some distance off.
>
> (Hardy, p. 97)

The two of them are finally drawn together, but not without the inevitable difficulties of social class and sexual experience to hinder their love. For it is Hardy who, upon discovering how much the other milkmaids are in love with Angel, stresses how 'self-sacrificing her [Tess's] mood' is and that she was well-aware 'to avoid compromising the happiness of either in the least degree' (Hardy, p. 110). It is clear that the notion of sacrifice has been engrained in her (if not all women of her generation if not all other generations) and the one thing that generally accompanies self-sacrifice is the guilt of not being able to sacrifice *more* or *not having sacrificed enough*. Tess, of course, suffers from the guilt of being Alec's woman and cannot accept Angel's love interest since he is essentially betrothed to another. 'And the thorny crown of this sad conception was that she whom he really did prefer in a cursory way to the rest, she who knew herself to be more impassioned in nature, cleverer, more beautiful than they, was in the eyes of propriety far less worthy of him than the homelier ones whom he ignored' (Hardy, p. 116).

But what we know of Clare is not altogether 'angelic' and his interest, if not Hardy's, in Tess's mouth borders on obsession.

> How very lovable her face was to him. Yet there was nothing ethereal about it: all was real vitality, real warmth, real incarnation. And it was in her mouth that this culminated. Eyes almost as deep and speaking he had seen before, and cheeks perhaps as fair; brows as arched, a chin and throat almost as shapely; her mouth he had seen nothing to equal on the face of the earth. To a young man with the least fire in him that little upward life in the middle of her red top lip was distracting, infatuating, maddening. He had never before seen a woman's lips and teeth which

forced his mind, with such persistent iteration, the old Eliza-
bethan simile of roses filled with snow. Perfect, he, as a lover,
might have called them off-hand. But no: they were not perfect.
And it was the touch of the imperfect upon the would-be perfect
that gave the sweetness, because it was that which gave the
humanity. Clare had studied those lips so many times that he
could reproduce them mentally with ease; and now, as they
again confronted him, clothed with colour and life, they sent an
aura over his flesh, a breeze through his nerves, which well-nigh
produced a qualm; and actually produced by some mysterious
physiological process, a prosaic sneeze.   (Hardy, p. 118).

And here we find a clear relationship between Angel and Alec. If
one recalls the scene of the British Queen strawberry these two
responses to Tess's mouth 'positions' her as not so much the *subject*
of desire, but the *object* of desire. For Alec, Tess and the strawberry
are, more or less, the same thing . . . some*thing* (emphasis on 'thing')
succulent and sweet. But Angel Clare too is not without his sexual
interests and the final passage of the phase indicates that and
inevitably leads up to the passage:

He had allowed her to free herself; and in a minute or two the
milking of each was resumed. Nobody had beheld the gravita-
tion of the two into one; and when the dairyman came round by
that screened nook, a few minutes later, there was not a sign to
reveal that the markedly sundered pair were more to each other
than mere acquaintances. Yet in the interval since Crick's last
view of them something had occurred which changed the pivot
of the universe for their two natures: something which, had he
known its quality, the dairyman would have despised, as a
practical man; yet which was based upon a more stubborn and
resistless tendency than a whole heap of so-called practicalities.
A veil had been whisked aside; the tract of each one's outlook
was to have a new horizon thenceforward – for a short time or
for a long.

(Hardy, p. 119).

Not only is there the reiteration of Tess's lips and mouth (that
which is both sensual and erotic), but also the reiteration of the
veil and all that the veil implies. That is, the veil being that gos-
samer threshold that exists between *the self* and *the other*, that
reduces the seduction, and keeps one pure. In ritualized marital

ceremonies the veil separates the betrothed from her suitor. She can be seen, but opaquely; she is cast in white; but, she cannot be touched. The man, of course, does not wear a veil since the veil is a curtain of sanctity, a register of property, which can only be raised after the proper vows have been administered. Ironically, as the veil is lifted, thus allowing the husband the right to 'kiss the lips' of the bride, he is also allowed, by the heavens, to take her virginity. In this case, the removal of the veil is also the right to take her virginity and with that the phase is concluded.

PHASE THE FOURTH: THE CONSEQUENCE

'The universe itself only came into being for Tess on the particular day in the particular year in which she was born' (Hardy, p. 121). This line relates to Hardy's notions of the incontrovertible and the accompanying authorial plot queries he uses throughout the novel, such as the lengthy, 'How then should he look upon her as of less consequence than himself; as a pretty trifle to caress and grow weary of; and not deal in the greatest seriousness with the affection which he knew that he had awakened in her – so fervid and so impressionable as she was under her reserve; in order that it might not agonize and wreck her?' (Hardy, p. 121) tend to reiterate what has been happening to her since the death of Prince and what is inevitably going to happen because of it.

In the romantic scheme of things, Clare renounces his interest in Mercy Chant for Tess; his family balks at the choice, but does not discount it, though Tess, still in her own guilt phase, declines his proposal which is only augmented by the fact: 'That she had already permitted him to make love to her and he read as an additional assurance, not fully trowing that in fields and pastures to "sigh gratis" is by no means deemed waste' (Hardy, p. 137). That she still considers herself a sacrificial being is reiterated when she says: 'I cannot bear to let anybody have him but me! Yet it is a wrong to him and may kill him when he knows! O my heart – O, O, O!' (Hardy, p. 140). Tess explains that the reason she cannot marry him is because of the D'Urberville ancestry since Clare has such disdain for the lineage and though she wants to tell him the truth, her mother says keep it a secret thereby extending the deception. Tess fully believes any one of the other milkmaids would, in fact, be a better choice since none of them, presumably, have an ancestral lineage equal to hers. So we find Tess in a very awkward predicament caught as she is between her heart and her guilt. But not only guilt: 'Her affection for him was now the breath and light of Tess's being: it enveloped her as a photosphere, irradiated her into forgetfulness of her past sorrows, keeping back the gloomy spectres that would persis in their attempts to touch her – doubt, fear, moodiness, care, shame. She knew that they were waiting like wolves just outside the circumscribing light, she had long spells of power to keep them in hungry subjection there' (Hardy, p. 153).

But Tess does not listen to her mother, since she cannot deceive 'and how she resolved with a bursting heart to tell her history to Angel Clare, despite her mother's command; to let him for whom she lived and breathed despise her if he would, and her mother regard her as a fool, rather than preserve a silence which might be deemed a treachery to him, and which somehow seemed a wrong to these' (Hardy, p. 157). So Tess, in being true to herself, would rather have her mother disdain her and her lover despise her than to live a lie. In that sense, she sacrifices herself once again for others.

Ironically, Hardy spends precious little time on the wedding itself. This is after Clare has proposed at least seven times to a reluctant Tess. Yet Hardy gives approximately one paragraph to the entire wedding ceremony and curiously avoids the consummating kiss. What Hardy does write is that: 'Clare knew that she loved him: every curve of her form showed that...' (Hardy, p. 167). The brevity of the ceremony is clearly in keeping with the tenor of phase, the consequence, and allows Hardy to register three distinct foreshadowings, all of which consume more space than the wedding, and which tend to extend that notion: the d'Urberville Coach, the crowing cock, the d'Urberville ancestral mansion.

Following the wedding, Clare tells Tess about the d'Urberville Coach. 'A certain d'Urberville of the sixteenth or seventeenth centuries committed a dreadful crime in his family coach; and since that time members of the family see or hear the old coach whenever –. But I'll tell you another day – it is rather gloomy. Evidently some dim knowledge of it has been brought back to your mind by the sight of this venerable caravan' (Hardy, p. 168). Anxious, Tess responds, 'Is it when we are going to die, Angel that members of my family see it? Or is it when we have committed a crime?' (Hardy, p. 168). Clare silences her anxieties with a kiss. As they leave the Crick farm we hear the cock crowing in the afternoon which, too, registers a bad omen and finally when they arrive at their honeymoon suite, Clare:

> found that the mouldy old habitation somewhat depressed his bride. When the carriage was gone they ascended the stairs to wash their hands, the charwoman showing the way. On the landing Tess stopped and started ... He looked up and perceived two life-size portraits on panels built into the masonry. As all visitors to the mansion are aware, these paintings represent women of middle age, of a date some two hundred years ago, whose lineaments once seen can never be forgotten. The long pointed features, narrow eye, and smirk of the one, so suggestive of merciless treachery; the bill-hook nose, large teeth, and bold eye of the other, suggesting arrogance to the point of ferocity, haunt the beholder afterwards in his dreams. (Hardy, p. 170)

These women, they are told, 'were ladies of the d'Urberville family', but it is also clear that Tess's 'fine features are unquestionably traceable in these exaggerated forms' (Hardy, p. 170). Certainly the combination of factors as Hardy has orchestrated them does not bode well for Tess. An abbreviated wedding ceremony, attended by no one in her family or his; allusions to the d'Urberville coach; a crowing cock in the afternoon; and, finally, the curious resemblance between the women on the wall and Tess. Certainly, there must be cause to pause at Hardy's sudden suggestion that in the beautiful Tess there are traces of the harridans in the portraits. Hardy is, in effect, suggesting his own physiognomy which may, in fact, relate to Lavater when he writes about the 'narrow eye', and 'smirk of the one', is suggestive of 'merciless treachery' and the 'bold eye of the other', suggesting 'arrogance to the point of ferocity'. As for the large teeth, neither Hardy nor Lavater have much to say about them directly. In Hardy's description one might tend to think of 'horse-teeth' and Lavater only discusses 'long teeth' and that those who have such teeth exhibit 'certain signs of weakness and pusillanimity' (Lavater, p. 395). Of the bill-hook nose Hardy says little, though by virtue of its shape (that is, not aquiline) the image, of course, is hawk-like. Lavater writes that 'noses which are much turned downwards are never truly good, truly cheerful, or noble, or great. Their thoughts and inclinations always tend to earth. They are close, cold, heartless, incommunicative; often maliciously sarcastic, ill humoured, or extremely hypochondriac, or melancholic' (Lavater, p. 472). Needless to say, the portrait Hardy paints of the d'Urberville women and the fact that Tess has traceable lines is a decidedly pointed attack on her character which runs counterpoint to how she thinks of herself.

The letter Tess writes to Clare, declaring all, is, of course, unread. 'There it was – sealed up, just as it had left her hands. The mountain had not yet been removed. She could not let him read it now, the house being in full bustle of preparation; and descending to her own room she destroyed the letter there' (Hardy, p. 165). Dramatically, the letter had to go unread because the mutual deception had to be revealed post- wedding. 'He then told her of that time of his life to which allusion has been made when, tossed about by doubts and difficulties in London, like a cork on the waves, he plunged into eight-and-forty hours' dissipation with a stranger' (Hardy, p. 177). This confession is met by 'O Angel – I am almost glad – because now *you* can forgive *me*! I have not made my confession. I have a confession, too – remember, I said so' (Hardy, p. 177). However, though Clare's deception and subsequent confession is countered with Tess's deception and confession, one discovers that all confessions are not equal; some are more equal than others, especially in terms of the power base. The phase concludes with Hardy, clearly projecting the visions of the d'Urberville portraits on Tess:

> A large shadow of her shape rose upon the wall and ceiling. She bent forward, at which each diamond on her neck gave a sinister wink like a toad's; and pressing her forehead against his temple she entered on her story of her acquaintance with Alec d'Urberville and its results, murmuring the words without flinching, and with her eyelids drooping down.   (Hardy, p. 177).

PHASE THE FIFTH: THE WOMAN PAYS

The Consequence of the previous phase is, presumably, Tess's confession while, curiously, the result of the confession is *The Woman Pays*. 'A sinister wink like a toad's' not only positions Tess as a part of that evil empire that is the d'Urberville family, but situates her as being something 'other worldly'. Hardy has clearly foregrounded the inevitable dessication of Tess's future and also makes of her a character totally unlike the one she is. To Tess's beseeching for forgiveness, Clare responds: 'O Tess, forgiveness does not apply to the case. You were one person: now you are another. My God – how can forgiveness meet such a grotesque – prestidigitation as that!' (Hardy, p. 179). And farther on he says, 'I repeat, the woman I have been loving is not you' but, 'another woman in your shape' (Hardy, p. 179). And if that were not enough: 'He looked upon her as a species of imposter; a guilty woman in the guise of an innocent one' (Hardy, p. 179). The association with 'magic' fits in precisely with Hardy's allusion to sinisterial frogs for Clare accuses Tess not only of 'prestidigitation' (and *grotesque* prestidigitation at that) but also of assuming another 'shape'. Both of these magical acts one can easily associate with witchcraft and the allusion to Tess as a witch or wicca is clearly apparent.

'It is claimed that a magician can be recognized by certain physical peculiarities, with which he is branded and by which his calling may be discovered should he attempt to conceal it. It is thought, for example, that the pupils of a magician's eyes have swallowed up the iris, or that his visual images are produced back to front... All over the world there are people who have a peculiarly cunning look, who appear odd or untrustworthy, who blink at one strangely. It is summed up in the idea of the "evil eye" and applies to persons who are feared and suspected' (Mauss, p. 27). In addition to the magician having power over objects, the magician has 'power over his own being and this is the prime source of his strength' (Mauss, p. 33). So the prestidigitation, the 'sleight of hand', is, of course, related to Tess's seeming ability to be something other than what she is which, in effect, relates to the notion of shape-shifting a process of witchcraft which Clare accuses her of enacting. Shape-shifting is, 'in fact, a kind of splitting in two which involves animal disguises, and while the metamorphosis seems to involve two formal beings, they are, in essence, still one... The metamorphosis among European witches does not involve indiscriminate shape-changing. They usually stick to one animal – a mare, a frog, a cat, etc. These facts lead us to suppose that shape-changing involves a regular association with a single species of animal' (Mauss, pp. 35–6). Granted, there is only the allusion to 'frogs' in the relationship between the diamonds and the toad's sinister wink, a metonymic device that is substituted for Tess, but it is evident that the metamorphosis is an evil one. Likewise, one finds that if Tess has shifted her shape, so too has Angel. In a curious set of circumstances, the fact that Tess is not Tess, but another woman results in Clare not being Clare, but another Clare. The former Clare, lover, confidant, has now been transformed into Clare the victim. What has been shifted is the nexus of victimization. Tess[a], who was victimized, becomes Tess[b] by virtue of telling the truth whereas Clare[a], who asks forgiveness by virtue of telling the truth, becomes Clare[b], the victim. As the shape-shifting witch, Tess has, in effect, transformed Clare into the victim and he is clear on this point as the notions of deceit are raised for Tess says: 'What have I done. What *have* I done? I have not told of anything that interferes with or belies my love for you. You don't think I planned it, do you? It is in your own mind, what you are angry at, Angel; it is not in me. O it is not in me, and I am not that deceitful woman you think me!' (Hardy, pp. 181–2) Clare hesitates, but rejoins with: 'H'm – well. Not deceitful, my wife; but not the same. No: not the same' (Hardy, p. 182).

And even though Clare admits, 'You were more sinned against than sinning' he cannot overcome his own prejudices. So, her confession is dismissed and she is looked upon as 'the belated seedling of an effete aristocracy'. So Clare's liberal views are a bit whitewashed. The fact that he sees her as an 'another woman in your shape' only augments the notion of perception at which time Hardy narrates a tale told by a cottager in which he says he overheard Tess saying: 'I don't see how I can help being the cause of much misery to you all your life. The river is down there: I can put an end to myself in it. I am not afraid ... I will leave something to show that I did it myself – on account of my shame. They will not blame you then.' (Hardy, p. 183) which continues her almost vital need to sacrifice herself for others.

As Clare descends the staircase, the refrain of the d'Urberville dames appears again with 'The Caroline bodice of the portrait was low – precisely as Tess's had been when he tucked it in to show the necklace; and again he experienced the distressing sensation of a resemblance between them' (Hardy, p. 184). What is curious here is how Hardy abrogates his stance on Tess's beauty from the moment she reveals herself as being 'tainted'. He alludes to her physical similarities with the d'Urberville dames which is completely inconsistent with the temperament of the descriptive prose up to that time. The fact he iterates the same position when Clare descends the stairs is a self-conscious failing.

Tess augments the notion of self-sacrifice when she alludes once again to suicide to which Angel responds: 'Now listen to this. You must not dare to think of such a horrible thing! How could you! You will promise me as your husband to attempt that no more.' 'I am ready to promise. I saw how wicked it was'. 'Wicked! The idea was unworthy of you beyond description' (Hardy, p. 187). Soon thereafter one reads the foreshadowing of what is to come when Clare says 'If he (Alec) were dead it might be different' (Hardy, p. 190). But two things are implied here: 1) things might be *different* if he were dead, but 2) things might not necessarily be *better*. So to Clare, Tess's confession detonates the *image* he has of her, her *form*, and changes it to something else. In terms of commodification, she becomes a 'used vessel' not unlike the utilitarian vessel Gudrun was to Gerald. Prior to her confession Tess is virgin, pristine, unused, a 'commodity' with enormous use-value; after the confession she becomes stained, sullied, used, and as such her value is attenuated. To look at her purely in terms of a double-standard misses the point. Women have historically been considered inferior and as such were to be used to the superior's advantage. For her *value* to be taken by someone else renders her practically useless to Clare since not only is Alec her natural husband, but her owner which accounts for the fact that Alec's interest in her is constant. Not for her sake, but for what she represents.

Subsequent to their separation, Tess, once again, returns home, to be greeted by: 'O you little fool – you little fool!' (Hardy, p. 201) Tess counters with: '"I know it, I know, I know!" she gasped through her sobs. "But O my mother, I could not help it, he was so good – and I felt the wickedness of trying to blind him as to what had happened. If – if – it were to be done again – I should do the same. I could not – I dared not – so sin – against him!"' (Hardy, p. 201). So once again the family, in the voice of Joan, has been disappointed by Tess. Encouraged to deceive, Tess tells the truth and 'pays the price'. Not only that, but the family has, in effect, banished her entirely from their collective life. 'Her old bed had been adapted for two younger children. There was no place here for her now' (Hardy, p. 202) and when her father appears Mrs Durbeyfield informs him that 'no letter [from Tess] has come, but Tess *unfortunately* [my emphasis] has come herself' (Hardy, p. 202).

Though Clare does provide for Tess financially (though rather niggardly in terms of forver) he encourages her to apply to his father if she needs to, but that is beyond Tess's ability and Clare should know that. Tess gives Joan half of the fifty pounds Clare has given to her then sets off yet again. This is the third time Tess has left home: 1) to visit the Stoke-D'Urbervilles; 2) to work for them; 3) to seek work with Marian and each time it has been for her to secure employment that would, primarily, assist the family and only marginally assist Tess. In subsequent correspondence, it is always Tess's mother who urges her to assist them financially and it is always Tess who somehow manages to pay. 'Tess had thirty pounds coming to her almost immediately from Angel's bankers; and the case being so deplorable, as soon as the sum was received she sent the twenty as requested. Part of the remainder she was obliged to expend in winter clothing; leaving only a nominal sum for the whole inclement season at hand' (Hardy, p. 214). Each time she is sent out once again to sacrifice herself for the sanctity of the 'domestic community'. It is not coincidental then that we get the scene:

> Under the trees several pheasants lay about, their rich plumage dabbled with blood; some were dead, some feebly twitching a wing, some staring up at the sky, some pulsating quickly, some contorted, some stretched out – all of them writhing in agony except the fortunate ones whose tortures had ended during the night by the inability of nature to bear more.   (Hardy, p. 218)

The scene only validates what has been happening to Tess all along and:

> With the impulse of a soul who could feel for kindred sufferers as much as for herself, Tess's first thought was to put the still living birds out of their torture, and to this end with her own hands she broke the necks of as many as she could find, leaving them to lie where she had found them till the gameskeepers should come, as they probably would come, to look for them a second time.
>
> (Hardy, p. 219)

Not only are these mercy killings, not only does she sacrifice her feelings to put the birds out of their own misery, but she is feeling guilty for her own woes and yet her woes continue since 'Tess hoped for some accident that might favour her; but nothing favoured her' (Hardy, p. 234) as she moves on to meet Marian.

At this point, Hardy sets up the stark contrast, contrived to be sure, 'forced' to use Stevenson's word, by presenting Farmer Groby and Flintcomb-Ash in counterpoint to Dairyman Crick and Talbothays. As Tess reaches the dairy farm Hardy writes of the place: 'These myriads of cows stretching under her eyes from the far east to the far west outnumbered any she had ever seen at one glance before. The green lea was speckled as thickly with them as a canvas by Van Alsloot or Sallaert with burghers. The ripes hues of the red and dun kine absorbed the evening sunlight, which the white-coated animals returned to the eye in rays most dazzling, even at the distant elevation on which she stood' (Hardy, p. 80). The meadow matches the mood and prefigures her meeting with Angel Clare. Subsequent to the separation as Tess approaches the farm we read: 'Here the air was dry and cold, and the long cart-roads were blown white and dusty within a few hours after rain. There were few trees, or none, those that would have grown in the hedges being mercilessly plashed down with the quickset by the tenant-farmers, the natural enemies of tree, bush, and brake' (Hardy, p. 220). Likewise, the intensity of the labour matches the mood of the respective manager: at Talbothays, milking was as docile as Crick himself; at Flintcomb-Ash, 'the stubborn soil' was as recalcitrant as Groby. In effect, Tess once again is sacrificed. The questions beg themselves: Cannot love be found in hazardous surroundings? Must love comply with the smooth gradations and soft contours of the land? Is pain and suffering the consequence of pain and suffering? According to Hardy: no, yes and yes.

PHASE THE SIXTH: THE CONVERT

This transfiguration of Alec from dandy to evangelist is purely superficial, a chicanery that only enhances the notion of deception that has been present throughout the novel; his quasi-religious rebirth (curiously inspired by Clare's father) is only fleeting since Alec soon abandons it. The entire chapter is devoted to Alec's attempts to regain Tess and he does so by any and all methods at his disposal. But one also sees a 'converted' Tess as well when she says: 'You, and those like you, take your fill of pleasure on earth by making the life of such as me bitter and black with sorrow; and then it is a fine thing, when you have had enough of that, to think of securing your pleasure in heaven by becoming converted. Out upon such – I don't believe in you – I hate it!' (Hardy, p. 242). She also says she does not believe in his conversion. She stares at him. ' "Don't look at me like that" he said abruptly ... Tess ... instantly withdrew the large dark gaze of her eyes' (Hardy, p. 243) which is a refrain of the 'evil eye' that Hardy alludes to earlier.

But Alec is not one to give up easily. Alec attempts to undermine Clare then intensifies 'the chase' when he plays on Tess's guilt feelings yet again: ' "Tess, my girl, I was on the way to, at least, social salvatin till I saw you again." He smiled, shaking her as if she were a child. "And why then have you tempted me? I was firm as a man could be till I saw those eyes and that mouth again – surely there never was such a maddening mouth since Eve's" ... "You temptress, Tess; you dear damned witch of Babylon – I could not resist you as soon as I met you again!" ' (Hardy, p. 254). It is at this point where Alec and Angel coalesce. Just as Angel perceived Tess as 'witchlike', so too does Alec perceive her as 'temptress'. Neither male is interested in assuming personal responsibility for his actions and Tess, once again, becomes a scapegoat for their individual failings.

Alec perseveres by constantly wanting to minister to her needs and her family's. But we know that his interests are purely selfish and if we have any question about it we should know better when Alec appears with pitch fork in hand and as 'the fire flared up' she beheld Alec's face. Hence the allusion to the Satanic which too fits in with the allusion to Milton and paradise (lost). Being Satanic, Alec finishes the tale of the D'Urberville Coach as if he were Angel's echo that 'It is that this sound of a non-existent coach can only be heard by one of d'Urberville blood, and it is held to be of ill-omen to the one who hears it. It has to do with a murder, committed by one of the family, centuries ago' (Hardy, p. 279); the telling of the tale truly seals his fate. His association with evil and death is shown again when the ubiquitous Alec shows up at the d'Urberville crypt eliciting Tess's exhortation, 'Why am I on the wrong side of this door!' It is not a question, but an exclamation. She is clearly caught between wanting to exist on her own terms and being sacrificed by 'destiny' to play out a role she does not want to play.

PHASE THE SEVENTH: THE FULFILMENT

Back from Brazil, Angel returns to rescue his bride from the evil Alec. Mrs Derbyfield reluctantly gives Clare Tess's whereabouts because she is not at all sure about what is going to happen by giving him the information. Joan candidly admits that 'I have never really known her [Tess]' (Hardy, p. 295) which is about as startling a bit of information as one has read in the novel. Presumably, she has known her well enough to use her, to sacrifice her, but, curiously, none of the other children are sacrificed. By this time Abraham is thirteen and Liza is over sixteen, yet, presumably, they are incapable of fulfiling the economic interests of the family as well as Tess. Presently, Joan and her family are financially secure owing to their sacrificial sell-out of Tess to Alec. Joan's reluctance is based solely on the possibility that leaking information to Clare may jeopardize financial solvency. Angel discovers Tess, but before Angel is dismissed, Tess exposes her heretofore hidden feelings which augment the notions of innocence and deception that have been played out in the entire novel. The motive for the murder becomes patently clear when Tess answers Alec's caustic reprisals:

'And then my dear dear husband came home to me...and I did not know it...and you had used your cruel persuasion upon me...you did not stop using it – no – you did not stop! My little sisters and brother, and my mother's needs....they were the things you moved me by...and you said my husband would never come back – never; and you taunted me, and said what a simpleton I was to expect him...And at last I believed you and gave way!...And then he came back! Now he is gone, gone! A second time, and I have lost him now for ever...and he will not love me the littlest bit ever any more – only hate me...O yes, I have lost him now – again because of you'.   (Hardy, p. 300)

The murder is inevitable since it has already been foreshadowed. 'do you know what I have been running after you for? To tell you that I have killed him!' (Hardy, p. 303) which is the answer to question Angel posed earlier. No aberration in the d'Urberville strain here, this is justifiable homicide which naturally leads to the ultimate of self-sacrifices and as such could only lead the reader to Stonehenge and the *fulfillment* of the sacrifice. Fulfillment of the sacrifice since fulfillment is to be filled and there is nothing but sacrifice to fill up Tess's life. Tess flings herself on an oblong slab (which recalls Alec on the tomb); Angel puts his cloak (shroud) on top of her as Tess says: 'She [Liza-Lu] is so good, and simple and pure...O Angel – I wish you would marry her, if you lose me, as you will do shortly. O if you would!...She has all the best of me without the bad of me; and if she were to become yours it would almost seem as if death had not divided us...' (Hardy, p. 311). The statement augments the totally self-sacrificing person Tess is and after the police discover her she is ready for what will happen to her. She has accepted her fate. She is hanged and in a rather macabre bit of irony, Angel joins Tess's sister.

What Hardy has done here is to create a 'pure' character and put her into a situation of earthly delights. Something akin to a painting by Bosch. It is the purity of evil that overtakes and destroys the purity of innocence. The phases in Tess's journey are clear:

1. The maiden – virgin innocence
2. Maiden no more – innocence lost; experience gained
3. The rally – the emergence of Clare
4. The consequence – of being a maiden no more
5. The woman pays – the confession
6. The convert – her conversion from innocence
7. Fulfillment – spiritual not physical

In terms of the Campbellian quest, we find there is a separation, initiation, and a return. The fact that Hardy has called these episodes 'phases' lends some credibility to that kind of movement. Certainly Hardy sets Tess on a quest. She begins as a maiden, is separated from that innocence and initiated into the world from which she gains the knowledge of good and evil and returns as someone else. But Hardy does not treat Tess kindly. Not only is she hanged for what could be perceived today as 'justifiable homicide' in relation to being physically abused, but after her death, Hardy has Clare marry her sister. On one level we can see that 'rebounded marriage' as Clare's attempt to recapture Tess, but on another level it can be seen as the ultimate irony in that Tess's sister got what she could never have despite her honesty, purity and self-sacrificing nature.

But Tess's threnodies are pervasive. Tess pleads plagently throughout. What one finds in much of Hardy criticism is some facile-minded notion that Tess is a mature woman. Hardy is clear on this point. She verges on womanhood in body only; she still talks, thinks and acts like an adolescent. Her 'sin' is the sin of ignorance, of the sublime adherence to trust, and the malady of being duped by someone like Alec. Certainly her execution is unjust despite the

Saturday Review article of 1892 in which the reviewer writes: 'Still, Mr Hardy did well to let her pay the full penalty, and not die among the monoliths of Stonehenge, as many writers would have done' (Hardy, p. 384). How express and admirable. She is, in fact, hanged because she is an uneducated working girl who, because she is seduced, raped, tormented and abused by the son of a retired manufacturer, decides to rid herself of being the object of subjugation and impose a sense of moral justice ignored by the social system that imposed it. Regardless of Hardy's admission that 'I could not help myself. I hate the optimistic grin which ends a story happily, merely to suit conventional ideas' (Hardy, p. 388) Hardy sacrifices her throughout the novel. Not only is she sacrificed by her family for financial interests, and by Alec and Clare for sexual or philosophical interests, but by Hardy for poetic interests. Hardy writes a poetics of the land, of social and religious casuistry, but there is an unmistakable, unmisprisionable poetics of sacrifice which renders Tess a victim of circumstance and the circumstance is clearly a product of her gender.

6

The Poetics of Peripatetics and Peripety in Hamsun's *Hunger*

Published in 1890, *Hunger* is probably Hamsun's best known and, arguably, his best written novel. Sizeably autobiographical, it deals with the time Hamsun existed in Kristiania (Oslo) and is extraordinary in terms of psychological depth and poetic temperament. But one cannot easily dismiss the effect starvation had on Hamsun and to that extent one cannot discount intentionality. As Robert Ferguson writes of *Hunger* in his biography, *Enigma: The Life of Knut Hamsun*: 'In writing it he drew on the experiences he underwent during his two most desperate periods in Kristiania in the winters of 1880–81 and 1885–86, and probably, also drew on the experiences of his winter in Chicago in 1886–87. The many small correspondences of fact and fiction – the narrator's visit to the castle, for example, and his address at Tomtegaten II – as well as the autobiographical details that crop up in letters to Erik Frydenlund and Johan Sørensen, indicate that the book is Hamsun's self-portrait in fiction' (Ferguson, p. 110). Implicit in that notion is that the voice of the protagonist is often the voice of Hamsun not only in terms of content, 'The things I have written about in Hunger I have experienced here – and many more worse things besides. God how I have suffered. But I live...' (Hamsun, Naess and McFarlane [hereafter *Letters*], 97), but in terms of poetics, 'My book! My book! About these delicate nuances. I would want to sift through the remotest nuances of the mind – I would let them listen to the mimosa's breathing – every word like brilliantly white wings – movements on the shining surface of language' (Hamsun, *Letters*, p. 88).

The course of the novel follows the nameless protagonist as he virtually wanders throughout the city while dwelling on the notions of life, death, homelessness, hunger and art all within the confines of the city's ethos. What one discovers about the character, if not with all people who are homeless, impoverished, and hungry, is that their *raison d'être* is a kind of survival, contingent on mobility. That is, without mobility they are effectively doomed to perish, death being the virtue of stasis. It is only this ability to move, to push a shopping cart, or carry a knapsack, or just be able to walk, that enables them to survive. In that course of that mobilization, at least in the protagonist's case, one sees two distinct features at work – peripatetics and peripety – since both notions are clearly formulated in Hamsun's *Hunger* and in his nameless hero.

What one knows of things peripatetic, (from the Greek *peripatetikos*, given to walking about), relate, of course, to Aristotle and to the school of the same name. The legend, fictional as it must be, registers that Aristotle taught and walked through the loggia of the school and hence the school became know as the Peripatos. But 'the extant "lives" are without exception late; they were written, or rather compiled, many centuries after Aristotle's death, in the late Roman period; their sources are uncertain and, at best, even these go back to Hellenistic times' (Grayeff, p. 13). But in a curious way there is a distinct relationship between the things peripatetic and with peripety (Greek *peripeteia*, a sudden change esp. that on which the plot of a tragedy hinges), and their connection between wandering and philosophizing. One discovers that the notion of things peripatetic, of things itinerant, applies with extended regularity to Hamsun's urban alienated protagonist who does, in fact, tend to philosophize whether hungry or temporarily sated. Likewise, he experiences peripety with a certain amount of regularity and the peripety sustains him in order that he may carry on with his work.

What is significant about the title of the novel is that the word, *hunger*, operates on several levels: hunger is obviously the physiologically painful sensation caused by lack of food, but it can also be strong desire or craving. So is the hunger a craving for food only or for something else? If the former, the food sates the hunger, but the hero is not satisfied with merely being sated. If the latter, what else is it? A hunger for death? Spirituality? Art? There is something to say for all of these things in *Hunger*, for all of them are attributable to it.

The novel begins as a memoir: 'It was in those days when I wandered about hungry in Kristiania, that strange city which no one leaves before it has set its mark upon him...' (Hamsun, p. 3). And the ellipsis, the leap or sudden passage from one topic to another, lets the reader know that the hero has not succumbed to starvation. From the opening lines one realizes that although it is a memoir, a recollection, the past events are revivified by the way Hamsun records them: 'Lying awake in my attic room, I hear a clock strike six downstairs' (Hamsun, p. 3). Even though this is a recollection of past events, the experience lingers on in the present. The relationship between past and present, between the events of the past and the re-experiencing of those events in the present is crucial in Hamsun's poetics. For in addition to the preoccupation the protagonist has with 'space' (he constantly tells us where he is going) he is also preoccupied with 'time' (he constantly informs us of the time of day) for in the daily exercise of someone who is homeless there are three main constituents: where one is, what time of day it is, and what one is thinking during the day. One's thoughts can be as desultory as one's movements and are as varied as the vagabond himself. But if one's thoughts revolve around one's station and how one got to be in that station, then the thoughts can be as varied as one's attitude towards philosophy or death or the absence of God. Perhaps one has a daily route one follows or perhaps one merely moves vagrantly, as one might expect from a wanderer. In any case, what is established is the necessity to establish cause and to dwell on one's reason for being.

As the novel opens, it is six in the morning. Our hero's wall is papered with old issues of the *Morning Times* and ads from both the Director of Lighthouses and Fabian Olsen, Baker as well as from 'Shrouds at Madam Andersen's'. Certainly the juxtaposition of these four items has not been made precipitously and the connection among 'light' and 'bread' and 'death' is not a serendipitous one on Hamsun's part. As a matter of fact, the foundation for the entire novel rests on the notions of light and bread and death since they are part of the wandering process that the protagonist experiences. 'Autumn had arrived, that lovely cool time of year when everything turns colour and dies...This empty room, where the floor rocked up and down at every step I took, was like a horrible, broken-down coffin' (Hamsun, p. 4). It is also early in the novel that the protagonist's appeals to the divine begin. These are appeals for either divine intervention or divine understanding or divine apprehension as in: 'God knows, I thought, if there is any point to my looking for work anymore!' (Hamsun, p. 4) and as the novel proceeds the supplications often become invectives though the protagonist never entirely loses faith even while he is in the process of denouncing it.

The conflicting notions of life and death persist as one also discovers that, 'All summer long I had haunted the cemeteries and
Palace Park, where I would sit and prepare articles for the news-
papers, column after column about all sorts of things – strange
whimsies, moods, caprices of my restless brain' (Hamsun, p. 5).
At this point one discovers that the act of writing is not peripheral
to the protagonist's hunger. As a matter of fact, the act of writing,
the art of writing, is fundamental to the novel since the novel is not
only about hunger, spiritual and physical, but about the art of
writing.

Then it is nine o'clock in the morning. Three hours have passed
and 'Nothing was further from my mind than just taking a morning walk in the fresh air' (Hamsun, p. 5). At this point the wandering begins in earnest. Only capable of thinking about his hunger 'If
only one had a bite to eat on such a clear day!' (Hamsun, p. 6) he
'looked up – the clock in the tower of Our Saviour's showed ten.
Continuing through the streets, I roamed about without a care in
the world, stopped at a corner without having to, turned and went
down a side street without an errand there. I went with the flow,
borne from place to place this happy morning, rocking serenely to
and fro among other happy people' (Hamsun, p. 6). The protagonist is very specific about where he goes and what he is doing there.
Whether it be trailing a cripple or hastening to a pawnbroker, each
movement is a calculated movement; each movement is done with
some measure of purpose; each movement is not done for the
simple sake of moving, but to accomplish some daily task and at
the same time to think about the measure of what one has accomplished. Yet as one reads on, the deleterious effects of hunger affect
him: aches in his ribs, pelvis, lower extremities; he is consumed by
nervous excitement, extreme irritability, there is the loosening of
social bonds, the lessening of morale; apathy appears, mental
depression, nausea, lack of concentration, lack of ambition, melancholy, submissiveness, all exhibit themselves as being directly
influenced by hunger. Curiously, sexual indifference is not
included. But one sees influences in the manner in which Hamsun
alters the focus of the paragraph:

> Once I had pulled through, I certainly didn't want to owe any-
> body a blanket; I might start an article this very day about the
> crimes of the future or the freedom of the will, anything what-
> ever, something worth reading, something I would get at least

> ten kroner for ... And at the thought of this article I instantly felt
> an onrush of desire to begin right away, tapping my chock-full
> brain. I would find myself a suitable place in Palace Park and not
> rest till it was finished.   (Hamsun, p. 7)

There is absolutely no causal connection between the blanket and
the article, nothing to stimulate the thought of it and just as quickly
the thought is dispelled. After finally getting a bite to eat at Palace
Hill 'my courage rose markedly; I was no longer satisfied with
writing an article about something so elementary and straightforward as crimes of the future, which anybody could guess, or
simply learn by reading history. I felt capable of a greater effort
and, being in the mood to surmount difficulties, decided upon a
three-part monograph about philosophical cognition' (Hamsun, p.
9). After he eats, he discards the idea of 'crimes of the future' for a
more difficult enterprise dealing with Kant and Renan. Naturally,
he says, he would 'deal a deathblow to Kant's sophistries' (Hamsun, p. 10) though one might be hard-pressed to decipher what
sophistries he is talking about; however, one may speculate that the
link between Kant and Renan appears to be their representative
positions on the existence of God and how those philosophies
relate to the protagonist. Then, with another ellipsis, he discovers
that his pencil is gone. He pleads to God again, 'God, how everything I touched seemed bent on going wrong' (Hamsun, p. 10) and
he attempts to recover the pencil forgotten at the pawn shop. As he
does, he decides not to attack Kant, and says 'I just had to make an
imperceptible detour when I came to the problem of time and
space' (Hamsun, p. 10), but he 'wouldn't have to answer for
Renan, that old parson' (Hamsun, p. 10). Hamsun's choice is not
serendipitous. Of course, the peripatetic hero not only philosophizes, but intends to write on philosophical issues (clearly an
un-commercial exercise) and the issues he chooses to write about
are integral to the hero's character and his journey. Hamsun's
choices here beg a kind of decomposition.

Certainly one of the things that brings both Kant and Renan
together are their approaches to the existence of God. Kant's *Der
einzig mögliche Beweisgrun* (*The One Possible Basis for a Demonstration
of the Existence of God*), is the fundamental underpinning of the
Critique of Pure Reason published two decades later. Simply formulated, the work consists of three sections which put forward the
ground of proof, the utility of the proof and the reasons which

demonstrate the existence of God, but Kant also leads with a dis-
claimer that 'The rule of thoroughness does not always require that
every concept, in even the most profound essay, be developed or
defined; particularly if one may be assured that the clear, common
concept can cause no misunderstanding where it is used' (Kant,
p. 53). But Kant's 'strategy is to show that God is necessary because
some things are possible' (Kant, p. 14). To that end, 'it is not possible
for there to be nothing, for the very possibility of total non-being
would itself have to be at least a possibility. If sheer non-being is
impossible, whatever is requisite as ground for even the possibility
of anything is necessary' (Kant, p. 14). That the protagonist talks
about Kant's sophisms can only be taken in the context in which he
is referring to Kant (that is, in relation to God). If Kant speaks in
sophisms it is purely in relation to the existence of God and since
God is fundamentally indifferent to the protagonist's welfare, the
existence of Kant's God is not co-existent with the protagonist's
notions of God. What is curious is that the protagonist eventually
recants and decides not to 'deal a deathblow to Kant's sophisms'
since it could be avoided by an imperceptible detour 'when I came
to the problem of time and space'. One might ask why he would
avoid dealing with issues of time and space since time and space are
all he owns. In terms of pure reason, philosophers in Kant's time
(Descartes, Spinoza, Leibniz) agreed that pure reason could prove
the existence of God and the nature of the soul. With Kant's *Critique
of Pure Reason* all Rational sciences came under scrutiny.

Perhaps the answer comes from Kant himself. In the *Critique of
Pure Reason, First Section of the Transcendental Aesthetic, §2. Of Space*,
he writes: 'Space is represented as an infinite given quantity. Now it
is quite true that every concept is to be thought as a representation,
which is contained in an infinite number of different possible representations (as their common characteristic), and therefore comprehends them: but no concept, as such, can be thought as if it
contained in itself an infinite number of representations. Nevertheless, space is so thought (for all parts of infinite space exist simultaneously). Consequently, the original representation of space is an
intuition a priori, and not a concept' (Kant, p. 63). In the *Second
Section of the Transcendental Aesthetic, §4. Of Time*, Kant writes:
'Time is not an empirical concept deduced from any experience,
for neither coexistence nor succession would enter into our perception, if the representation of time were not given *a priori*. Only when
this representation *a priori* is given, can we imagine that

certain things happen at the same time (simultaneously) or at different times (successively)' (Kant, p. 67). Clearly both of these examples indicate why Hamsun's protagonist (or anyone else starving to death) would indeed make a detour around Kant's notions of space and time especially in how it relates to notions of the divine; however, Renan is another story.

Renan did not believe in a transcendent and personal God. Borrowing the 'three age' theory from Cousin, Renan believed in the final age of man to be both scientific and religious and believed in the clear scientific action of a universe in which there was no perceptible action of a free will superior to man. According to Renan, mankind 'had been pictured by classical historians in terms of an absolute, fixed, static being, the great advance of the nineteenth-century historical thought lies in "substituting the category of *becoming* (*devenir*) for that of *being* (*être*), the conception of the *relative* (*relatif*) for that of the *absolute* (*absolu*), and movement for immobility"' (Chadbourne, p. 50). Renan 'conceives of God no longer as a personal being, absolute and eternal, but as a spiritual reality emerging from human history. "What else is God for humanity except the transcendent sum of its spiritual needs, the category of the ideal, the form under which we conceive the ideal, just as space and time are categories or forms under which we conceive physical bodies"' (Chadbourne, p. 50). Renan objected to the transcendental because, for him, knowledge of reality was obtained through observation and the verification of empirical hypotheses. Positive knowledge of reality must have an experimental basis and that was why the enlightened man could not believe in God since a being who does not reveal himself by any act is for science a being that does not exist. The occurrence of divine intervention has never been proved yet the empirical evidence does not preclude the act of faith and this is exactly the conundrum the character is faced with and that is why he decides to avoid dealing with Kant and take issue with Renan. On the face of it the selection appears quite arbitrary, but subsequently the true significance of choosing these two philosophers becomes quite clear.

But whatever the choice, 'what had to be done was to write an article filling so and so many columns; the unpaid rent and my landlady's long looks when I met her on the stairs in the morning, tormented me all day and popped up even in my happy moments, when there wasn't another dark thought in my head' (Hamsun; p. 10).

In order to finish his article he needs the pencil and with that pencil he had 'written my monograph about philosophical cognition in three volumes' (Hamsun, p. 14). Hadn't the pawnbroker heard of it? So not only does the 'lie' establish the protagonist as a kind of literary provocateur, it also establishes the need, the hunger, he has to write. By now it is twelve noon and as he walks down Karl Johan Street, by the University, and wanders up Palace Hill he begins to think about his present circumstances in relation to the 'happy' people he sees on the street. At this point the apparent philosophical digression becomes specific and the ambivalence comes to fruition.

Coddling myself with this thought I found that a terrible injustice had been done to me. Why had these last few months been so exceedingly rough on me?... What was the matter with me? Had the Lord's finger pointed at me? But why exactly me?... why precisely I should have been chosen as a guinea pig for a caprice of divine grace...I wandered about debating this matter, unable to get it out of my mind; I discovered the weightiest objections to the Lord's arbitrariness in letting me suffer for everybody else's sake...What if God simply intended to annihilate me? I stood up and paced back and forth in front of my bench...The thought of God began to occupy me again. It seemed to me quite inexcusable of him to meddle every time I applied for a job and thus upset everything, since all I was asking for was my daily bread...I felt increasingly bitter toward God for his continual oppressions. If he meant to draw me closer to himself and make me better by torturing me and casting adversity in my way, he was simply mistaken, that I could vouch for. *And* nearly crying with defiance, I looked up toward heaven and told him so once and for all, inwardly...Had not my heavenly Father provided for me as he had for the sparrows of the air, *and* had he not shown me the grace of pointing at his humble servant? God had stuck his finger down into the network of my nerves *and* gently, quite casually, brought a little confusion among the threads. *And* God had withdrawn his finger *and* behold! there were fibres *and* delicate filaments on his finger from the threads of my nerves. *And* there was a gaping hole after his finger, which was God's finger, *and* wounds in my brain from the track of his finger. But where God had touched me with the finger of his hand he let me be *and* touched me no more, *and* allowed no evil to befall me. He let me go in peace, *and* he let me go with that gaping hole. *And* no evil shall befall me from God, who is the Lord through all eternity . . . (my emphasis)   (Hamsun, pp. 16–17)

The paragraph is noteworthy in that there is a subtle shift from being divinely accusative, filled with imprecations, to being divinely contrite which is totally consistent with his own moral ambivalence. In other words, ultimately he embraces Kant and dismisses Renan since he initially refuses to take personal responsibility, but, rather, blames his condition on the Lord. But the blame does not last. Soon the Lord gains a 'reprieve', hostage as the protagonist is to his childhood and the 'cadences' of the Bible, and the protagonist assumes some kind of personal responsibility for his actions.

But, stylistically, the paragraph is unique in that what Hamsun is attempting to achieve here through the use of *polysyndeton* is a kind of Biblical rhythm and in the poetics of that Biblical rhythm there is a clear valorization not only of the Biblical discourse itself, but the subject of the Biblical discourse. The use of *polysyndeton* is equivalent to the *leitwort* that Robert Alter speaks of in *The Art of Biblical Narrative*. 'A *leitwort* is a word or a word- root that recurs significantly in a text, in a continuum of texts, or in a configuration of texts: by following these repetitions, one is able to decipher or grasp a meaning of the text, or at any rate, the meaning will be revealed more strikingly . . . The measured repetition that matches the inner rhythm of the text, or rather, that wells up from it, is one of the most powerful means for conveying meaning without expressing it' (Alter, p. 93). Hence the shift in style from the accusative to the contrite; from the implied acceptance of Kant to the implied condemnation of Renan and all of this is done peripatetically. By now, it is two o'clock in the afternoon.

But it is not only the relationship of the protagonist to his God that is significant, but the relationship of the writer to his work. In that sense he is to his work what God is to him. One cannot easily attribute his rapid digressions to the fact he is starving since the narrator is not starving. The narrator is recalling what it was like to starve which is a completely different version of starvation indeed. Hamsun clearly captures the physiological and psychological privation inherent in the condition, but precisely because it is a reconstruction of the incidents makes it such a unique work especially when one considers that he was completing the novel in Copenhagen where he was often not lacking. But woven within the fabric of the novel one clearly distinguishes that it is, as in the works of Austen or Smart or Lispector, a novel about writing as well. The entire Happolati incident is just such an example in which lies appear 'full-fledged in my head on the spur of the moment' (Hamsun, p. 20) and as he continues fabricating the tale of the fictitious Happolati he himself becomes carried away with the fiction. 'This was beginning to get interesting. The situation was running away with me, and one lie after another sprang up in my head...The little dwarf's gullibility made me reckless, I felt like stuffing full of lies come what may, driving him from the field in grand style. Had he heard about the electric hymn book that Happolati had invented?'...I was completely taken up with my own tales, wonderful visions hovered before my eyes, the blood rushed to my head and I lied like a trooper' (Hamsun, pp. 21–3). These are not the thoughts of a 'madman'; they are the thoughts of a fiction writer absorbed in the details of his fabrication as the fabrication takes over the writer and, in a way, the writing itself. The passage: 'Quite instinctively, I had gotten paper and pencil into my hands, and I sat and wrote mechanically the date 1848 in every corner of the page. If only a single scintillating thought would come, grip me utterly, and put words in my mouth! It had happened before after all, it had really happened that such moments came over me, so that I could write a long piece without effort and get it wonderfully right. I sit there on the bench and write 1848 dozens of times; I write this number crisscross in all possible shapes and wait for a usable idea to occur to me. A swarm of loose thoughts is fluttering about in my head' (Hamsun, p. 25), is clearly and precisely a summary of the entire writing process.

What is significant about this passage is that it begins talking about writing and segue-ways into writing about autumn and death then shifts back to writing:

And I sat down again, picked up my pencil once more and was ready to attack my article in earnest. It would never do to give up when the unpaid rent was staring me in the face. My thoughts gradually began to compose themselves. Taking great care I wrote slowly a couple of well-considered pages, an introduction to something; it could serve as the beginning to almost anything, whether a travelogue or a political article, depending on what I felt like doing. It was an excellent beginning to something or other.   (Hamsun, pp. 25–6)

Then, he perceives a 'gaping emptiness' followed by ' "Lord, my God and Father!" I cried in agony, and I repeated this cry several times in succession without adding a word' (Hamsun, p. 26). With one last appeal to God he prays 'silently to God for this job' (Hamsun, p. 27) he has discovered. 'Then I went back up to my room and sat down to think in my rocking chair, while the darkness grew more and more impenetrable. It was beginning to be difficult to stay up now' (Hamsun, p. 27). And so ends the first day.

The second day begins much as the first. Time, as well as space, continues to be of critical concern. He notes that it is five o'clock. What he is preoccupied with at that time of day is neither physical hunger nor the existence of God, but writing:

Suddenly one or two good sentences occur to me, suitable for a sketch or story, nice linguistic flukes the likes of which I had never experienced before. I lie there repeating these words to myself and find that they are excellent. Presently they are joined by others, I'm at once wide-awake, sit up and grab paper and pencil from the table behind my bed. It was as though a vein had burst inside me – one word follows another, they connect with one another and turn into situations; scenes pile on top of other scenes, actions and dialogue well up in my brain, and a wonderful sense of pleasure takes hold of me. I write as if possessed, filling one page after another without a moment's pause. My thoughts strike me so suddenly and continue to pour out so abundantly that I lose a lot of minor details I'm not able to write down fast enough, though I am working at full blast. They continue to crowd in on me, I am full of my subject, and every word I write is put in my mouth.

(Hamsun, p. 28)

Hamsun continues in this fashion for several more paragraphs as if possessed by the writing process until 'Elated with a sense of fulfillment and puffed up with joy, I feel on top of the world' (Hamsun, p. 28) and reckons the piece to be worth at least five, maybe ten kroner. Coterminous with the completion of the story, 'it was growing lighter and lighter in the room' (Hamsun, p. 28) even though he could read 'the fine, skeleton-like letters concerning Madam Andersen's shrouds' (Hamsun, p. 28). By now it is past seven, but not quite eight. And as he leaves his room with a 'glorious feeling' making me thankful to God and everyone, and I kneeled down by the bed and thanked God in a loud voice, for his goodness toward me this morning. I knew – oh yes, I knew that the exalted moment and the inspiration I had just experienced and written down was a wonderful work of heaven in my soul, an answer to my cry of distress yesterday. 'It's God! It's God!' I cried to myself and I wept from enthusiasm over my own words...

(Hamsun, p. 30)

There is, of course, the relationship between God and inspiration and when the protagonist is 'inspired' to produce he thanks God in the same way he blasphemes against God when he is not inspired. The word 'enthusiasm' means 'to be filled with God' and the relationship is clear. This attitude is a bit understated by Hamsun himself when he was asked to describe his attitude towards religion and he replied 'Almost indifferent. I am not godless, but like all my friends and acquaintances, indifferent to questions of religion. No, no change whatsoever. I am not much good at praying to God, but warmly grateful to him when he has been merciful, and saved me from something or other' (Ferguson, p. 399). His letters as well as his novel belie that attitude.

At ten o'clock he drops off the manuscript he has been toiling over. The editor is not there. He must return at four. He begins to walk. Then the doubts begin to enter. He walks to Our Saviour's Church and daydreams. Time passes. He reconsiders the manuscript, questions his ability; his hope moves to despair: 'Could I be absolutely certain that my story was truly inspired, a little artistic masterpiece? God knows it might have some faults here and there... What if it was quite mediocre or perhaps downright bad; what guarantee did I have that it wasn't at this very moment lying in the wastepaper basket already?' (Hamsun, p. 33). It is now twelve. He continues to walk and to ponder. Suddenly he realizes it is past four and returns, sees the editor who says he will be in touch. The piece has not been rejected. 'My hopes are fired up again, nothing was lost yet – on the contrary, I could still win everything, for that matter. And my brain began to fantasize about a great council in heaven where it had just been decided that I should win, win capitally, ten kroner for a story... (Hamsun, p. 35). He walks to the harbour and ponders. It is nine. He falls asleep, awakes. He walks some more. It is ten when he finally reaches the Bogstad Woods and so ends the second day.

When the third day begins there is no sun when he awakes at about three in the afternoon. He continues to walk and as he walks, as he ponders his condition, he says 'All in all, it was simply absurd to live like this. Holy Christ, what had I done to deserve this special persecution anyway! I simply couldn't understand' (Hamsun, p. 39). The rest of the day is spent in idle wandering moving from one venue to another, thinking the same, yet different, thoughts. At seven he goes to the Oplandske Café waiting for someone from whom he can borrow money. At eight the person arrives, but he has nothing to lend. 'Oh God, I'm so miserable! Oh God, I'm so miserable' (Hamsun, p. 46) and he continues walking again. He finally returns to his room, to the place he'd never return to and discovers a letter:

> A stream of light seems to surge through my breast, and I hear myself giving a little cry, a meaningless sound of joy: the letter was from the editor, my story was accepted, it had gone directly to the composing room! A few minor changes... corrected a few slips of the pen... promising work... to be printed tomorrow... ten kroner. Laughing and crying, I made a running start and raced down the street, stopped to slap my thighs and flung a solemn oath into space for no particular reason. And time passed.
>
> (Hamsun, p. 48)

At the conjunction of depression and wandering, peripeteia appears: the ten kroner. By the end of Part I, the protagonist has been on a perpipatetic journey that has taken him at least one time to the following places: Our Saviour's Church, Grænsen Street, Palace Park, Palace Hill, Pascha's Bookstore, Pilestrædet Lane, Cisler's Music store, University Street, St. Olaf Place, Karl Johan Street, the Students' Promenade, Stortorvet Square, Aker Street, Ullevaal Road, St. Hanshaugen, Kirke Street, Haegdenhaugen district, Majorstuen, Bogstad Woods, Jærnbanetorvet Square, the Steam Kitchen, Grønlandsleret Street, Møller Street, Christ's Cemetery, Oplandske Café, Torv Street, the Arcades. But it has also taken him on a peripatetic journey as well since his situation has been changed by virtue of selling an article. Hence this is how the protagonist survives: the peripatetic wanderer dependent on the peripeteic investment of others.

As part two begins, a fortnight has passed and the narrator is back in the cemetery again, before leaving for Jærnbane Pier. It is ten at

night, he is disconsolate and he is broke again, but what is of
interest here is the relationship between his hunger and his art.
As he attempts to 'kill time' at the pier he is also in the process of
creating fiction. 'I sat there with tears in my eyes gasping for breath,
quite beside myself with feverish merriment. I began to talk aloud,
told myself the story of the cornet, aped the poor policeman's
movements, peeped into the hollow of my hand and repeated
over and over to myself: He coughed when he threw it away! He
coughed when he threw it away! I added new words, with titillat-
ing supplements, changed the whole sentence and made it more
pointed' (Hamsun, p. 53). In this feverish excitement of the 'revisionary' process, the protagonist segue-ways into the relationship
between ships and voyages before the transition into the discourse
on Ylajali, the fictional name of a woman he meets on the street. But
the poetics of the mental journey take him via the 'silent monsters'
and their 'black hulls', resting in the harbour, across the sea to
Ylajali's castle in which he writes in detail how both she and the
space appear as he employs such figurative language as: a sparkling hall (light); amethyst walls (blue); a throne of yellow roses
(light); twenty summers (light); every white night (light); bright
orchards (light); brilliant emerald hall (sparkling green); sun shines
(light); choral music (harmony); waves of fragrance (sweetness);
wild beauty of enchantment; red hall of rubies; and among all
this light, they kiss. When he thinks of love, he thinks in images
of brilliance, of light. She is a fictional redeemer. She and her love
redeem him (at least at the fictive level) from the darkness associated with death. He comments on his blood perceiving a subtle
greeting from her (Hamsun, p. 13) and feels 'the wild beauty of
enchantment race through my blood' (Hamsun, p. 54). She
becomes, in effect, the queen goddess of the world for the woman
is life who saves him from the darkness. It is not coincidental that in
describing his meeting with Ylajali in the castle, the protagonist
begins in the yellow chamber, progresses through a corridor to
another, green chamber, then through another corridor to the inner-
most recesses of the red chamber before he is thrust back into a
'hurricane of light' after which he returns to wakefulness 'mercilessly called back to life and my misery' (Hamsun, p. 54). But, of
course, the image of the woman is not the woman and the fictive
quality of woman is much greater than her presence in the flesh.
   Whereas the Ylajali Episode is almost totally contingent on
notions of light, the Tangen Episode is almost totally contingent

on darkness. The Tangen Episode (so called because the protagonist when offerred by the police a place to spend the night because
of his 'homelessness' uses the pseudonym, Andreas Tangen, jour-
nalist) works as a counterpoint to the Ylajali Episode. He thinks
spending the night as an indigent in the warm confines of the
police station is a good idea since it will afford him a place to
rest. But what happens during the night is he becomes captive to
his own fear and that is reflected in his language. After the lights
are turned out he says:

> But I wasn't sleepy and couldn't fall asleep. I lay awhile looking
> into the darkness, a thick massive darkness, without end that I
> wasn't able to fathom. My thoughts couldn't grasp it. It struck me
> as excessively dark and I felt its presence as oppressive. I closed
> my eyes, began to sing in an undertone, and tossed back and
> forth in the bunk to distract myself, but it was no use. The
> darkness had taken possession of my thoughts and didn't leave
> me alone for a moment. What if I myself were to be dissolved
> into darkness, made one with it? I sit up in bed and flail my arms.
>   (Hamsun, p. 60)

'Darkness' of various intensity seems to be the operative word here
as Tangen struggles against it. And in his battle against the darkness he suddenly chances upon a word – *Kuboaa*.

> The word stood out sharply against the darkness before me. I sit
> with open eyes, amazed at my find and laughing for joy. Then I
> start whispering: they might be spying on me, and I intended to
> keep my invention a secret.   (Hamsun, p. 61)

He struggles to make some sense of the word.

> No, the word was really suited to mean something *spiritual*, a
> feeling, a state of mind – couldn't I understand that? And I try
> to jog my memory to come up with something spiritual. Then
> it seems to me someone is speaking, sticking his nose into my
> chat, and I answer angrily, What was that? Oh my, you'll get
> the prize for biggest idiot! Knitting yarn? Go to hell! Why should
> I be under an obligation to let it mean knitting yarn when I was
> particularly opposed to its meaning knitting yarn?.
>   (Hamsun, p. 61–2)

But then the darkness returns but with more intensity and he uses such phrases as 'brooding darkness', 'the same unfathomable black eternity', both of which lead him into thoughts of dying. 'This is what it's like to die, I said to myself, and now you're going to die!' (Hamsun, p. 63) until he spots a 'grayish square in the wall, a whitish tone, a hint of something – it was the daylight' (Hamsun, p. 63) and it is only then that he 'returns to his senses' and falls asleep from exhaustion. Not coincidentally, it is the manifestation of the word Kuboaa and its sundry meanings that rescues him from the darkness and sustains him until the first meagre morning light as it has been the word that has sustained him throughout the course of the novel when he has been on the brink of starvation.

The remainder of Part II continues in much the same way as it has up to Part II consisting of: his imprecations to God; his wanderings (especially to the harbour); his chats with himself; his acts of self-torture and persecution; his acknowledgement of the powers of darkness; his suffering from the ache of honour all of which lead eventually to Part III which opens with 'a week went by in joy and gladness' (Hamsun, p. 91). After which the narrator talks of two specific items: his writing and *The Nun*, which was ready to sail from Kristiania. The allusion to the ship and to sailing has already been established and essentially has laid the groundwork for the narrator's imminent departure which one reads at the conclusion of Part IV. But the major portion of the opening pages of Part III is devoted exclusively to his writing. 'I toiled at my work day after day, barely allowing myself time to gulp down my food before going on with my writing again' (Hamsun, p. 91). He finishes an article and takes it to the Editor and while he is there he looked about me in the small office: busts, lithographs, clippings, and an immense wastebasket that looked as though it could swallow a man whole. I felt sad at the sight of this huge maw, these dragon's jaws which were always open, always ready to receive fresh scrapped writings – fresh blasted hopes' (Hamsun, p. 92). Of course his article, on Correggio, is politely rejected by the editor with the statement, 'Everything we can use must be so popular... You know the sort of public we have. Couldn't you try to make it a bit simpler? Or else come up with something that people will understand better?' (Hamsun, p. 93), but he refuses to take an advance and decries his 'unlucky stars' (dis/aster) before he meets a young woman, Marie, and the narrative shifts to sexually explicit events, yet he is presumably impotent. 'Alas, I had no real bounce in me these days. Women had become almost like men to me. Want had dried me up. But I felt I was cutting a sorry figure vis-à-vis this strange tart and wanted to save face' (Hamsun, p. 98). He preaches to her under the pseudonym of Pastor such and such then sends her off in favour of his writing, of revising. Standing outside of his room, in the lamplight he tries to write, 'But the words wouldn't come. I read through the entire piece from the beginning, read each sentence aloud, but I just couldn't collect my thoughts for this crashing climax' (Hamsun, p. 99).

What is of significance here is the relationship the narrator has with writing and how the act of writing sustains him. From the Tangen Episode one recalls that it was the 'word' that kept the oppressive darkness from consuming him; in the Marie Episode, he dispatches the woman in favor of his writing. Clearly, there is a relationship between what the novel is about and the writing of the novel itself. What the novel is about is hunger, but it is also about the act and process of writing. Writing under the influence of hunger, writing and the writing process. There are several levels of writing at work. On one level it is the narrator talking about his own writing, but it is also Hamsun writing about the narrator writing as well. So we have the narrator writing about his trials as a writer under the influence of hunger and of Hamsun's writing of *Hunger* under the influence of hunger. Which brings up the experience of hunger and its psychology. The cumulative effects of hunger inevitably lead to emotional instability. There are protracted periods of depression; the inability to sustain mental or physical effort; the discouragement due to one's relative inability to cope with daily life; there is increased irritability; a lack of self-discipline and self-control; an increased sensitivity to noise; marked nervousness; and personal neglect. Hamsun himself writes in a letter dated 2 December 88:

> I cannot work – not well, not with the right touch. I am sitting here in a garret with the wind blowing through the walls. There is no stove, almost no light, only one small pane in the roof… The food situation has also been quite desperate; many times last summer it seemed all up with me. Edvard Brandes saved me several times; so I used what I got from Brandes to write a little for *Politiken*, but in the meantime the money has gone and my position is no different from what it was. In the end you really

become quite wretched, quite faint. Then you can't write; and
you just start crying when you can't get things to go
(Naess & McFarlane, p. 71).

One finds that the presumed 'madness' experienced by the narrator
is often the same as the presumed 'madness' of his creator. From
the Tangen Episode one reads:

> I had passed over into the sheer madness of hunger; I was empty
> and without pain and my thoughts were running riot. I debate
> with myself in silence. With the oddest jumps in my line of
> thought, I try to ascertain the meaning of my "new word".
> (Hamsun, p. 61)

And from a letter dated 1888 one reads:

> I cannot get away from it. My book! my book! About these
> delicate nuances. I would want to sift through the remotest
> nuances of the mind – I would let them listen to the mimosa's
> breathing – every word like brilliantly white wings – movements
> of the shining surface of language. My mind cries out in its
> longing to begin! I haven't time to wait – the devils of my work
> will not leave me in peace! Now is the fullness of time! Now my
> book should be out!   (Naess and McFarlane, p. 88)

Certainly, the relationship between narrator and creator is there in
the language, in the structure of the language and in the passion of
the language. Just as the language is there to help sustain the
narrator in times of financial and physical crisis, the language is
there for Hamsun to sustain him in the same dilemma. Women do
not sustain him. The image of Ylajali he has in Part II is not the
same as his eventual 'revelation' of her, which concludes in Part III
with:

> She came quickly over to me and held out her hand. I looked at
> her full of distrust. Was she doing this freely, with a light heart?
> Or was she doing it just to get rid of me? She put her arm around
> my neck, tears in her eyes. I just stood and looked at her. She
> offerred me her mouth but I couldn't believe her, it was bound to
> be a sacrifice on her part, a means of getting it over with.
> (Hamsun, p. 143)

Certainly the realization of the woman is not the same as the fascination of the woman and the subject of one's desires cannot in any meaningful way sustain in the narrator the same way the fascination of the subject can. In other words, any realization of an event cannot be as redeeming as the fictionalizing of the event. The realization of the event is purely in the power of the manifested word and not in the manifestation of the event. That is the reason why the narrator constantly returns to his writing, to the manuscript at hand, to the words. And with the conclusion of the 'amorous affair' with Ylajali in both mind and matter, the narrator returns to his writing in Part IV.

As Part IV opens, winter has arrived. The narrator has been living in Vaterland district for several weeks attempting to avoid the landlady over the rent. Though he is out of money, his situation has improved somewhat and he continues to pursue his writing though he has reached a kind of 'writer's block' on a piece he started that was supposed to be 'an allegory abut a fire in a bookstore'. At that time there comes a confrontation with the landlady in which the following dialogue ensues:

> 'I'm working on an article, as I mentioned to you before,' I said, 'and as soon as it's finished you'll get your money. There's no need to worry.'
>
> 'But you won't ever finish that article, will you?'
>
> 'You think so? I may feel inspired to write tomorrow, or maybe even tonight; it's not all impossible that the inspiration will come sometime tonight, and then my article will be finished in a quarter of an hour, at the most. You see, it's not the same with *my work* (my emphasis) as with other people's; I can't just sit down and get so much done every day, I have to wait for the right moment. And nobody can tell the day or the hour when the spirit will come upon him. It must take its course.
>
> (Hamsun, p. 150)

The admission is not convincing and not only does the landlady walk away, but later in the chapter she tells him it will be his last night there. But what is different about this part of the novel is that the narrator has made an admission that heretofore has not been admitted; namely, he is a writer. He establishes that it is his work and that admission focalizes the chapter in a significant way, a significant writerly way, since he now associates himself with his writing. The difficulties arise when the landlady and her tenants give the narrator a difficult time by not allowing him to 'write in peace'.

> 'While I think of it, I must tell you that I simply can't afford to let people have board and room on credit,' she said. 'I have told you this before, remember.'
> 'But please, it's only a matter of a couple of days, till my article gets finished,' I answered. 'Then I'll gladly give you an extra five-krone bill, yes, very gladly.'
> But she obviously had no faith in my article, I could see that.
> (Hamsun, p. 156)

What one finds in this section of the fourth part is that the narrator does not wander. In previous sections, he has wandered about, often aimlessly, in search of something to quell his 'hunger'. But in this section his needs have been sated, at least for the short term, and he is able to devote his attention, albeit divided, to writing. Except for several excursions from his room, the narrator is constantly absorbed with two things: paying his rent and finishing the article which is eventually abandoned in favour of a drama titled ''The Sign of the Cross'' with a theme from the Middle Ages'. It is with the play that the narrator deals with a number of aspects of the writing process and it is well to quote in full what he says:

> In particular, the central character was fully worked out in my mind – a gorgeous fanatical whore who had sinned in the temple, not out of weakness or lust, but from a hatred of heaven, had sinned at the very foot of the altar with the altar cloth under her head, simply from a voluptuous contempt of heaven.
> 'I became more an more obsessed by this character as the hours went by. She stood vividly alive before my eyes at last, exactly the way I wanted to portray her. Her body was to be misshapen and repulsive: tall, very skinny and rather dark, with long legs that showed through her skirts at every step she took. She would also have big, protruding ears. In short, she would not be easy on the eyes, barely tolerable to look at What interested me about her was her wonderful shamelessness, the desperate excess of pre-meditated sin that she had committed. I was actually too much taken up with her, my brain was downright swollen with this

queer monstrosity of a human being. I worked for two whole hours at a stretch on my play.

When I had done about ten pages, or perhaps twelve, often with great difficulty, at times with long intervals during which I wrote to no avail and to tear up my sheets, I was tired, quite numb with cold and weariness, and I got up and went out into the street.   (Hamsun, p. 157)

The narrator has exercised his mind and his creative skill to the limit and only when he has finished does he leave his room and even then he still thinks about the work he has to finish. The focus of Part IV vacillates between the two conditions of revising the work-in-progress and the inability to work without interruption, the latter of which constantly impinges on the former. If it is not the landlady who interrupts him, then it is the noise and agitation of the other residents. Frustrated with the attempt, he leaves the house again and returns to the docks a venue which works on two levels: first, the docks are a kind of 'refrain' in the storyline since the narrator is constantly returning to the docks as if it will be his final salvation; and two, it offers him a place to continue his writing, albeit for a short period of time.

I came down to the docks. A big barque with a Russian flag was unloading coal; I read its name, *Copégoro*, on the ship's side... The sun, the light, the salty breath from the ocean, all this lively, bustling activity stiffened my backbone and set my heart throbbing. All at once it occurred to me that I might do a couple of scenes of my play while sitting here. I took my sheets of paper from my pocket.

I tried to shape up some line from the lips of the monk, lines that ought to swell with intolerance and power, but I didn't succeed. So I skipped the monk and tried to work out a speech, that which the judge addressed to the desecrator of the temple, and I wrote half a page of this speech, whereupon I stopped. My words just wouldn't evoke the right atmosphere. The bustling activity around me, the sea shanties, the noise of the capstans, and the incessant clanking of the railcar couplings agreed poorly with that thick, musty air of mediaevalism which was to envelop my play, like fog. I gathered up my papers and got up.

(Hamsun, p. 168)

It is not surprising that Hamsun has set up the narrator for his inevitable departure in this way. There is the relationship between the departure from Kristiania (the return) and the satiation of the narrator's hunger (his writing). The narrator has often come to the docks before, but the docks had a distinctly onerous and oneiric quality to them distinct from the rather exhuberant quality he experiences in Part IV. The reason for the change is apparent: he has found his work. Once he has found his work, the reason for staying in Kristiania is over. Just as Hamsun had to experience hunger to write about it, so too does his narrator need to experience hunger to write about it.

He returns to his room and, as in previous parts, a peripety awaits when 'A few steps outside the entrance the messenger catches up with me, says hello once more and stops me. He hands me a letter. Angry and reluctant, I tear it open – a ten-krone bill falls out of the envelope, but no letter, not a word' (Hamsun, p. 173). Saved once again, the narrator pays off his debt to his landlady and strikes off again knowing that he has no money to eat on. But the physical hunger is displaced as he once again turns his attention to his work:

> It was probably around four by now, in a couple of hours I might get to see the theatre manager if my play had been finished. I take out the manuscript on the spot and try to put together the three or four last scenes, by hook or by crook. I think and sweat and read it through from the beginning but can't get anywhere. No nonsense, now! I say, no bullheadedness there! And so I work for dear life on my play, writing down everything that comes to mind just to finish quickly and be off. I tried to convince myself I was having another big moment, lying to my face and openly deceiving myself while scribbling away as though there was no need to look for the right words. That's good! That's a real find! I whispered every so often, just get it down! Eventually, however, my most recent lines of dialogue began to sound suspicious to me: they contrasted too sharply with the dialogue in the early scenes. Besides, there wasn't the slightest tinge of the Middle Ages about the monk's words. I break my pencil between my teeth, jump up, tear my manuscript to bits, every single sheet, toss my hat in the gutter and trample it. 'I'm lost,' I whisper to myself. 'Ladies and gentlemen, I'm lost!' I say nothing except these words as I stand there trampling my hat. (Hamsun, p. 175–6)

The passage expresses the anguish which accompanies the revisionary process, but the narrator has achieved what he set out to achieve in the opening movements of the novel: the journey has taken him from a non-committed space to a committed one. Regardless of what he has done to the manuscript, he has finally entered the terrain of the writer and the experiences coterminous with it. It is not unusual, then, for his last wandering to be towards the pier where he asks the captain of the *Copégoro* if he can use a deck-hand. The captain says yes, yet another peripety, and the novel ends with 'Once out in the fjord I straightened up, wet with fever and fatigue, looked in toward the shore and said goodbye for now to the city, to Kristiania, where the windows shone so brightly in every home' (Hamsun, p. 182).

The discussion of the novel has revolved around the notions of peripatetics and peripety; however, there are some very interesting things about this co-mingling of Aristotelian philosophizing, the manner of its presentation and the way in which we find the narrator wandering in philosophical, spiritual and topographic ways. In a sense, the whole notion of peripatus, even beginning with Aristotle, deals with 'quest' and quests, all quests, have a number of things in common all of which pertain to the notion of movement, of wandering: that is, the movements of separation, initiation, and return. These movements can be seen in *Hunger* as well as in other rites of passage on both spiritual and intellectual levels. Though there are certain places the narrator visits more frequently than others, he is on a journey, a peripatetic journey, and, like all homeless people, exists for the purpose of walking. Being ambulatory gives them some significance. They have a purpose for being since they are walking to somewhere, purposefully. Their days are measured by their walking and in that walking there is some substance to their lives. Like Aristotle, 'Tangen,' constantly philosophizes while he walks, while he sits, while he wanders. His thoughts are truly philosophical thoughts, thoughts that often escape the boundaries of logical, reasonable thoughts, but are none the less philosophical. It is only when he rests and writes that he can synthesize what he has been thinking about. Though Hamsun declines to acknowledge the work is 'a novel', it is, arguably, one of his best works since it deals forthrightly with the demonic nature of writing, the writing process, the 'hunger' of writing and the anguish of writing under duress.

The peripatetic and peripeteic nature of the narrator's quest can best be seen in relation to the routes taken and the reward given for such. By the beginning of Part III one sees how Hamsun has 'intentionally' fashioned the narrative as being 'not a novel'. Part I deals primarily with the narrator's wanderings ending with the peripety of ten kroner; Part II continues, after a two-week respite, with the peripatetic hero essentially repeating the same yet different experiences he had in Part I with the peripety of five kroner; Part III begins in an iterative manner with 'a week went by in joy and gladness' (Hamsun, p. 91) and continues in the fashion established in Parts I and II (i.e. wandering, philosophizing, wandering, writing, wandering) the main difference being he spends considerably more time writing. 'I toiled...left' (pp. 91–2). In Part IV the narrator continues his writing as his situation has improved. The financial problems with his landlady are alleviated with a peripety of ten kroner which allows him to settle up with the landlady, end the journey and begin another. Even when he has given up his ten kroner to his landlady, he is saved again at the end of the novel by the captain, thus closing the quest. From the initial separation in which we find the narrator, through the initiation which constitutes the novel itself, to his final departure and return, the narrator has experienced the suffering of growth through the prevailing notions of peripatetics and peripety finally resulting in the recognition that his life's work is his words and the facilitation of them.

ADDENDUM

The addendum gives a detailed account of the narrator's peripatetic movements and the accompanying peripety.

Part I

As the quest commences, the 'separation' has already been established as the journey begins in a place other than his home. The entire novel deals with his 'initiation' into the role of 'writer'.

Peripatetic Journey – Day One

Point of Departure: His attic room

Wanders a nameless street
Arcades
Wanders nameless streets

Grænsen Street
Palace Park
Pilestrædet Lane
Palace Hill
Pascha's Bookstore
Cisler's Music Store
University Street
St Olaf Place
Side street
Karl Johan Street
University
Palace Hill
The Students' Promenade
Wanders down nameless streets
Returns to his room

Peripatetic Journey – Day Two

Point of Departure: His attic room

Wanders nameless streets
Semb's
Stortorvet Square
Newspaper office
Grænsen Street
Karl Johan Street
Our Saviour's Cemetery near the chapel
Aker Street
Ullevaal Road
St. Hanshaugen
Sagene section
Empty lots and cultivated fields
Wanders a nameless country road
St. Hanshaugen
Newspaper office
Semb's
Kirke Street
Ingebret's
Nameless theatre
Lodge Building
Water and the Fortress

Haegdehaugen section (in memory)
Karl Johan Street
Storting
Tordenskjold Street
Wanders nameless streets
University clock
Haegdehaugen area
Majorstuen
Bogstad Woods
Falls asleep there

Peripatetic Journey – Day Three

Point of Departure: Bogstad Woods

The Steam Kitchen
Jærnbanetorvet Square
Grønlandsleret Street,
Møller Street
Stortorvet Square
Newspaper office
The Arcades
Christ's Cemetery
Oplandske Café
Torv Street
Between the church and the Arcades
Attic room

Peripety: Ten kroner

END PART I

Part II

Peripatetic Journey: – Two weeks later

Point of Departure: Cemetery
Wanders aimlessly
City Jail
Harbour

Jærnbane Pier
Nameless streets
City Jail

Peripatetic Journey – Next day

Point of Departure: *City Jail*

Youngstorvet Square
Home
Newspaper office
Homansbyen section
Toldbod Street
Bernt Anker Street No. 10
Wanders nameless streets
Jærnbanetorvet Square/Clock at Our Saviour's
Jaernbane Pier
Newspaper office
Pilestaedet Lane
Fire station
Pascha's Bookstore
Pastor Levion's
Stortorvet Square
Home
Stener Street
Wanders nameless streets
Church of Our Saviour
Wanders nameless streets
Bakery
Ropewalk
Cisler's Music Store
Wanders nameless streets
Yarn Store
Wanders nameless streets
Church of Our Saviour
Wanders nameless streets
Pawnbroker

Peripety: Ten kroner

END PART II

PART III

Peripatetic Journey – A week went by

Point of Departure: His room

Newspaper office
Several evenings pass
Room
Wanders nameless streets
Oplandske Café
Palace
Karl Johan Street
Grand Hotel
Blomquist's entranceway
Storting Place
Returns home
Wanders nameless streets
Dry goods store

Peripety: Five kroner

Storgaten Way; eats
Wanders nameless streets; vomits
Café
Home
Walks woman home
St. Olaf Place

Peripatetic Journey – Next day

Point of Departure: His room

Clothing stalls
Stortorvet Square
Elephant Pharmacy
Grænsen Street
Storting Place
37 Ullevaal Road
11 Tomte Street
Vognmand Street

Grønland section
Wanders nameless streets
His room

Peripatetic Journey – Next day

Point of Departure: *His room*

Torv Street
Arcades
Smiths' Passage
Youngsbakken Lane
Jaernbane Pier
Jaernbanetorvet Square
Havn Street

Peripety: Ten kroner

Wanders nameless streets
11 Tomte Street

Peripatetic Journey – Tuesday

Point of Departure: *Tomte Street*

2 St Olaf Place
Karl Johan Street
University Street
2 St Olaf Place

                              END PART III

PART IV

Peripatetic Journey – Many weeks later

Point of Departure: Room in Vaterlan

Stays in his room

Peripatetic Journey – A few days went by

Point of Departure: *His room*

Drammen Road
Karl Johan Street near Jaernbanetorvet Square
His room

Peripatetic Journey – Next day

Point of Departure: *His room*

Kirke Street
Fortress
Docks
His room
Peripety: Ten kroner
Tomte St and Jaernbanetorvet Square
Wanders nameless streets
Royal Hotel
Arcades
Our Saviour's
Vognmand Street
Jaernbane Pier

Peripety: Job aboard the Copégoro

When one breaks down the parts into their individual journeys, one finds the following:

Part I	56 areas mentioned plus nameless streets
Part II	27 areas mentioned plus nameless streets
Part III	39 areas mentioned plus nameless streets
Part IV	13 areas mentioned plus nameless streets

One might think that as the novel progress, the narrator would minimize his wanderings and, in fact, the numbers do decrease from Part I to Part II, increase slightly in Part III and dramatically decrease by Part IV. By Part IV, the narrator has, in a way, become initiated into that 'writer's space' which he has longed to find throughout the novel. By virtue of finding that space, the need to wander diminishes. Once he has found his 'calling', the narrator can then embark on another journey, hence the decrease in interest in the surroundings and the eventual departure from Kristiania. But be that as it may, the narrator rarely wanders far from the centre of the city. The included map (*circa* 1909) of Kristiania, indicates that the narrator's wanderings were well within a defined area of circumscription. The geometric space within which the narrator chooses to isolate himself, is not unlike the geometric space of the novel. Just as the narrator wanders from place to place within the city, apparently with no other motive but to wander, the narrative displaces a linear kind of narrative in favour of a kind of narrative that, too, wanders.

7

The Poetics of Prose Poetry in Elizabeth Smart's *By Grand Central Station I Sat Down and Wept*

In her insightful introduction to Elizabeth Smart's *By Grand Central Station I Sat Down and Wept*, the late, poetically gifted, Brigid Brophy writes that it is one of the 'half dozen masterpieces of poetic prose in the world'. Clearly, after reading the novella, one understands what Brophy may mean by 'poetic prose', but Brophy's statement also begs numerous questions. For example, what makes it poetic prose? What is poetic prose read like? And how does it differ from non-poetic prose? And, more important, what makes it poetic prose?

When negotiating with notions of poetic prose, one usually marks the Symbolist poets as the point of departure, Baudelaire as the poet of departure and, specifically, his text *Le Spleen de Paris* as the text of departure for it is in *Le Spleen de Paris* that we clearly see the origins of poetic prose and how that style becomes the foundation for the majority of prose poetry that is subsequently written.

In his essay 'Vibratory Organism: crise de prose', Roger Shattuck proposes that 'the opening paragraphs from "*De la couleur*" represent Baudelaire's first *poème en prose*... After the two initial paragraphs the rest of the chapter on color breaks down into short paragraphs mostly of one sentence and of a discursive nature' (Caws and Riffaterre, p. 26). Shattuck then quotes Baudelaire's dedication of *Petits poèmes en prose* to Arsène Houssaye in which he writes, 'Quel est celui de nous qui n'a pas, dans ses jours d'ambition, rêvé la miracle d'une prose poétique, musicale sans rythme et sans rime, assez couple et assez heurtée pour s'adapter aux mouvements lyriques de l'âme, aux ondulations de la rêverie, aux soubresauts de la conscience?' Shattuck also suggests that Baudelaire's writing in the colour poem 'attends to the fact that this is

his first treatment of the theme of correspondences' (Caws and
Riffaterre, p. 27). In short, Shattuck maintains Baudelaire's reliance
on painting, especially Impressionist painting, genuinely casts the
prose poem in the light of colour and sense. In Baudelaire's synaesthetic poetry we see a number of these correspondences or analo-
gies with the senses, this a commingling of the senses. 'Good
poetry, invoking a special language, provokes a special vision:
childlike, mystical, macabre, humorous, fanciful, illogical, myopic
or whatever, but never prosaic'. (Broome, p. 41) How then do we
get to something like poetic prose? Something that one could
categorize as oxymoronic.

J. S. Simon writes of the prose poem that 'not only are prose
poems observably 'short' (and autonomous) but they must be so
for beyond a certain length, the tensions and impact are forfeited
and [the prose poem] becomes – more or less – poetic prose' (Caws
and Riffaterre, p. 40). To that extent, Monique Parent writes 'this
energy which becomes manifest through music and images, and
which is self-sufficient, soaring to the rank of an absolute and
seeking only to express itself in an appropriate language, is indeed
the lyrical state of mind, it is lyricism itself; this state of mind
creates the poem' (Caws and Riffaterre, p. 41).

What we can synthesize from these diverse approaches to the
prose poem is the relationship among colour, image, sound and
autonomy. This synaesthetic amalgam could be said to be included
in *Le Spleen de Paris* and of the work itself Michel Beaujour suggests
'it is not a long poem, but rather like any collection of poems held
together by some sort of topical, modal or generic similarity' (Caws
and Riffaterre, p. 46). What is unique about *Le Spleen de Paris*
(among many things) is the picture it represents, a compendium
of the city as Baudelaire, the Parisian *flanêur*, documents what he
sees as he strolls from scene to scene in much the same way we
picture what Moussorgsky paints in sound (yet another
correspondence) in *Pictures at an Exhibition*.

Since Hugo 'French poetry has been concerned more with seeing
than with thinking, and in general it has aimed at provoking an
imaginative rather than an intellectual response. The poet's imagination is his vital attribute, "la reine des facultés" as Baudelaire said,
a kind of sixth sense which commands and binds together all the
others ... The prosaic rendering of reality offers only boredom; the
poetic task is to kindle through a supremely creative use of language a new vision of things. What is seen or felt to lie in or beyond

reality will depend on the individual poet . . . poetry is there to open one's eyes, even to the invisible' (Broome, pp. 39–40). Broome continues that, 'The natural vehicle for this vision is the poetic image, by which is meant a figure of speech which draws together two ideas, two elements or two areas of association by comparison and holds them there suggestively poised between difference and identity. Imagery has always been an essential of poetry adding an ornamental glitter to the banal, explaining the intangible in terms of the tangible, persuading by the unexpected appropriateness of its parallels or seducing by its magical extensions and transformations of reality' (Broome, p. 42).

Out of this coalescence of imagination and the poetic image emerges the origins of free verse which are two of the most important developments of modern poetry and one is clearly indebted to poets such as Baudelaire and Rimbaud for what they contributed to the sonority of free verse poetry for both of them have utilized that form in their prose poems.

It becomes clear that 'poetic vision' has become more important than poetic sentiment, imagery more important than description, rhythm more important than prosody. The respect for the sonority and texture of words and the love of the powers of suggestion have their fundamental roots in the French Symbolist poets. But whereas the prose poems in *Le Spleen de Paris* are held together by the fabric of the city and the urbanity of the peripatetic *flanêur*, we find in *By Grand Central Station* a similar kind of peripatetic wandering, but woven into a text which lays claim to being both an extended prose poem and a novel. Both claim allegiance to the prose poem which Beaujour suggests 'is a text where the verse density approaches that of regular material forms, while eschewing the anaphoric servitudes of prosody' (Caws and Riffaterre, p. 55), yet they diverge into differing poetics.

What Smart has done in *By Grand Central Station* is to incorporate the main components of the prose poem (Baudelairean, if you will), and expand the situational, episodic nature of the text into a unified novella. As Brophy says, 'the story goes scarcely beyond the bare three lines of a love triangle, and even those have to be inferred from the narrator's rhapsodizing or lamentation over them' (Preface). So the events and the action within the novel are peripheral to the poetic quality of the prose. So too are time and place only important in relation to the narrator's feelings or 'act as backdrops for the emotional drama unfolding in the heart of the narrator' (Van

Wert, p. 39). Extending the notion of the Parisian Prowler, the *flanêur*, Smart moves her autobiographical protagonist from the paradisical nature of California to the urban squalor of New York. Whereas Baudelaire's notions of urbanity were expressed from the point of view of the poet responding to the masses and their meagre attempts at survival, their bourgeois attitudes to things pedestrian, and all conducted with a kind of poet's subjective contempt, but with the illusion of objectivity, Smart too incorporates her personal pain into the prose. Whereas Baudelaire's pain is a pain mitigated by virtue of the masses themselves, their hirsute attitudes to art, as in *Le chien et le flacon*, Smart has altered the venue which 'only acts as a correlative to the narrator's internal state: the consummation of the love affair occurs in the lush California landscape; her lover's betrayal, however, takes place against the cheap hotels and cafés of New York' (Van Wert, p. 39).

Just as the structure of the prose poems has a clear beginning, middle and end, so too does the novel which is divided into ten sections with each section being rather autonomous, yet unified through the themes of love, faith, death and betrayal. The frame of the story begins with the narrator, the lover and his wife and ends with the narrator betraying the lover for his wife. But whereas the peripatetic wanderings of Baudelaire are relegated to the ruelles and boulevards of Paris, Smart is led on a journey that crosses the breadth of the United States with excursions into Canada. It is, therefore, no coincidence that the 'journey' which she takes is documented in what Smart has written in a 'novel-journal' both of which relate to the 'diurnal', the day's travel, the day's entry. As Dee Horne writes, 'The flexibility of the journal form enables Smart to examine her experiences in different ways and to explore different forms of writing. This link is such that what she writes influences how she uses each journal. The fact she often writes in several journals simultaneously also indicates that she uses each one for different purposes... As a writer's notebook, Smart's journals reveal the seeds and evolution of her style; her journals evolve from external to internal observations and from personal writing to a more developed form in which Smart begins to speak in her own voice and portray her life as crafted art' (Horne, p. 131).

And for Smart, writing wasn't merely the physical application of applying pen to paper; the personal anguish she felt in discovering the exact word and in structuring an art form is clear from many of her entries. In June, 1933, for example, Smart writes, 'What is writing?

Isn't it just getting things on paper? What things? Just putting them down? but there is an art. Yes. But doesn't that make artifice. Can that be truth too? The truth, the truth – but there's too much of it. Self-consciousness. Self-analysis. Even writing this. I am saying – am I pretending? Trying to be truthful and soul-sighing!...Why can't I write the truth – and if I do, why isn't it right? What bores? – surely long windy artifices signifying nothing' (Horne, p. 133). The conflict between writing the *word* and writing the *truth*, of merely adapting to paper and crafting into art were conflictive gestures for Smart. And, perhaps, the 'journey' she takes in *By Grand Central Station* as a wanderer runs parallel to the 'journey' she takes as a writer in the process of discovering a style and of crafting her art.

If one decomposes her peripatetic 'journey', what we have are the following phases: phases 1 to 3 take place in California: Monterey/Big Sur; phase 4, in Arizona; phases 5 to 6, in Canada; and phases 7 to 10 in New York. I use the term 'phase(s)' rather than chapters because the journey is a journey of self-enlightenment and the term 'phase', as Hardy has used in *Tess*, is more reflective of the experimental journey than are mere 'chapters'. In terms of setting, there are four venues: California, Arizona, Ottawa, New York; in terms of time, the autumn, advances to winter in Canada and New York then moves to spring and summer in New York. The names of the characters are not as important as the characters themselves, all of whom we see through the narrator's eyes. So, on the basis of the primary narratological items we might find in standard Realistic novels we are a bit 'short-changed' here since there is no clear formula present that would distinguish it as a 'novel' in the sense that E. M. Forster would distinguish it as a novel.

Without the usual accoutrements of the Realistic novel we are left with something altogether different, something that distinguishes the novel more than plot, character and setting and that is language. Smart, like Baudelaire before and Lispector after, is in love with words. She uses figurative and imaginative language throughout the novel in a way that often 'explodes' the senses. As in Baudelaire, the narrator remains the sole lyrical voice within the work. Even the dialogue is mediated by the lyrical narrator who applies no quotation marks to the speech. In Smart, the other characters only act as counterpoint to the role of language in the decisive journey of the narrator through the perils of a love found and lost within the confines of an apparently indifferent world and Smart also uses a variety of tropes throughout the novel; tropes that engender the novel with a special attitude and tonality which situate the text as something that is both novel-journal and extended prose poem. As Riffaterre writes, in a prose poem, 'the unifying factor will have to be generated by the text itself' (Caws and Riffaterre, p. 118). And the notion of intertextuality designates 'a function involving three factors: text, intertext and context with text being understood as the poem under the reader's eye; intertext being the indefinite and invariable corpus of literary works, written either before or after the text, perceived by the reader as having some relation to his own text; and context which designates surroundings within either the text or the intertext of that text' (Caws and Riffaterre, pp. 118–19). Each of these elements is found in Smart's work on microliterary and macroliterary levels. That is to say, either within the sentence or within the paragraph of the selected phases.

With these approaches as a foundation to Smart's text, one can then explore specific examples in the text which will enable us to appreciate better the poetics of her novel. For example, in Phase Four, while she is being detained by the police in Arizona for running away with 'him', she's asked questions about her lover to which she parenthetically responds in an allusion to Psalm 137 by counterpointing the interrogation with the intertextual discourse of *Song of Songs:*

What relation is this man to you? (My beloved is mine and I am his: he feedeth among the lilies).
How long have you known him? (I am my beloved's and my beloved is mine: he feedeth among the lilies).
Did you sleep in the same room? (Behold thou art fair, my love, behold thou art fair: thou hast dove's eyes).
In the same bed? (Behold thou art fair, my beloved, yea pleasant, also our bed is green).
Did intercourse take place? (I sat down under his shadow with great delight and his fruit was sweet to my taste).
When did intercourse first take place? (The king hath brought me to the banqueting house and his banner over me was love).
Were you intending to commit fornication in Arizona? (He shall lie all night betwixt my breasts).
Behold thou art fair my beloved, behold thou art fair: thou has dove's eyes.
Get away from there! cried the guard, as I wept by the crack of the door.

(My beloved is mine).

Better not try any funny business, cried the guard, you're only making things tough for yourself.

(Let him kiss me with the kisses of his mouth).

Stay put! cried the guard, and struck me. (Smart, pp. 47–8).

This particular passage is significant because it works on several levels in relation to both the prose and to the story itself. First, it counterpoints the mundanity of the interrogation with the sensitivity of the narrator's feelings; second, it exhibits a number of rhetorical techniques which abound in the novel; and third, it establishes a link (which is done throughout the novel) between the spirituality of love and the spirituality of religion. In that sense, love becomes likened to a religion and it is often dealt with that way.

But in addition to the intertextual Biblical allusions, there are numerous other intertextual allusions to mythical and literary figures. Regarding the notion of intertextuality, especially in relation to prose poems, Riffaterre has written that 'In a prose poem...the unifying factor will have to be generated by the text itself...The meaning cannot play this role, since meaning will not differentiate the poem's peculiar idiolect from language, from common usage. The unifying factor must be the significance. I propose to find the latter in a constant invariant relationship between text and intertext, in an invariable intertextuality. This much-abused and fashionable term designates a function involving three factors: text, intertext and context' (Caws and Riffaterre, p. 118). Riffaterre then goes on to categorize text 'as the poem under the reader's eye', the intertext as 'the indefinite and variable corpus of literary works, written either before or after the text, perceived by the reader as having some relation to his own text' and the context as that which designates 'these surroundings within the text or the intertext of the text'. Of the three, Riffaterre clearly privileges the impact of the intertext on the poem since once the reader has 'caught sight of the detail, episode, or image as the link to his text, he cannot help being influenced by what lies all around that connective in the intertext. Nor can he help comparing or trying to match up the impact of the connective's surroundings in the intertext with the impact of its surroundings in the poem he is reading' (Caws and Riffaterre, p. 118).

To that extent, the reader (she or he) intertext abounds in the novel. 'Like Macbeth, I keep remembering that I am their host. So it is tomorrow's breakfast rather than the future's blood that dictates fatal forbearance' (Smart, p. 18) and 'I went into the redwoods brooding and blushing with rage, to be stamped so obviously with femininity, and liable to humiliation worse than Venus' with Adonis, purely by reason of my accidental but flaunting sex (Smart, p. 20)[1] and 'He kissed my forehead driving along the coast in evening, and now, wherever I go, like the sword of Damocles, that greater never-to-be-given kiss hangs above my doomed head' (Smart, p. 22).[2] and 'It is written. Nothing can escape. Floating through the waves with seaweed in my hair, or being washed up battered on the inaccessible rocks, cannot undo the event to which there were never any alternatives. O lucky Daphne, motionless and green to avoid the touch of a god! Lucky, Syrinx, who chose a legend instead of too much blood! For me there was no choice. There were no cross-roads at all' (Smart, p. 22)[3] We also read of Antaeus, 'Like Antaeus, when I am thrust against this earth, I bounce back recharged with hope' (Smart, p. 56).[4] and 'By the Pacific I wander like Dido, hearing such a passion of tears in the breaking waves, that I wonder why the whole world isn't weeping inconsolably' (Smart, p. 94).[5] 'The repeated allusions to mythical and literary traditions reinforce the metaleptic (imagistic) framework and create an associative pattern that thematically and structurally unifies the novel. Allusions are an integral part of the narrator's thought, and they delineate her emotional struggle as she experiences the vicissitudes of love; in fact, she says her thoughts are "archives full of archetypes"' (Van Wert, p. 43). Finally we get, 'Every brick was blood. The spire gored her for christening, even while her upturned face expected the kiss of Christ. The stones are smooth because her agony rolled them out. She was spilt as offering. Three times she was martyred, but the third time she truly died' (Smart, p. 108).

Curiously, Smart's reliance upon biblical literature and mythology predates that of Hélène Cixous whose 'predilection for the Old Testament is obvious, but her taste for classical antiquity is no less marked. Her capacity for identification seems endless: Medusa, Electra, Antigone, Dido, Cleopatra – in her imagination she has been them all. In fact, she declares that "I am myself the earth, everything that happens on it, all the lives that live me there in my different forms": This constant return to biblical and mythological imagery signals her investment in the world of myth: a world that, like the distant country of fairy tales is perceived as pervasively meaningful, as closure and unity. The mythological or religious discourse presents a universe where all difference, struggle and discord can in the end be satisfactorily resolved' (Moi, p. 116). Yet Smart has not been valorized for this uniqueness by Cixous (as Cixous valorizes Lispector, for example) nor by many others.

All of these intertextual figures are used as additional commentary on the mental/emotional state of the lyrical narrator; they also counterpoint the rather mundane world in which she lives and in which she suffers. These figures serve the purpose of detachment and escape from the everyday and the stark indifference she finds in how the 'elders' perceive love. 'Essentially, the narrator finds solace and relief in the world of heroic lovers, and in the world of literature where the erotic desire and pain unite natural passion and the imagination. The transformation of the lovers into archetypes thematically links the lovers of the particular world with the legendary world of heroic ideals'. (Van Wert, p. 44)

But beyond the textual intercalations we are presented with the writing itself. The writing *qua* writing and as such it begs the question (again): What makes the prose poetic? Or is it something other than poetic prose *à la* Baudelaire, but, rather, the craft of a presumed *écriture féminine*? And what then distinguishes poetic prose from *écriture féminine*? When one thinks of an *écriture féminine* one tends to think of Hélène Cixous; however, depending on one's choice of feminist critics, Cixous either affirms or denies the actual existence of an *écriture féminine*. According to Verana Andermatt Conley, (circa '92) Cixous' 'turning toward a feminine future and an écriture féminine lead her toward a rich, abundant, exalted phase of writing' (Conley, p. 54) and that 'she searches for a feminine writing whose mass defies retention, repression and [the logic of] meaning' (Conley, p. 55). On the other hand, Verana Andermatt Conley (circa '84) writes that 'Cixous is adamant that even the term '*écriture féminine* or "feminine writing" is abhorrent to her, since terms like "masculine" and "feminine" themselves imprison within a binary logic, within the "classical vision of sexual opposition between men and women"' (Conley 129). Is the ambivalence intentional? Unintentional? Logically illogic? For Cixous, speaking for herself, a woman physically materializes that she's thinking; that is, she signifies with her body. And with that vision, Christine Makward indicates there 'are twelve different kinds of style in Cixous' novel *LA*: seven poetic and five narrative levels. Five of the seven poetic levels can be characterized as in some way biblical, liturgical or mythological. These high poetic inflections find their way into Cixous' more theoretical writing as well' (Moi, p. 115). In other words, the manner in which Cixous is writing (at least in terms of the biblical or the mythological) is not unlike what Smart was writing three decades earlier.

This diachronic malady presents a problematic situation in that if one can read Baudelaire in Smart and one can read Smart in Cixous then one might expect to read Baudelaire in Cixous. If so, was an *écriture féminine* actually invented by Baudelaire? And does that really reduce the notion of an *écriture féminine* to a variant (if not an analogue) of the prose poem in which case Smart would be the progenitrix of an *écriture féminine* that was Baudelaire-born an irony that Baudelaire (if not Jeanne Duval) would have had a difficult time countenancing. Or, in Duval's case, if one can believe Baudelairean biographers, even understanding.

But how does one recognize this kind of writing? Clearly one is dealing with a systemic overflow of images, metaphor, metonymy, metastasis, of repetition, permutation, trope. But can one distinguish one from the other? Male–Female. Irigaray writes 'the connotations of women's discourse are primarily expressed in privileged ways – through adjectives, for example' (Irigaray, p. 36) which would lead one to believe in a kind of Gramscian 'hegemony of adjectives' in which we, as readers, are somehow implicit partners in this coercion of language since 'female' adjectives must somehow take precedence over 'male' adjectives. Obviously, this approach leads us nowhere. Without going into exhaustive detail of *By Grand Central Station* (and here I pay obeisance to Todorov's approach to the entire notion of poetics in general) one might be better served by presenting representative passages from Smart to illustrate her poetics in practice. For example:

> The long days seduce all thought away, and we lie like the lizards in the sun, postponing our lives indefinitely. But by the bathing pool, or on the sandhills of the beach, the Beginning lurks uncomfortably on the outskirts of the circle, like an unpopular person whom ignoring can keep away. The very silence, the very avoiding of any intimacy between us, when he, when he was only a word, was able to cause me sleepless nights and shivers of intimation, is the more dangerous.   (Smart, pp. 19–20).

By restructuring the passage at the sonic level we can poeticize the prose (at least in form) to look like the following:

1. The long days seduce all thought away
2. and we lie like the lizards in the sun
3. postponing our lives indefinitely.
4. But by the bathing pool
5. or on the sandhills of the beach
6. the Beginning lurks uncomfortably
7. on the outskirts of the circle
8. like an unpopular person
9. whom ignoring can keep away.
10. The very silence
11. the very avoiding
12. of any intimacy between us
13. when he
14. when he was only a word
15. was able to cause me sleepless nights
16. and shivers of intimation
17. is the more dangerous.

With this kind of a scheme we can measure the lines in terms of variable syllabics in which we get the following seventeen line pattern:
9–10–10–6–8–10–8–8–8–5–6–10–2 –7–9–8–6
which breaks down into the following measured syllabics:

octosyllabic (5)
decasyllabic (4)
hexasyllabic (3)
nonosyllabic (2)
heptasyllabic (1)
pentasyllabic (1)
disyllabic (1)

We read alliteration in lines 2 and 4; similes in lines 2 and 8; repetition is lines 10 to 11 and 12 to 13; we have stichs and enjambment and liaisons and the synaesthestic metaphor in line 16 all of which 'coagulate' into a kind of prose that clearly lends itself poetry, but poetry of a different kind. Again from Smart:

> For clues to all calamity I have the painful lovemaking of alley-cats along the roofs outside my window; the quarter-hour chiming of a clock whose notes partly never strike; the wheezing of the coils,

cheerful and regular like crickets. The elevator, though, clatters a
promise of event never fulfilled, and sometimes the plumbing
shrieks remotely like the message of a falling comet. (Smart, p. 80).

1. For clues to all calamity
2. I have the painful lovemaking
3. of alleycats along the roofs
4. outside my window;
5. the quarter-hour chiming
6. of a clock whose notes partly never strike;
7. the wheezing of the coils,
8. cheerful and regular like crickets.
9. The elevator,
10. though,
11. clatters a promise of events never fulfilled,
12. and sometimes the plumbing shrieks remotely
13. like the message of a falling comet.

Once again in terms of variable syllabics we get the following
pattern in thirteen lines:
8–8–8–5–6–10–7–9–4–1–11–9–10
with the constituent syllabics of:

octosyllabic (3)
decasyllabic (2)
nonosyllabic (2)
pentasyllabic (1)
hexasyllabic (1)
heptasyllabic (1)
tetrasyllabic (1)
monosyllabic (1)
hendecasyllabic (1)

Smart appears to have a preference for the octosyllabic measure in
her prose, but regardless of her preference (conscious or not) there
is a strong element of the poetic alive. Using the same kind of
formatting, one can see some startling similarities with some of
Baudelaire's work specifically in *Spleen* LXXXV in which he writes:

Pluviôse, irrité contre la ville entière,
De son urne à grands flots verse un froid ténébreux

Aux pâles habitants du voisin cimetière
Et la mortalité sur les faubourgs brumeux.

Mon chat sur le carreau cherchant une litière
Agite sans repos son corps maigre et galeux;
L'ame d'un vieux poète erre dans la gouttière
Avec la triste voix d'un fantôme frileux.

Le bourdon se lamente, et labûche enfumée
Accompagne en fausset la pendule enrhumée
cepdenant qu'en un jeu plein de sales parfums,

Héritage fatal d'une vielle hydropique,
Le beau valet de coeur et la dame de pique
Causent sinistrement de leurs amours défunts.

(Pluviose, irritated with the entire city,
Pours a torrent of tenebrous cold from his great urn,
Over the pale inhabitants of the neighboring graveyards
And on the mortality of the foggy suburbs.

My cat walking on the flagging searching for his litter
Agitated and without repose, his body mangy and malnourished;
An old poet's soul wanders in the gutter
With the sad voice of a chilling phantom.

The bourdon laments and the firelog smokes
Accompanied by the falsetto of a pendulum that wheezes
While in a card game of vile smelling perfumes,

The fatal heritage of an aging dropsical
The handsome Jack of Hearts and the Queen of Spades
Chat sinisterly of their defunct love).

If one breaks down the poem into English prose, the variable syllabics are not of as much concern in the analysis (though clearly the twelve syllable Alexandrine lends itself to a panoply of rhythmical divisions) as is the content similarity related to the love experience and how such similar images are used in such different ways: love unrequited, love lost. But the fabric of Smart's prose and Baudelaire's poetry is clearly evinced in the texts though one is considered 'prose' and the other 'poetry'. The question as to whether Smart read Baudelaire is immaterial. If she did read him, in French, then she was able to synthesize the poetic virtue of the prose into English. If she read him in English, then she was able to synthesize the poetic virtue of the prose into her own idiom. Perhaps a better example of showing the similarities in the poetic style of both is the following:

> I am over-run, jungled in my bed, I am infested with a menagerie of desires: my heart is eaten by a dove, a cat scrambles in the cave of my sex, hounds in my head obey a whipmaster who cries nothing but havoc as the hours test my endurance with an accumulation of tongues. Who, if I cried, would hear me among the angelic orders? I am far, far beyond that island of days where once, it seems, I watched a flower grow, and counted the steps of the sun, and fed, if my memory serves, the smiling animal at his appointed hour. I am shot with wounds which have eyes that see a world all sorrow, always to be, panoramic and unhealable, and mouths that hang unspeakable in the sky of blood. (Smart, p. 23)

And from Baudelaire's *Paris Spleen* he writes in, 'One O'Clock in the Morning':

> Dissatisfied with everything, dissatisfied with myself, I long to redeem myself and to restore my pride in the silence and solitude of the night. Souls of those whom I have loved, souls of those whom I have sung, strengthen me, sustain me, keep me from the vanities of the world and its contaminating fumes; and You, dear God! grant me grace to produce a few beautiful verses to prove to myself that I am not the lowest of men, that I am not inferior to those whom I despise.   (Varèse, p. 16)

Both of these excerpts clearly engage the personal, the journal-istic, the spiritual, the poetic. Without attempting to compare the pieces at the sonic level, one is struck with their similarity, not only in the way they approach the 'I' and the 'other' (and there are numerous instances in which the 'I' and the 'other' are manifest as the writer as '*flaneûr or flaneûse*' observes the world around him/her), but in how they allow the prose to reflect poetically the moment both in content and context. The form of the prose, the manner in which the prose is written, then becomes a kind of versification itself and that versification is clearly a hallmark of poetic prose. To that end, a notion of an *écriture féminine* has little basis. What one deals with, whether in French or English (or any other language, for that matter) is the writer's ability to poeticize language. One can either do that or not do that, but to lay claim that an *écriture féminine* exists and is distinguished (as Irigaray suggests) by the use of 'adjectives' seems specious at best. Though one can universalize, as Irigaray does, that 'women's discourse designates men as subjects' (Irigaray, p. 35) and men's discourse is 'designated as inanimate abstractions integral to the subject's world' (Irigaray, p. 35), her point of departure is seemingly predicated on a kind of discourse that includes all cultural identities and excludes all imaginative writing.

However, beyond the prose versification there is the constant repetition of certain images that clearly play into a notion, if not of an *écriture féminine* then certainly of a kind of 'feminine ethos'. The images of blood and water are everywhere apparent and the repetition of blood seems inextricably bound with love as both a birth principle and a death principle: birth in relation to the creation; death in relation to the ultimate betrayal. There are constant allusions to blood. From Phase two where she says 'and who will drown in all this blood' (Smart, p. 31) to Phase ten where she writes that 'he also is drowning in the blood of too much sacrifice' (Smart, p. 111) the images of blood and water play a major role in the novel. From the line 'O the water of love that floods everything over, so that there is nothing the eye sees that is not covered in. There is no angle the world can assume which the love in my eye cannot make into a symbol of love. Even the precise geometry of his hand, when I gaze at it, dissolves me into water and I flow away in a flood of love' (Smart, p. 39) to 'Not all the poisonous tides of the blood I have split can influence these tidals of love' (Smart, p. 39), Smart constantly coagulates blood with water. Unlike Cixous whose 'mythical and biblical allusions are often accompanied by – or interspersed with – 'oceanic' water imagery, evolving the endless pleasures of the polymorphously perverse child' (Moi, p. 116), Smart's images of water and blood have no reliance on the 'comforting security of the mother's womb' (Moi, p. 117), but, rather, rely on the more primordial solvents of blood and water as representative of birth and death.

In the end, she is betrayed by her lover and all that remains is her language, a language of love and he, love, is now a legend in which he is 'beautiful and allegory. He is as beautiful as the legend the imagination washes up on the sand' and she concludes with the line 'I prefer corncobs to the genitals of the male' (Smart, p. 112) which seems to be as clear a notion of feminine empowerment as anything written by either Cixous or Irigaray. What ultimately remains in Smart's poetics is the notion of the invincible, the immortal, the sacrosanct which butts up against the ogre of reality in the guise of the metal and marble of Grand Central Station, and which relishes in the poetic prose perpetuated by pain.

8

The Poetics of Mortality in Lispector's *The Hour of the Star*

Lispector's *The Hour of the Star* (*A Hora da Estrela*) was her final novel and was published one month before her death. One could write a great deal about 'terminovels', those novels which become the last living testament of the author and the author's 'purpose' but that would be beyond the scope of this testament. Obviously, Lispector was well aware of the fact she was dying of cancer which may, in fact, account for what Giovanni Pontiero has written that 'Clarice Lispector began to experience an almost obsessive nostalgia for Recife in the North-eastern State of Pernambuco, where she had spent her childhood' (Lispector, p. 89). Certainly the main protagonist of the novel, Macabéa, a 'nordestina' whose quest for a better life takes her from provincial squalor to a more metropolitan squalor is much like Lispector herself who knew what it was like to journey from a venue of abject safety to one of abject mystery and 'knew, too, what it meant to be immediately bombarded with a plethora of utterly new sights, sounds and ideas. She knew what it meant to find herself suddenly among strangers and to have to make up her life as she went along' (Fitz, p. 202); however, even though the prevailing social conditions are important in *The Hour of the Star*, what is patently clear about the novel is that it functions on two distinct levels: 1) as a quasi-biographical novel and implicit in that autobiography, a testament to her life; and 2) as a novel about the act of novel-writing.

In one of her more insightful comments, Hélène Cixous has written 'In Clarice, happiness is always secret. Perhaps at a certain level the beautiful, which belongs to aesthetics, is replaced by truth. The beautiful is annulled in a kind of neutralization of the beautiful and the ugly. At the limit, instead of the too beautiful, we have what is too much alive, even mortally alive. Something is so much alive that one can die of it, or it can die' (Cixous, p. 83). And if one decomposes what Lispector has done in this 'poetics of mortality' one can see that from the very outset of the novel she is not equivocating in her 'song of death'. *The Author's Dedication (alias Clarice Lispector)* is anything but equivocating, though it is Lispectorly deceptive. There is no illusion of an 'implied author' in the Dedication; there is no need for one since it is not only her epitaph about which she is writing, but a fundamentally substantive poetics for the 'novel' that is to follow. It is, in a way, reminiscent of Musil's *Posthumous Papers of a Living Author* in which Musil writes: 'I at any rate have decided to forestall publication of my own last literary effects before the time comes when I no longer have a say in the matter. And the most dependable way to make sure of this is to publish it myself while still alive, whether this makes sense to everyone or not' (Musil, p. ix).

Like Musil, Lispector is a *Dichter*, a term which has no real English equivalent, but encompasses both poetic/prose stylists and one would be foolish indeed to believe that Lispector would fashion her own epitaph as a Dedication to her text without the same rigour that she would apply to the work of fiction itself. To that end, one needs to quote the Dedication in full to appreciate the rigor of the poetics she positions:

> I dedicate this narrative to dear old Schumann and his beloved Clara who are now, alas, nothing but dust and ashes. I dedicate it to the deep crimson of my blood as someone in his prime. I dedicate it, above all, to those gnomes, dwarfs, sylphs, and nymphs who inhabit my life. I dedicate it to the memory of my years of hardship when everything was more austere and honourable, and I had never eaten lobster. I dedicate it to the tempest of Beethoven. To the vibrations of Bach's neutral colours. To Chopin who leaves me weak. To Stravinsky who terrifies me and makes me soar in flames. *To Death and Transfiguration*, in which Richard Strauss predicts my fate. Most of all, I dedicate it to the day's vigil and to day itself, to the transparent voice of Debussy, to Marlos Nobre, to Prokofiev, to Carl Orff and Schoenberg, to the twelve-tone composers, to the strident notes of an electronic generation – to all those musicians who have touched within me the most alarming and unsuspected regions; to all those prophets of our age who have revealed me to myself and made me explode into: me. This me that is you, for I cannot bear to be simply me, I need others in order to stand up, giddy and

awkward as I am, for what can one do except meditate in order to plunge into that total void which can only be attained through meditation. Meditation need not bear fruit; meditation can be an end in itself. I meditate without words or themes. What troubles my existence is writing.

And we must never forget that if the atom's structure is invisible, it is none the less real. I am aware of the existence of many things I have never seen. And you too. One cannot prove the existence of what is most real but the essential thing is to believe. To weep and believe. This story unfolds in a state of emergency and public calamity. It is an unfinished book because it offers no answer. An answer I hope someone somewhere in the world may be able to provide. You perhaps? It is a story in technicolour to add a touch of luxury, for heaven knows, I need that too. A men for all of us.   (Lispector, pp. 7–8)

And so begins and ends Lispector's poetics of mortality, her *coda* to mortality, if you will, since the prevailing focus in the Dedication is clearly the *adieu* to the music that had influenced her life, but the Dedication is devoted not just to music, but *music, meditation and molecularization* a not altogether disparate trio of items and one which needs to be decomposed individually to see how they link both thematically and poetically.

Lispector literally leaves us with Beethoven's tempest and Bach's neutral colours; Stravinsky's flames and Strauss's transfigurational tone-poems; Debussy's transparent voice and the music of Marlos Nobre, Prokofiev, Orff and Schoenberg all of whom, in somewhat equal measure, have afforded the writer material for her life. To what extent these different composers have rendered Lispector, Lispector is not clear; she does not specify what composition(s) of Debussy, Marlos Nobre, Prokofiev, Orff or Schoenberg she has in mind, though one could presume perhaps they could be Debussy's diaphanous *Lent et rêveur* ('The Odours of the Night' from *Ibéria*); Prokofiev's Toccata, as homage to Schumann's own Toccata; Orff's *Carmina Burana* and Schoenberg's *Variations for Orchestra, op. 31* all of which, in their own way, tend to encourage a kind of non-traditional sound to them, a sound that would appeal to Lispector's sense of the non-traditional, of the non-linear. The inclusion of Marlos Nobre among all these other composers is significant. Not only is the only Latino composer among them (he was a fellow Brazilian, also born in Recife) but his work is particularly important in relation to Lispector's own work by virtue of its unique style in which he tried to create a new musical language based on a kind of free serialism, incorporating aleatory structures and indigenous touches as in *Variaçoes rumicas* and *Ukrinmakrinkrin*.

But regardless of what compositions Lispector may have been thinking, the composers are both similar and disparate as the range of their music might indicate including, for example, both Stravinsky and Schoenberg. And in a curious way, Lispector is somewhat indebted to Adorno for her Dedication, for it is in Adorno's *Philosophy of Modern Music* (1948) that two instrumental essays appear dealing with both Stravinsky and Schoenberg both of which lend themselves to a clearer understanding of Lispector's novel itself.

The Stravinsky essay 'Stravinsky and Restoration' is 'the shorter of the two, and was conceived specifically to round out the nevertheless comprehensive view of modern music incorporated into "Schoenberg and Progress", which had been written seven years previously as an independent study. Adorno saw the two figures as representing necessarily linked, yet diametrically opposed, aspects of musical modernism in the West' (Franklin, p. 58). But what Adorno addresses specifically in relation to Schoenberg is in his section titled 'Dialectics of Loneliness' where he writes 'What radical music perceives is the untransfigured suffering of man. His impotence has increased to the point that it no longer permits illusion and play...In the expression of anxiety as 'forebodings', the music of Schoenberg's Expressionistic phase offers evidence of this importence' (Adorno, p. 42). But Adorno also speaks to the issue of Progress and considers Schoenberg the model of the progressive artist 'in that all change in art depends to some extent – positively or negatively, self-consciously or intuitively – upon an attitude adopted to the culturally determined products that were available to the nascent artist, then in all art, according to its relative acquiescence to or rejection of tradition, we have that stance which Adorno sees as essentially a "philosophic" one' (Franklin, p. 61).

Though this study makes no attempt at dealing with the poetics of Adorno's *Philosophy of Modern Music*, it does attempt to show how the composers that Lispector chose to include in her Dedication are not in any way aleatory selections, though they may appear to be and that *appearance* of being aleatory though not aleatory is, in great measure, the crux of Lispector's overall poetics and which leads to the second topic implicit in the Dedication: meditation and, presumably, Zen meditation.

Lispector says that she 'meditates without words or themes' and as one reads in *The Four Statements of Zen*, 'A special transmission outside the Scripture; No dependence on words or letters; Direct pointing at the Mind of man; Seeing into one's Nature and attainment of Buddhahood' (Suzuki, p. 1). This notion of meditating, and especially of Zen meditation, fits very nicely into the presumably ambiguous patterns that one reads in *The Hour of the Star*, patterns which lend themselves directly to this kind of Zen thought in which the whole notion of truth is called into question. As Suzuki writes, 'A truth that is definite is a truth that can be defined. Such a truth has a *finis*. But life itself being forever a matter of unfinished business, the truth that life must be a truth that is unbounded, without a *finis*, in-finite rather than de-finite. Zen is not a doctrine, nor a set of ideas nor a position. It is not subsumable under any sort of "ism". It cannot be classified as either theism, atheism or agnosticism. It is affiliated with no particular school of philosophy; it is no closer to idealism than to materialism. It has no view about the nature of reality; it formulates no system of ethics, propounds no political ideology ... Zen will be found not in the words themselves, but only in penetrating the living source from which come these words and from which an infinity of other wordings could come' (Suzuki, p. xxii). The novel is replete with allusions to being and non-being, a state of humanness that is a fundamental part of the Zen (non)philosophy.

Which brings us to the last of the three foci in the Dedication which is 'molecularization', which is a kind of *mélange* of meditation and atomization since Lispector writes 'we must never forget that if the atom's structure is invisible, it is none the less real'. In that statement we not only have a Zen refrain, but a Kabbalistic one as well. As a Jew, Lispector would doubtlessly have been familiar with the Kabbalah and would certainly have been familiar with the Zohar and the Zohar states that the 'human being consists of the following elements: 1) a spirit which represents the highest degree of his existence; 2) a soul which is the seat of good and evil, of good and evil desires – in short, of all moral attributes; and 3) a coarser spirit which is closely related to the body and is the direct cause of lower movements – that is, the actions and instincts of animal life' (Franck, p. 124). As Lispector 'begins' the novel 'Everything in the world began with a yes. One molecule said yes to another molecule and life was born' (Lispector, p. 11). And so begins a Zoharic connection between the 'coarser spirit' and molecular biology. But the Kabbalah is a means for education, for one's quest, one's journey in life which, among many things, is clearly a trial, a trial that readers of Kafka may even overlook. According to Kabbalah, 'the soul has a need, inherent in its finite nature, to play a part in the universe and to contemplate the spectacle offered by Creation, in order to attain awareness of itself and its origin; and to return without becoming entirely identified with it, to that inexhaustible source of light and life called divine thought' (Franck, p. 127). Lispector concludes the Dedication by saying that 'One cannot prove the existence of what is most real but the essential thing is to believe. To weep and believe'. To which she finally adds, 'Amen for all of us'. To that end, the Dedication is not merely a page-and-a-half of aleatory salutations, adieus and importunate renderings, it is a residual effect of a life led in discovery and does, by its very nature, amalgamate mortality, meditation and the molecule in an extraordinary way and, at the same, time establishes a poetics that will become the foundation for the entire novel to follow, a novel which does not purport to begin with something as 'eccentric' as a presumed table of contents.

A table of contents is, by definition, meant to edify. In the best tradition of Brazilian tables of contents, from Machado de Assis to Márcio Souza, Lispector has altered where the table of contents should be and substituted the title(s), which acts as a table of contents without being labelled as such and which yields not one single and definitive title, but a dozen titles which are both typographically and orthogenetically crucial to the text.

THE HOUR OF THE STAR
The Blame is Mine
or
The Hour of the Star
or
Let Her Fend for Herself
or
The Right to Protest
Clarice Lispector

.As for the Future.
or
Singing the Blues
or
She Doesn't Know How to Protest

or

A Sense of Loss

or

Whistling in the Dark Wind

or

I Can Do Nothing

or

A Record of Preceding Events

or

A Tearful Tale

or

A Discreet Exit by the Back Door

Lispector, using a series of possible (yet presumably not usable titles), presents the reader with a kind of compendium that exacts the nature of the novel, its heroine, and the heroine's progenitor since each 'title' has a bearing upon the outcome of the text both within the confines and outside the confines of the covers. And though all the titles have, in one way or another, a bearing on the novel, what distinguishes each of them is the link between them: 'or'. To have an 'or' one must have an 'either'; to have an either/or implies a choice which implies a decision to be rendered. But when one uses 'or' in the manner in which Lispector uses it, the writer is not clear about what choice there is to make. In that ambiguity rests the fact that something both 'is' and 'is not'. And one finds that that ambiguity, which was seen in the Dedication and now in the presumed 'table of contents', runs throughout the entire novel. For Lispector is constantly saying what is and what isn't. She will write something only to write the opposite sometime later as if things are, but are also not at the same time a movement that is both Zen and Kabbalistic. Examples abound. One reads 'But emptiness, too, has its value and somehow resembles abundance. One way of obtaining is not to search, one way of possessing is not to ask; simply to believe that my inner silence is the solution to my – to my mystery' (Lispector, p. 14); 'To probe oneself is to recognize that one is incomplete' (Lispector, p. 16); 'what is fully mature is very close to rotting' (Lispector, p. 17) and so on.

Clearly the title '.*As for the Future.*' plays a pivotal role in the text since it is the *only* title to have periods at the beginning and the end preceded by Lispector's signature thus privileging itself as a kind of semiotic referent to the future that has no future beyond the confines of the page. What is clear is that her signature, placed where it is, is revealing for it is typographically placed between 'the right to protest' and '.As for the future.' There is no 'or' between them. Merely periods. End points. Stops. On page 13 she specifically addresses the title, 'As for the future', and it is the only title on which she specifically comments though she alludes to one of the other titles when she writes 'Yet I am prepared to leave quietly by the door' (Lispector, p. 21) an 'exit' which doubtlessly passes to someplace else. She also writes 'Will this story become my own coagulation one day?' (Lispector, p. 12) which clearly defines itself as a haemophilia of different origins and which leads a reader to see how the story of Macabéa is true even though it is invented.

The role of invention is, of course, the fabric of Lispector's fiction whether the invention comes in the form of the Dedication or in the form of an ambiguous narrator or in the form of alternative truths in the fiction itself since the novel is also a novel about novel writing. From the self-conscious Dedication to the replete interventions of the author *qua* narrator (and here there is little doubt about the fact) one is witnessing the writing of a novel and the novel of writing. *The Hour of the Star* is replete with allusions to writing or the writing process: Yet I have no intention of adorning the word, for were I to touch the girl's bread, that bread would turn to gold...so I must express myself simply – without making too much fuss about my humility for then it would no longer be humility – I confine myself to narrating the unremarkable adventures of a girl living in a hostile city (Lispector, p. 15). Or: 'Coming back to myself: what I am about to write cannot be assimilated by minds that expect much and crave sophistication. For what I am about to express will be quite stark. Although it may have as its background – even now – the tormented at night. Do not, therefore, expect stars in which follows for nothing will scintillate. This is opaque material and by its very nature it is despised by everyone. This story has no melody that could be rightly termed *cantabile*' (Lispector, p. 16) which begs a comparison with Duras's *Moderato cantabile*, but without the restraint. Or: 'In writing this story, I shall yield to emotion and I know perfectly well that every day is one more day stolen from death. In no sense an intellectual, I write with my body'. (Lispector, p. 16). Or: 'Why do I write? First of all because I have captured the spirit of language and at times it is the form that constitutes the content. I write, therefore, not for the girl from the North-east but for the much more serious reason of

force majeure, or as they say in formal petitions by "force of law" '
(Lispector, pp. 17–18). She also asks the question: 'How do I write?'
(Lispector, p. 18) and that she is 'scared of starting' [to write]
(Lispector, p. 19) that 'The action of the story will result in my
transfiguration [my emphasis] into someone else and in my ultimate
materialisation into an object' (Lispector, p. 20) statements which
refer not only to the Dedication, but to the 'future'. Lispector is
constantly intervening in the story of the story in the thinly dis-
guised Rodrigo. She makes authorial comments at will without
regard for the 'normal way of writing' as she writes 'So I shall
attempt, contrary to my normal method, to write a story with a
beginning, middle, and a "grand finale" followed by silence and
falling rain' (Lispector, p. 13). Throughout the novel she will inter-
vene to give the reader a comment about the character or about the
writer or about writing which is a constant reminder that someone
is in control of the characters, and the writer, and the writing and
what happens to them. Her relationship to Macabéa is the same
relationship of Lispector's to God and, as one reads later, the constant allusions to God and Jesus are not serendipitous.

The question naturally arises: What exactly do we know about the
narrator? And who is the narrator? The narrator moves in and out
of the narrative; is often contradictory; does not necessarily know
the truth; and spends a great deal of time telling us about what it
[the novel] is going to be like, when it [the novel] is going to start,
the causes for its [the novel's] delay, when, in fact, it already has
begun and is continuing. This is done continually even as late as
page 23 when she writes 'I see that I have almost started telling my
story . . . ' and on page 24 one discovers that the actual story part of
the story begins in earnest. But one detects the narrator too is as
ambiguous as the philosophy and as such plays into the founda-
tions established in the Dedication and alluded to in the fundamental distribution of the 'laws' of Zen. Lispector writes: 'I suspect that
this lengthy preamble is intended to conceal the poverty of my
story, for I am apprehensive. Before this typist entered my life, I
was a reasonably contented chap despite my limited success as a
writer. Things were somehow so good that they were in danger of
becoming very bad because what is *fully mature is very close to rotting*
[my emphasis]' (Lispector, p. 17); however, two paragraphs later
'he' writes that 'It seems that I am changing my style of writing. Not
being a professional writer, I please myself what I write about – and
I must write about this girl from the North-east otherwise I shall

choke' (Lispector, p. 17). Not only does one detect the ambiguity of Zen in the writing, but one must question the authority of the author. Is the author a 'limited successful writer' or '[not a] professional writer'? Does limited success mean one who has received money for one's work? If so, then one is, at least to some degree, modest as it may be, a professional writer. If one is a professional writer, regardless of the quantity of cash one receives, then why state one is not a professional writer unless the ambiguity is part of the poetics of the piece?

Which, too, begs the question as to the authority of the author's gender. Can one be convinced that, in fact, the author, Rodrigo S. M., is a male since as 'he' writes 'There is no way of escaping facts' (Lispector, p. 16). Beyond the admission that the writer 'write[s] with my body' (Lispector, p. 16) (a very curious thing for a male writer to write), the novel records a number of instances in which 'the body' is the main referent [for example, 'I know there are girls who sell their bodies' and 'the person whom I am about to describe scarcely has a body to sell' (Lispector, p. 14)] all of which leads one back to the notions of *écriture féminine* or 'writing the body' or as Cixous has said 'it is the woman who is more the writer, by the very fact that she creates an idiom; and the poet well knows that it is the mother tongue he speaks and no other' (Eagleton, p. 313) and that 'the woman is close to the body, the source of writing: "it is obvious that a woman does not write like a man, because she speaks with the body, writing is from the body"' (Ibid). Without reinventing the chapter on Elizabeth Smart (which deals extensively with the notion of *écriture féminine*,) nor dealing with the work of Artaud who, in his own way, wrote the body, one can look at Lispector's text with an eye towards whether the work 'reflects' the writing of a man or a woman which to a great extent plays into Lispector's frame of ambiguity.

One knows, for instance, that she wrote the Dedication as 'The Author's Dedication (alias Clarice Lispector)', but she writes the novel as Rodrigo S. M. So how, then, does the male implied author write? Does he write like a man or does he write like a woman? If he writes like a man what does that look like? And if he writes like a woman is that an example of *écriture féminine?* There are key passages in the novel which do, in fact, tend to yield to a Cixousian instance of *écriture féminine* if that is to mean 'writing the body' the way a woman would write the body. 'It reminds me of a former girl friend. She was sexually experienced and there was such darkness inside her body. I have never forgotten her: one never forgets a person with whom one has slept. The event remains branded on one's living flesh like a tattoo and all who witness the stigma take flight in horror' (Lispector, p. 18). Or: 'I must reproduce myself with the delicacy of a white butterfly. The idea of the white butterfly stems from the feeling that, should the girl marry, she will marry looking as slender and ethereal as any virgin dressed in white' (Lispector, p. 20). Or: 'Meanwhile, the clouds are white and the sky is blue. Why is there so much God? At the expense of men' (Lispector, p. 26). Or: 'Although her tiny ovules were all shrivelled. So hopelessly shrivelled' (Lispector, p. 33). Or: 'By contrast, Olímpico was a demon of strength and vitality and who had fathered children. He possessed the precious semen in abundance. And as was said or left unsaid, Macabéa had ovaries as shrivelled as overcooked mushrooms' (Lispector, p. 58). Or: 'A woman's destiny is to be a woman. Macabéa had perceived the almost painful and vertiginous moment of overwhelming love. A painful and difficult reflowering that she enacted with her body and that other thing you call a soul and I call – what?' (Lispector, p. 84). And finally: 'When I consider that I might have been born her – and why not? – I shudder. The fact that I am not her strikes me as being a cowardly escape. I feel remorse, as I explained in one of my titles for this book' (Lispector, p. 38).

One can certainly lay claim, in a Cixousian manner, that these excerpts are written truly from the body and that several of them do, seemingly, sound incongruous coming from a male point of view. It is certainly possible that a man might never forget all the wo/men with whom he has slept and it is certainly possible that a man might be interested in Macabéa's ovules and their shrivelledness and it is certainly possible that a man might refer to his semen as 'precious', but all of these possibilities seem highly unlikely. And the final example where Lispector feels remorse as she explained in 'one of my titles for this book' is revealing since it is Rodrigo who is narrating this passage and not Lispector. Or is it Lispector writing as Rodrigo writing as Lispector? Or might this be a type of literary *la cage aux folles*? What transpires throughout the work itself, through the words themselves, is that the narrator is not male, but female which begs the question why? But this too plays into the notion of ambiguity in her writing. The novel is written by a woman who has even signed the title page with her name, yet she claims to be Rodrigo S. M. the use of initials acting as yet another example of poetic ambiguity and therefore identity. And through-out the novel both Macabéa, through the narrator, and the narrator are questioning the notion of being and non- being, of who they are and what they are.

So even before one gets into the 'thicket' of the story itself a number of different aspects have been established: irony, black humour, the presence of an intrusive narrator who uses paradox-ical language and ambiguous phrasing. But Lispector does not merely let the poetics of the text maintain a kind of literary balance. She also infuses the text with an irony incumbent in the names of her characters as well: Macabéa and Olímpico. Olímpico from Mt Olympos, the residence of the gods, and Macabéa after Judas Maccabeus who recovered the temple in 165 BCE or after one of the family of Maccabees who, because they were obedient to the commandments of God, had been given victory over those who would undermine the teachings of Torah. Clearly, the character of Olímpico as 'one who inhabits Olympos' is irony enough since 'He came from the backwoods of Paraíba. His determination to survive stemmed from his roots in a region noted for its primitive, savage way of life, its recurring spells of drought. Olímpico had arrived in Rio with a tin of perfumed vaseline and a comb, his sole posses-sions purchased at an open market in Paraíba. He rubbed the vaseline into his hair until it was wet and glossy. It never occurred to him that the girls in Rio might be put off by that lank, greasy hair. He had been born looking more shrivelled and scorched than a withered branch or a stone lying in the sun' (Lispector, p. 57). Which, of course, is in direct contrast to: 'Olímpico was a demon of strength and vitality and who had fathered children. He possessed the precious semen in abundance' (Lispector, p. 58). In either case, Olímpico is not a character whose name revivifies times and heroes of a nobler age. One could make a case that Lispector's poetics here are merging on the theological in some kind of parasyntactic rela-tion between the Jews and the Hellenistic tradition out of which the Maccabean uprising occurred since 'inherent in Hellenism was an inexorable challenge to the particularity of the Torah' (Franck, p. 50), but Lispector was not after that kind of theoliterary dynamic. What she was after is the distinctly ironic way in which she uses the process of (un)naming and in the role Fortune plays especially in the case of Macabéa.

To the former, one discovers that Macabéa had no name at birth and names, of course, relate to identity. So from birth, she had no identity, no way of knowing who she was or what she was. In an odd state of affairs, when she does discover who she is, she is an ugly virgin who drinks coke and listens to the radio; who does not know she is impoverished, who is always thinking about who or what she is as mediated by the narrator who is constantly thinking about who or what she is. This suggestion, of course, brings up the notion of identity since identity and naming are inextricably bound. Lispector even writes: 'Forgive me if I add something more about myself since my identity is not very clear, and when I write I am surprised to find that I possess a destiny. Who has not asked himself at some time or other: am I a monster or is this what it means to be a person'? (Lispector, p. 15). This, of course, relates to the writer Rodrigo S. M. which is the facile alias of Lispector herself clearly implicated in the destiny of the Dedication. But Lispector also goes on to talk about Macabéa in identi(cal) terms. 'First of all, I must make it clear that this girl does not know herself apart from the fact that she goes on living aimlessly. Were she foolish enough to ask herself 'Who am I?', she would fall flat on her face. For the question 'Who am I?' creates a need. And how does one satisfy that need? To probe oneself is to recognize that one is incomplete' (Lispector, pp. 15–16). Such an attitude towards incompleteness seems to imply a kind of duality between body and other. The Hegelian resolution would be to recognize the other as the spirit, though Hegel would contend (*vis-à-vis* the *Phenomenology of Spirit*) that the spirit would usurp the body and, therefore, be one spiritual being. But Macabéa has no Hegelian credentials. For Macabéa, who was born without a name and hence without an immediate identity, spirituality gains no parcel. One can conjoin Locke's view that personal identity consists in a sameness of consciousness and the fact that Macabéa had no name at birth would not preclude her from remembering. Without going into a kind of dualist v. materialist account of personal identity (which is beyond the scope of this book) the fact that Macabéa is nameless at birth and that as an adult she hardly exists for those around her is tied in with the notion of her name. The use of the name Macabéa, after one of the heroes of the Jews, is doubly ironic in that 1) Macabéa has no leadership capabilities at all and 2) she is more a product of the 'fickleness' of Fortune than was Maccabeus whose Fortunes smiled kindly on the leader of 'the chosen people'.

One discovers as early as page 26 that Macabéa was 'born with a legacy of mis-Fortune' and that natal encumbrance is repeated again on page 27. A foundation of *mis*-Fortune for Macabéa is thus established which is augmented throughout the novel not in her relationship with Olímpico and Gloria, but in her daily life. But the selection of the Goddess Fortuna to be the slave of conveyance for Macabéa shows a kind of ambiguity as well since the Goddess Fortuna has evolved from the early Roman ideal of her as an independent ruling power to the medieval Christian ideal of her as a power subservient to a higher power, namely God. The Roman ideal of Fortune was based on her appearance as a goddess of chance whose character implied pure fate. At that time, Fortune came into her own and her fickleness, instability and irrationality in both attitude and appearance can be seen in Ovid when he writes that changeable Fortune wanders abroad with aimless steps, abiding firm and persistent in no place; now she comes in joy, now she takes on a harsh mien, steadfast only in her own fickleness'. In other words, 'from meaning simply "the one who brings our destiny," the term later came to signify the one who performs that act in a capricious way – [the] original deity was simply known as "Fors," to which "fortuna" was added as a cognomen, later only to break off and become independent' (Patch, p. 10).

As the Romans came to regard themselves at the mercy of Fortune, so did they try to save themselves by limiting her powers. The one way to minimize Fortune's powers was through the implementation of reason and the arrival of Christianity gave validity to reason. 'A period which saw the universe ruled by order used "Fors Fortuna", or simply, "Fortuna", as the equivalent of "Fate"; another, which rejected order and emphasized (at least from the human point of view) caprice, used the term to mean "chance"' (Patch, p. 11). The Church fathers made it clear that Fortune had no actual existence and her works were not realistic, but illusory, thus subduing her might. 'Fortune is highly variable and scarcely knows her own mind. She is in doubt; she is sometimes asleep, but wakes up when she pleases; she goes along changing her style, or turning her face like a weathercock' (Patch, p. 49). And this calls into question the relationship between Fortune and the faces of beauty and ugliness, of Fortune and unreason. Just as the Romans came to regard themselves as at the mercy of Fortune they tried to limit her powers by opposing reason to her unreason. But Macabéa is ruled by mis-Fortune, Fortuna Mala, in other words, the goddess of Fortune gone awry. If reason prevails over Fortune, which in its best state is unreasonable, then unreason in its most unmitigated state must prevail over mis-Fortune for it would seem that things that were unfortunate could not be ruled by reason. Witness, for example, world catastrophes, social holocausts, whimsical tragedies. MisFortunes cannot stand the test of reason. The theme of 'Fortune's course' 'suggests that to attain any gift of Fortune we must follow her though she flee. The same idea is found in the conception of Fortune as leading mankind on a way of her own choosing, and so giving men the various adventures they experience. Fortune, and not Reason, thus becomes the guide of life' (Patch, p. 99). And so it is with Macabéa.

This is also alluded to when Lispector writes, 'There were certain words whose meaning escaped her. One such word was *ephemeris*' (Lispector, p. 39). And with the word 'ephemeris' we discover a number of possibilities all of which fit into the 'Fortune' scheme of the text as ephemeris can be associated with:

1. an astronomical almanac;
2. a table that gives co-ordinates of the heavenly bodies;
3. in Latin, a diary or chronicle of daily events; and,
4. in Greek, the associated word 'ephemeral' or 'fleeting'.

Each of these possibilities associated with Fortune and with the ephemeris relate to Macabéa's life, the substance of her life and, eventually, to her death. When we get to the Fortune teller she tells Macabéa that 'As for your immediate future, my child, that's miserable as well. You're about to lose your job just as you've already lost your boyfriend, you poor little thing. If you haven't got the money to pay me, don't you worry. I'm a woman of some means' (Lispector, p. 76). She then follows that up with 'Oh there is something else! You are about to come in for a great fortune that a foreign gentleman will bring to you in the night' (Lispector, p. 76). So within two paragraphs the ambiguity reappears. Then of course Macabéa is killed 'for my hour has come' (Lispector, p. 79).

So the notions of ephemeris (fleeting/daily), Fortune/mis-Fortune (Latin can be both good/bad luck) and dis-aster (ill-starred) all coalesce. Here we get the link between Fortune and the 'hour of the star'. All of this ties in with notions of free will, or the lack of it, of things happening beyond our control, of things cosmic. Recall Lispector's beginning 'Everything in the world began with a yes', but the affirmations of the molecules were set in motion by a mediator who has no second. Which ultimately leads us to the prevailing uses of God and Jesus in the text.

The ambiguity about God is replete throughout the novel. In discussing Macabéa's appearance, Lispector writes: 'Her eyes were enormous, round, bulging and inquisitive – she had the expression of someone with a broken wing – some deficiency of the thyroid gland – questioning eyes. Whom was she questioning? God? She did not think about God, nor did God think about her. God belongs to those who succeed in pinning Him down. God appears in a moment of distraction. She asked no questions. She divined that there were no answers' (Lispector, p. 26). But death does not exist apart from the exigencies of the poetics of mortality in the text because the last half-dozen pages of the text not only link the tripartite relationship among God–Macabéa–Death, but link the tripartite relationship among God–Lispector–Death. After Macabéa's fatal accident the Rodrigo pose is abandoned when Lispector writes 'Is this melodrama? What I can say is that melodrama was the summit of her life. All lives are an art, and hers inclined towards an outburst of restless weeping with thunder and lightning.'

A scrawny fellow appeared on the street-corner, wearing a threadbare jacket and playing the fiddle. I should explain that, when I was a child and living in Recife, I once saw this man as dusk was falling. The shrill, prolonged sound of his playing underline in gold the mystery of that darkened street. On the ground, beside this pitiful fellow, there was a tin can which received the rattling coins of grateful bystanders as he played the dirge of their lives. It is only now that I have come to understand. Only now has the secret meaning dawned on me: the fiddler's music is an omen. I know that when I die, I shall hear him playing and that I shall crave for music, music, music' (Lispector, p. 82) a paragraph that recalls the lines, 'Tout à coup, entendit sur le trottoir un bruit de gros sabots, avec le frôlement d'un bâton; et une voix s'éleva, une voix rauque, qui chantait:

> Souvent la chaleur d'un beau jour
> Fait rêver fillette à lamour.

Emma se releva comme un cadavre que l'on galvanise, les cheveux dénoués, la prunelle fixe, béante.

> Pour amasser diligemment
> Le épis que la faux moissonne,
> Ma Nanette va s'inclinant
> Vers le sillon qui nous les donne.

−"L'Aveugle!" s'écria-t-elle.

Et Emma se mit à rire, d'une rire atroce, frénétique, désespéré, croyant voir la face hideuse du misérable, qui se dressait dans les ténèbres éternelles comme un épouvantement.

> *Il souffla bien fort ce jour-là*
> *Et le jupon court s'envola!*

Une convulsion la rabattit sur le matelas. Tous s'approchèrent. Elle n'existait plus (Flaubert, pp. 412–13).

In a way, Macabéa is like Emma Bovary in the sense that she has been 'victimized' by the 'riches' of urbanity and like the blind man who sings of Emma's demise, Lispector's fiddler plays not only the dirge for Macabéa, but for Lispector as well and the refrain of 'music, music, music' closes the circle begun in the Dedication.

Though death is alluded to throughout the novel, it is dealt with directly at the end as Lispector invokes, 'Death is my favorite character in this story' (Lispector, p. 83) and on page 85 we read 'She is finally free of herself and of me. Do not be frightened. Death is instantaneous and passes in a flash. I know, for I have just died with the girl. Forgive my dying. It was unavoidable. If you have kissed the wall, you can accept anything. But suddenly I make one last gesture of rebellion and start to howl: the slaughter of doves! To live is a luxury.

Suddenly it's all over.

Macabéa is dead. The bells were ringing without making any sound. I now understand this story. She is the imminence in those bells, pealing so softly.

The greatness of every human being' (Lispector, p. 85).

And almost as an homage to Macabéa, Lispector leaves a white space, a gap of silence, between the end of her protagonist and the end of her own life. The novel ends:

'And now − now it only remains for me to light a cigarette and go home. Dear God, only now am I remembering that people die. Does that include me?

Don't forget, in the meantime, that this is the season for strawberries. Yes' (Lispector, p. 86).

The novel thus ends where it began with a 'yes'. Perhaps that closes the circle on Lispector and her poetics of mortality. One can decompose the novel into sections, quadrants, portions, as one wishes, which highlights a number of interdependent subjects:

novelwriting, God, death, Jesus, fortune, etc. all of which form a kind of nexus of creation. It is incumbent on a reader to negotiate with these issues in a way that renders them novel yet at the same time renders the text a kind of homage to a life lost. Certainly *The Hour of the Star* is an autobiographical novel not unlike Smart's *By Grand Central Station* or Duras' *The Lover* or Beckett's *Company*. But what gives it a different posture than the others is the immediacy of the immanent moment, that as she writes the story of the rise and fall of Macabéa she writes the rise and fall of herself, her life, and the history of her being. The novel is, in fact, an epitaph for Lispector, a poetics of mortality.

9

The Poetics of Voice in Beckett's *Company*

It is curious that a novella such as *Company*, one of Beckett's last prose works, would get such limited attention. Perhaps that is because of the autobiographical nature of the piece or because it is too short or because most of his prose writing tends to be subsumed by his dramatic pieces. Yet *Company* is a rather startling bit of prose and the poetics of the piece, especially in relation to 'voice', are certainly as dynamic as any of Beckett's other prose writing.

The structure of *Company* is simple, the prose, laconic: in fewer than twelve-thousand words there are 58 paragraphs in 56 pages, with extra-wide margins and numerous gaps of paragraphical white space, in which he presents a microbiography of the narrator's life. The paragraphs seem to follow two forms: a bit more than three dozen, 42 to be exact, tell about a figure 'lying on his back in the dark' and 15 relate to the microbiography. The man is silent and is referred to as the listener or hearer; he is mute while the voices he hears compete for a kind of mental domination. But the best point of departure for a study of Beckett's poetics of voice in *Company* is to refer to *Three Dialogues with Georges Duthuit* in which he says: 'The expression that there is nothing to express, nothing with which to express, nothing from which to express, no power to express, together with the obligation to express' (Beckett, *Three Dialogues*, p. 103). The operative word here is 'expression', the act of transforming ideas into words and the words are mediated by voice, voice rendered. 'The voice has been dramatic since its appearance in *Molloy*, and the possibilities of staging it were enhanced in 1965 when Beckett assisted two friends in such an enterprise' (Acheson, p. 193).

Beckett's dramatic pieces have, by and large, been the most salient examples of voice in his *oeuvre* and the play, *Not I*, possibly the most salient example of the salient examples. It is worth paying attention to what Beckett has done in *Not I* as a kind of prelude to what he does in *Company*. If one looks at the opening note of the play it reads: 'Movement: this consists in simple sideways raising of arms from sides and their falling back, in a gesture of helpless compassion. It lessens with each recurrence tills scarcely perceptible at third. There is just enough pause to contain it as MOUTH recovers from vehement refusal to relinquish third person' (Beckett, *Ends and Odds*, p. 12). This note is then followed by extensive stage directions which include the following:

> *Stage in darkness, but for MOUTH, upstage audience right, about 8 feet above stage level, faintly lit from close-up and below, rest of face in shadow. Invisible microphone.*
> *AUDITOR, downstage audience left, tall standing figure, sex indeterminable, enveloped from head to foot in loose black djellaba, with hood, fully faintly lit, standing on invisible podium about 4 feet high shown by attitude alone to be facing diagonally across stage intent on MOUTH, dead still throughout but for four brief movements where indicated. See Note.*
> *As house lights down MOUTH's voice unintelligible behind curtain. House lights out. Voice continues unintelligible behind curtain, 10 seconds. With rise of curtain ad-libbing from text as required leading when curtain fully up and attention sufficient into:'*
> (Beckett, *Ends and Odds*, p. 13).

For the duration of the play, approximately eight pages, MOUTH then speaks in a series of 'chaotic' ellipses replete with staggered words, repetitions, fragments, queries, the stock in trade of Beckettian discourse. But it is the MOUTH that speaks these words, not I, though the not I is, presumably, not s/he, but Beckett himself, 'nothing of note till coming up to sixty when – ... what? ... seventy? ... good God! ... coming up to seventy ...' (Beckett, *Ends and Odds*, p. 13) the not I, MOUTH, substituting for the I, Beckett, the he of the 'small beak' whose voice one hears as a substitution for the s/he on stage. The comparison with *Company* is not serendipitous. Beckett's obsession with the semiotics of the stage in *Not I* (and elsewhere) is somehow transferred to the semiotics of the 'stage' in *Company*. In other words, what we find in terms of how the MOUTH is staged (i.e. vertically, in the dark with arms to the sides, etc.) we see with the ONE ON HIS BACK (i.e. staged horizontally, in the dark and, presumably, with arms at his sides). Just as MOUTH expresses itself vertically and vocally, ONE ON HIS BACK expresses himself horizontally and sub-vocally yet the subject of the discourse remains fairly constant since the subject of the discourse becomes his 'company' which are the inventions and memories that inhabit the narrator's mind as he lies sub-vocalizing, in the darkness, a condition he maintains throughout the novella.

The dramatic potential of *Company* was exploited by Gontarski and staged at the Los Angeles Actor's Theater in 1985. But rather than keep the voice on his back in the dark, Gontarski and Pierre Chabert, the director, with the blessings of Beckett himself, chose to sit the figure in a chair with the addition of a floating head. What Gontarski discovered 'from the earliest rehearsals was that even as a prose work *Company* already contained a fundamental dramatic structure, a dichotomy between second- and third-person voices, and Beckett's characterization of the two voices reflected the contrapuntal relationship not only between each section but within them as well' (Acheson, p. 196).

Beyond the semiotics of how the 'voice' is staged, there is the signifying aspect of the voice itself sounded in sub-vocalization. There is the suppression of the subjective 'I' and the intermingling of both second and third person. Gontarski says, 'The third-person voice, he noted, was "erecting a series of hypotheses, each of which is false." The second-person voice was "trying to create a history, a past for the third-person", each episode of which the third-person rejects, insisting, in effect, "that was not I"' (Acheson, 196). So once again we find a relationship between voices. But whose voice is it? Where does it come from? A voice, presumably his own voice, then, from his memory, comes to him in the dark. To one on his back in the dark. To one on his ass in the dark. We see the shift in person as when he states: 'As for example when he hears, You are on your back in the dark' (Beckett, p. 7) when he, the silent figure, hears, the silent figure, is on his back in the dark as mediated by his thoughts. That can be validated, but not all can be validated. As for example when he hears, 'You first saw the light on such and such a day and now you are on your back in the dark' (Beckett, p. 7). Why this can not be validated is because it is not mediated by his memory alone, but is mediated by someone else whom he remembers mediated by his memory alone. He then repeats (something for which Beckett is famous): 'To one on his back in the dark a voice tells of a past' (Beckett, p. 7). With occasional allusion to a present and more rarely to a future as for example, 'You will end as you are now. And in another dark or in the same another devising it all for company. Quick leave him' (Beckett, p. 8).

Here is the first use of the word 'company', but in the entire
novella it is mentioned approximately 30 times. But one might ask
how is this particular phrase and the associated word 'company'
related to the title? We read on page 9: 'Yet a certain activity of
mind however slight is a necessary adjunct of company. That is
why the voice does not say, You are on your back in the dark and
have no mental activity of any kind. The voice alone is company
but not enough. Its [the voice] effect on the hearer is a necessary
complement... But company apart this effect is clearly necessary'
(Beckett, pp. 9–10). Gontarski submits that there are two 'fundamental themes of the word: first, the strength and potential solace
of the imagination as company; and second, the weakness and
failure of the imagination as company, that is, its failure to alleviate
man's most fundamental condition, loneliness' (Acheson, p. 197).

Likewise, there is an alteration between past and present. In total
there are 15 memories of the past – 7 of childhood, 2 of adulthood
and 6 of old age. But it is the manner in which the paragraphs are
constructed that are of interest which I quote at length:

> A small boy you come out of Connolly's Stores holding your
> mother by the hand. You turn right and advance in silence
> southward along the highway. After some hundred paces you
> head inland and broach the long steep homeward. You make
> ground in silence hand in hand through the warm still summer
> air. It is late afternoon and after some hundred paces the sun
> appears above the crest of the rise. Looking up at the blue sky
> and then at your mother's face you break the silence asking her if
> it is not in reality much more distant than it appears. The sky that
> is. The blue sky. Receiving no answer you mentally reframe your
> question and some hundred paces later look up at her face again
> and ask her if it does not appear much less distant than in reality
> it is. For some reason you could never fathom this question must
> have angered her exceedingly. For she shook off your little hand
> and made you a cutting retort you have never forgotten.
>
> (Beckett, pp. 10–11)

The way this paragraph is written in relation to the others is
markedly different. One discovers that the discourse is clearly
more representational. Gone is the rhetoric of anadiplosis, etc.
and what one reads is something keenly biographical a clear shift
in the poetics of the passage. In relation to the following passage:

If the voice is not speaking to him it must be speaking to another. So with what reason remains he reasons. To another of that other. Or of him. Or of another still. To another of that other or of him or of another still. To one on his back in the dark in any case. Of one on his back in the dark whether the same of another. So with what reason remains he reasons and reasons ill. For were the voice speaking not to him but to another then it must be of that other it is speaking and not of him or of another still. Since it speaks in the second person. (Beckett, pp. 12–13)

The poetics of the following passage are replete with the fundamental rhetoric that is Beckett. The repetitions of words and phrases go completely against the kind of representational passage he wrote the paragraph before. Yet the contextual voice changes once again in the subsequent paragraph with a description of the labour and the father's reasons for avoiding it:

It being a public holiday your father left the house soon after his breakfast with a flask and a package of his favourite egg sandwiches for a tramp in the mountains. There was nothing unusual with this. But on that particular morning his love of walking and wild scenery was not the only mover. But he was moved also to take himself off and out of the way by his aversion to the pains and general unpleasantness of labour and delivery. Hence the sandwiches which he relished at noon looking out to sea from the lee of a great rock on the first summit scaled.
(Beckett, *Company*, p. 13).

The voice here is less poetic than it is nostalgically representational. In other words, Beckett seems to modify his voices moving from a kind of representational discourse which is generally associated with the nostalgic moment and a poetic discourse (which often utilizes Beckettian rhetoric) that is generally associated with the present moment. These voices rarely coincide. For example after the representational passage on page 13 Beckett follows with:

'You are an old man plodding along a narrow country road. You have been out since break of day and now it is evening. Sole sound in the silence your footfalls. Rather sole sounds for they vary from one to the next...So many since dawn to add to yesterday's. To yesteryears'. To yesteryears... (Beckett, 14–15)

The use of the 's' alliteration and the repetitive phrase 'Sole sound(s)' is something Beckett generally avoids with the representational/nostalgic voice, but not in the poetic present voice. 'You' is the voice the narrator calls himself, especially in those micro-texts in which the refrain 'on your back in the dark' is written.

There is an alternation of voices and voices within the voice. The refràin of 'on your back in the dark' belongs to the voice other than the representational nostalgic voice. This is the poetic voice which alternates with the nostalgic and is often given more 'space' than the latter. He will juxtapose a representational passage with a poetic one, but with the poetic passages being more abundant. A passage which recalls his youth with: 'He calls to you to jump. He calls, Be a brave boy. The red round face. The thick moustache. The greying hair'. (Beckett, p. 18) is followed by a passage in which the poetic movement is much more apparent with the line: 'Some soft thing softly stirring soon to stir no more'. (Beckett, p. 19)

The poetic passages interlocute with the nostalgic passages. Not only is there a distinction of voice, but there is a clear differentiation between the interlocutors. The poetic voice establishes itself as such and the rhetorical techniques Beckett prefers anadiplosis, polysyndeton, anaphora are prevalent throughout the novella while the representational/nostalgic passages have little in the way of poetic measure in and of themselves. The poetic tends to disenfranchise itself from the nostalgic. Non-representational writing also precludes the narrator from remembering the past. The poetic movements only allow for a cognitive expression of what is and what may be. Speculation. The discourse, frenzied, chaotic in harmonious ways, only reinforces the Beckettian silence like a mouth, opened, but expressiveless. Throughout it all, the tropes eventually lead one to the solitary and final word 'Alone' which dignifies the frame set up at the beginning of the novella.

Likewise, the narrator is both querulous and querying and the voice in which he is both is the voice of the present, not that of the past. As early as page 9 the narrator asks: 'May not there be another with him in the dark to and of whom the voice is speaking? ... You saw the light on such and such a day and now your are alone on your back in the dark? Why?' (Beckett, p. 9) And the voice is constantly questioning, questioning in a way not unlike Faust. 'With what feeling remains does he feel about now as compared to then?' (Beckett, p. 22) or 'Till the eye closes and freed from pore the mind inquires, What does this mean? What finally does this mean that at first sight seemed clear?' (Beckett, p. 23). The questions are always asked within the framework of the poetic present and always questioning one's being as in: 'For why or? Why in another dark or in the same? And whose voice is asking this? Who asks, Whose voice asking this? And answers. His soever who devises it all. In the same dark as his creature or in another. For company. Who asks in the end, Who asks? And in the end answers above?' (Beckett, p. 24) This is the anti-Faustian narrator, not necessarily interested in 'the light', but in 'the dark' and the dark is a much more poignant and lugubrious associate than the light for in the end, the deviser of devisers is 'Nowhere to be found. Nowhere to be sought. The unthinkable last of all. Unnamable. Last person. I. Quick leave him' (Beckett, p. 24).

But the questions and the questioning are replete with allusions to several items: posture, imagination and breath. 'But physically? Must he lie inert to the end?...Might he not cross his feet?' (p. 28); 'Finally what meant by his own unrelieved? What possible relief?' (p. 31); 'Which of all imaginable postures least liable to pall? Which of motion or of rest the more entertaining in the long run? And in the same breath too soon to say and why after all not say without further ado what can later be unsaid and what if it could not? What then?' (p. 43); 'Would it be reasonable to imagine the hearer as mentally quite inert?...For what if not it and his breath is there for him to hear?... Does he hear the crawl? The fall?...What if not sound could set his mind in motion? Sight?...Taste? The taste in his mouth?...Touch?...Might not a notion to stir ruffle his apathy?...Smell? His own?...Might the crawling creator be reasonably imagined to smell?...Inexplicable premonition of impending ill? Yes or no? No. Pure reason? Beyond experience. God is love. Yes or No? No.' (pp. 50–1); and finally 'Which of all the ways of lying supine the least likely in the long run to pall?' (p. 56). The three notions of posture, imagination and breath act like a leitmotif through the novella if not through Beckett's work. The constant questioning of the human condition, of the narrator's human condition, of the narrator's condition is a measure of the narrator's reason for being. As the present encroaches on the nostalgic past, displacing it with the inexorable movement of the present, the questions all tend to be questions of an existential desire to know, but without answer.

What is significant about the alternation of the past as present and the present as present mediated by the same yet different voice is the notion of memory. Ceartainly the narrator is clear about remembrance of things past. There is no ambiguity, nothing equivocal. The descriptions of the past are not opaque descriptions. For the most part, they are precise descriptions, albeit brief, of some other time. Curiously, the only time the narrator appears to be ambiguous or forgetful about his recollections of the past is in the case of the doctor who delivered him, 'Dr Hadden or Haddon'. This ambiguity is not serendipitous. Recalling Freud's suggestion that 'When we recapitulate the conditions for forgetting a name with faulty recollection we find: 1) a certain disposition to forget the name; 2) a process of suppression which has taken place shortly before; and 3) the possibility of establishing an *outer* association between the concerned name and the element previously suppressed' (Freud, p. 11). Certainly there is a clear association between the physician and the narrator's present state 'on his back in the dark' and all that relates to that posture. The 'voice alone is company but not enough' is akin to the narrator's memory and the notion of memory is a substantive one in the novella not only because the voice is memory and memory alone is not enough to someone on his back in the dark, but the fact that memory becomes a character of company that is constantly present. As Bergson states, 'Memory, as we have tried to prove, is not a faculty of putting away recollections in a drawer or of inscribing them in a register. There is no register, no drawer; there is not even, properly speaking, a faculty, for a faculty works intermittently, when it will or when it can, whilst the piling up of the past upon the past goes on without relaxation. In reality, the past is preserved by itself, automatically. In its entirety, probably, it follows us at every instant; all that we have felt, thought and willed from our earliest infancy is there, leaning over the present which is about to join it, pressing against the portals of consciousness that would fain leave it outside' (Bergson, pp. 4–5).

But there is a limit to that notion in that through time the special dispensation of memory dwindles. Unlike Descartes who writes 'I can use both my memory, which connects present experiences with preceding ones, and my intellect, which has by now examined all the causes of error' (Descartes, p. 122), the narrator's memory is fraught with ambiguity and the narrator longs for other company perhaps to affirm the memory. He longs for company from without since the voice is not necessarily an accurate voice and the voice is not the company one would choose to be with. When we are confronted with an issue of memory we are confronted with an issue of remembering, an act which is not merely recuperative since memory involves editing and revising; fragmentation and dismemberment; it brings one closer to experience, but distances one as well as when he writes 'Deviser of the voice and of its hearer and of himself. Deviser of himself for company' (Beckett, p. 26) The 'deviser' of the voice is memory and memory cannot be trusted over time.

This notion of the deviser appears again on page 46 in paragraphs 1 and 2. Which leads to the techniques of repetition and permutation for which Beckett is so notorious. As a matter of fact, on page 16 paragraph 2 it is even written about. 'Another trait its repetitiousness. Repeatedly with only minor variants the same bygone.' This repetition is not done for the sake of repetition, but for the purpose of reiterating the daily, the mundane, the repetition of the moment until the moment no longer exists and is displaced by some other, less imaginable, present. It is curious that the only mention of God comes in the phrase 'God is love. Yes or No? No.' It is an unequivocal statement much like the subtextual statement on Beckett's tomb. Resting between two families in the cemetery at Montparnasse, both of which voice recourse to God's good intentions, Beckett's tomb bears nothing but his name and the name of his wife. Nothing else. Nothing more laconic. No voice where none intended.

Notes

CHAPTER 1 – *DON QUIXOTE*

1. An age that is not serendipitously chosen as it is an age that has significant spiritual implications and is found in such characters as Mann's Von Aschenbach (*Death in Venice*), Hesse's Harry Haller (*Steppenwolf*), and Axelrod's Blase Kubash (*Posthumous Memoirs of Blase Kubash*) just to name a few. Though there is no exact date, the most plausible speculation as to the time Cervantes first began to write *Quixote* would be subsequent to his release from prison in 1598 which would have made him 51.

CHAPTER 4 – *MADAME BOVARY*

1. Definition from the *Dictionary of Accepted Ideas*.

CHAPTER 7 – *BY GRAND CENTRAL STATION I SAT DOWN AND WEPT*

1. Venus, while playing with her son Cupid, wounded her breast with one of his arrows. Before the wound healed she saw Adonis and, captivated by him, gave up everything for him charging him not to do anything dangerous. Being Adonis he cannot abide by that and, ultimately, is killed by a boar.
2. Damocles, a flatterer, having extolled the happiness of Dionysius' tyrant of Syracuse, was placed by him at a banquet with a sword suspended over his head by a hair to impress upon him the perilousness of that happiness.
3. Daphne. Here we have the love of the narrator and her paramour aligned with Daphne which relates to the myth of Daphne and Apollo who, struck by Cupid's arrow, did everything he could to capture her. In his quest to obtain her, Daphne pleads with Peneüs, her father the river god, to save her in order to escape Apollo; he changes her into a laurel tree which Apollo covets and makes a laurel crown to wear.
4. Antaeus, son of Poseidon and Gaea, was a Libyan giant and wrestler whose strength was invincible so long as he remained in contact with his mother Earth; those whom he defeated, died. Though he was strangled by Hercules while holding him off the ground.
5. Dido, daughter of Belus, King of Tyre. Her husband was secretly murdered by her brother Pygmalion for his money. She went to

Africa, founded Carthage and became its queen. When Aeneas came
to Carthage, Dido fell in love with him. Dido tried to keep Aeneas
with her and used every allurement and persuasion; when he left she
uttered a curse against the Trojans, stabbed herself and died on a
funeral pyre.

References

Foreword

Albalat, Antoine, *Le travail du style enseigné par les corrections manuscrites des grands écrivains*. Paris: Librairie Armand Colin, 1913.

Arnheim, Rudolf, *Entropy and Art: An Essay on Disorder and Order*. Berkeley: University of California Press, 1971.

Axelrod, Mark, Personal Interview. Paris, 1984.

Barthes, Roland, *New Critical Essays*. New York: FSG, 1980.

Benjamin, Walter, *Illuminations*. New York: Schocken Books, 1969.

Brooke-Rose, Christine, 'Whatever Happened to Narratology'. *Poetics Today*, Vol 11, Number 2 (Summer 1990): 281–93.

Burke, Kenneth, *The Philosophy of Literary Form*. Berkeley: University of California Press, 1973.

Derrida, Jacques, (ed. Attridge, Derek) *Acts of Literature*. New York: Routledge, 1992.

Flaubert, Gustave, *Intimate Notebook 1840–1841*. Introduction, Trans. Steegmuller, Francis, New York: Doubleday, 1967.

Gleick, James, *Chaos: Making a New Science*. New York: Viking Press, 1987.

Guillén, Claudio, *Literature as System: Essays Toward the Theory of Literary History*. Princeton, NJ: Princeton University Press, 1971.

Hytier, Jean, *The Poetics of Paul Valéry*. Garden City, NY: Doubleday, 1966.

James, Henry, *The Art of Fiction and Other Essays*. New York: Oxford, 1948.

Lemon, Lee T. and Reis, Marion J. *Russian Formalist Criticism: Four Essays*. Lincoln: University of Nebraska Press, 1965.

McHale, Brian, *Postmodernist Fiction*. New York: Routledge, 1987.

Orr, Leonard, *Problems and Poetics of the NonAristotelian Novel*. Lewisburg, PA: Bucknell University Press, 1991.

Prigogine, Ilya, and Stengers, Isabelle, *Order Out of Chaos*. New York: Bantam Books, 1984.

Preminger, Alex, and Brogan, T. V. F. (eds), *Princeton Encyclopedia of Poetry and Poetics*. Princeton, NJ: Princeton University Press, 1993.

Rimmon-Kenan, Shlomith, *Narrative Fiction: Contemporary Poetics*. New York: Methuen, 1983.

Sebeok, Thomas, (ed.), *Style in Language*. Cambridge, MA: Technology Press of Massachusetts Institute of Technology, 1960.

Spilka, Mark, (ed.), *Towards a Poetics of Fiction*. Bloomington: Indiana University Press, 1977.

Sukenick, Ronald, *In form, digressions on the act of fiction*. Carbondale, IL: Southern Illinois University Press, 1985.

Todorov, Tzvetan, *The Poetics of Prose*. Translated from the French by Richard Howard. Ithaca, NY: Cornell University Press, 1977.

Toril, Moi, *Sexual/Textual Politics*. London and New York: Routledge, 1985.

Walter, Benjamin, *Illuminations*. Translated by Harry Zohn. New York, NY: Schocken Books, 1969.

Chapter 1 – *Don Quixote*

Hans Ulrich Gumbrecht, *South Atlantic Quarterly*, Durham, NC(SAQ). 1992 Fall, 91:4, 891–907.
Campbell, Joseph, *The Hero With a Thousand Faces*. New York: Pantheon Books, 1949.
Cervantes, Miguel, *Don Quixote*. Translated by J. M. Cohen. New York: Penguin Books, 1950. [source of English extracts.]
Cervantes, Miguel, *Don Quixote*. Barcelona: Editorial Juventud, S. A., 1968. [Source of Spanish extracts.]
Foucault, Michel, *Madness and Civilization: A History of Insanity in the Age of Reason*, translated from the French by Richard Howard, New York: Random House, 1965.
Frazer, Sir James George, *The Golden Bough: A Study in Magic and Religion*. New York: Macmillan, 1978.
Gilman, Stephen, *The Novel According to Cervantes*. Berkeley: University of California Press, 1989.
Hamel, Peter Michael, *Through Music to the Self*. Translated from the German by Peter Lemesurier, Boulder: Shambhala, 1979.
Hegel, G. W. F., *Reason in History*. Translated, with an introduction by Robert S. Hartman. Indianapolis: Bobbs-Merrill, 1976.
Mancing, Howard, *The Chivalric World of Don Quixote; Style, Structure and Narrative Technique*. Columbia: University of Missouri Press, 1982.
Riley, E. C., *Cervantes's Theory of the Novel*. Newark, Delaware: Juan de la Cuesta, 1992.
Underhill, Evelyn, *Mysticism: A Study in the Nature and Development of Man's Spiritual Consciousness*, New York: E. P. Dutton, 1961.
van Gennep, Arnold, *The Rites of Passage*, translated by Monka B. Vizedom and Gabrielle L. Caffee, Chicago: University of Chicago Press, 1960.
Zimmerman, J. E. *Dictionary of Classical Mythology*. New York: Bantam, 1968.

Chapter 2 – *Northanger Abbey*

Austen, Jane, *Northanger Abbey*, New York: Signet/Penguin, 1980.
Bakhtin, Mikhail, *Problems with Dostoevsky's Poetics*. Ed. and Trans. by Caryl Emerson. Manchester: Manchester University Press, 1984.
Chapman, R. W., (ed.) *Jane Austen's Letters to her sister Cassandra and others*, 2nd edn. London: Oxford University Press, 1952.
Grey, David, (ed.) *Jane Austen Handbook*. London: The Athalone Press, 1986.
Haggerty, George E., *Gothic Fiction/Gothic Form*. University Park: Pennsylvania State University Press, 1989.
Hutchinson, Peter, *Games Authors Play*. London: Methuen & Co. Ltd., 1983.
Iser, Wolfgang, *The Act of Reading: A Theory of Aesthetic Response*. London: Routledge & Kegan Paul, 1978.

Lauber, John, *Jane Austen Twayne Series*. New York: Oxford University Press, 1993.

Lerner, Laurence, (ed.) *Reconstructing Literature*. Oxford: Basil Blackwell, 1983.

Leavis, F. R., *A Selection from* Scrutiny. Vol 2, Cambridge: Cambridge University Press, 1968.

Radcliffe, Ann, *The Mysteries of Udolpho*. Oxford: Oxford University Press, 1970.

Radcliffe, Ann, *A Sicilian Romance*. Oxford: Oxford University Press, 1993.

Rose, Margaret, *Parody/Meta-Fiction: An Analysis of Parody as a Critical Mirror to the Writing and Reception of Fiction*. London: Croom Helm, 1979.

Sage, Victor, (ed.) *The Gothick Novel*. Basingstoke: The Macmillan Press, 1990.

Watt, Ian, *The Rise of the Novel*. London: Peregrine Books, 1963.

Fowles, John, *The French Lieutenant's Woman*. New York: New American Library, 1969.

Chapter 3 – *Wuthering Heights*

Cheresh Allen, Elizabeth, (ed.) *The Essential Turgenev*. Evanston, IL: Northwestern University Press, 1994.

Bal, Mieke, *Narratology: Introduction to the Theory of Narrative*. Trans. Christine van Boheemen. Toronto: University of Toronto Press, 1985.

Brontë, Emily, *Wuthering Heights*. Edited by Linda H. Peterson. Boston: Bedford Books of St. Martin's Press, 1992.

Duthie, Enid L., *The Brontës and Nature*. New York: St. Martin's Press, 1986.

Freeborn, Richard, *Turgenev: The Novelist's Novelist*. Oxford: Oxford University Press, 1960.

Lodge. David, *Language of Fiction: Essays in Criticism and Verbal Analysis of the English Novel*. New York: Columbia University Press, 1966.

Powell, Claire, *The Meaning of Flowers: A Garland of Plant Lore and Symbolism from Popular Custom and Literature*. Boulder, CO: Shambhala, 1979.

Turgenev, Ivan Sergeevich, *The Essential Turgenev*. Elizabeth Chenesh Allen (ed). Evanston, DC: Northwestern University Press, 1994.

Turton, Glyn, *Turgenev and the Context of English Literature 1850–1900*. London: Routledge, 1992.

Vogler, Thomas A., (ed.) *Twentieth Century Interpretations of* Wuthering Heights. Englewood Cliffs, NJ: Prentice-Hall, 1968.

Chapter 4 – *Madame Bovary*

Barthes, Roland, *The Pleasure of the Text*. Trans. Richard Miller. New York: Hill and Wang, 1975.

Baudelaire, Charles, *Selected Writings on Art and Artists*. Trans. P. E. Charvet. New York: Penguin Books, 1972.

Flaubert, Gustave, *Madame Bovary*. Paris: Éditions Gallimard, 1972.

Flaubert, Gustave, *Madame Bovary*. Trans. Paul De Man. New York: Norton, 1965.

Flaubert, Gustave, *The Letters of Gustave Flaubert 1830–1857*. Trans. Francis Steegmuller. Cambridge, MA: Belknap Press, 1981.

Chapter 5 – *Tess of the D'Urbervilles*

Checkland, S. S., *The Rise of Industrial Society in England*, 1815–1885. New York: St. Martin's Press, 1964.
Douglas, Tom, *Scapegoats: Transferring Blame*. London: Routledge, 1995.
Dworkin, Andrea, *Intercourse*. London: Secker & Warburg, 1987.
Girard, René, *Violence and the Sacred*. Trans. Patrick Gregory. Baltimore and London: Johns Hopkins University Press, 1972.
Hardy, Thomas, *Tess of the D'Urbervilles*. New York: W. W. Norton, 1991.
Hubert, Henri, and Mauss, Marcel, *Sacrifice: Its Nature and Function*. Trans. W. D. Halls, London: Cohen and West, 1964.
James, E. O., *Sacrifice and Sacrament*. New York: Barnes & Noble, 1962.
Lavater, John Caspar, *Essays on Physiognomy*. Trans. Thomas Holcroft. London: Ward, Lock, & Bowden, Nineteenth Edition (No date given).
Mauss, Marcel, *A General Theory of Magic*. Trans Robert Brain. London: Routledge and Kegan Paul, 1972.

Chapter 6 – *Hunger*

Chadbourne, Richard M. *Ernest Renan*. New York: Twayne Publishers, 1968.
Ferguson, Robert, *Enigma: The Life of Knut Hamsun*. New York: Farrar, Straus & Giroux, 1987.
Grayeff, Felix, *Aristotle and His School*. London: Gerald Duckworth & Company, 1974.
Hamsun, Knut, *Hunger*. Trans. Sverre Lyngstad. Edinburgh: Rebel, Canongate Books Ltd, 1996.
Kant, Immanuel, *The One Possible Basis for a Demonstration of the Existence of God*. Trans. and Introduction by Gordon Treash. New York: Abaris Books, 1979.
Kant, Immanuel, *The Essential Kant* introduction by Arnulf Zweig (ed.). New York: New American Library, 1970.
Naess, Harald and McFarlane, James, *Knut Hamsun: Selected Letters, Volume I, 1879–98*. Norwich: Norvik Press, 1990.

Chapter 7 – *By Grand Central Station I Sat Down and Wept*

Alter, Robert, *The Art of Biblical Narrative*. New York: Basic Books, 1981.
Baudelaire, Charles, *Oeuvres Complètes*. Paris: Éditions Robert Laffont, 1980.
Baudelaire, Charles, *Paris Spleen*. Trans. Louise Varèse. New York: New Directions, 1970.
Broom, Peter, and Chesters, Graham, *The Appreciation of Modern French Poetry 1850–1950*. Cambridge: Cambridge University Press, 1976.
Caws, Mary Ann and Riffaterre, Hermine, *The Prose Poem in France: Theory and Practice*. New York: Columbia University Press, 1984.

Conley, Verena Andermatt, *Hélène Cixous*. Toronto: University of Toronto Press, 1992.

Conley, Verena Andermatt, *Hélène Cixous Writing the Feminine*. London & Lincoln: University of Nebraska Press, 1984.

Horne, Dee, Elizabeth Smart's Novel Journal. *Studies in Canadian Literature*. 16:2, Fredericton, New Brunswick, Canada, 1991.

Irigaray, Luce, *je, tu, nous*. Trans. Alison Martin. New York, London: Routledge, 1993.

Moi, Toril, *Sexual/Textual Politics*. New York, London: Routledge, 1985.

Smart, Elizabeth, *By Grand Central Station I Sat Down and Wept*. London: Paladin, 1986.

Van Wert, Alice, 'By Grand Central Station': The Novel as Poem. *Studies in Canadian Literature*, 11:1, Fredericton, New Brunswick, Canada, 1986, Spring.

Chapter 8 – *The Hour of the Star*

Cixous, Hélène, *Readings: The Poetics of Blanchot, Joyce, Kafka, Kleist, Lispector and Tsvetayeva*. Ed. trans. and introduced Veren Andermatt Conley. Hemel Hempstead: Harvester Wheatsheaf, 1992.

Eagleton, Mary, (ed.) *Feminist Literary Theory: A Reader*. Oxford: Blackwell Publishers, 1986.

Fitz, Earl E., 'Point of View in Clarice Lispector's *A Hora da Estrela*'. *Luso-Brazilian Review*, XIX, 2. Madison, WI: University of Wisconsin, 1982.

Franck, Adolphe, *The Kabbalah: The Religious Philosophy of the Hebrews*. New York: Bell Publishing Company, 1940.

Franklin, Peter, *The Idea of Music: Schoenberg and Others*. Basingstoke: Macmillan, 1985.

Musil, Robert, *Posthumous Papers of a Living Author*. Trans. Peter Wortsman. Hygiene, CO: Eridanos Press, 1987.

Patch, Howard R., *The Goddess Fortuna in Mediaeval Literature*. London: Frank Cass & Co. Ltd., 1967.

Suzuki, D. T., *The Essentials of Zen Buddhism*. Ed. and Introduction Bernard Phillips. London: Rider and Company, 1963.

Clarice Lispector. *The Hour of the Star*. Trans. by Giavanni Pontiero. New York: Carcanet Press, 1986.

Theodor Adorno. *Philosophy of Modern Music*. Trans. by Anne G. Mitchell & Wesley V. Blomster. New York: Seabury Press, 1973.

Chapter 9 – *Company*

Acheson, James, and Arthur, Kateryna (eds) *Beckett's Later Fiction and Drama*. Basingstoke: Macmaillan, 1987.

Beckett, Samuel, *Proust and Three Dialogues with Georges Duthuit*, London: Calder, 1965.

Beckett, Samuel, *Company*. New York: Grove Weidenfeld, 1980.

Beckett, Samuel, *Ends and Odds*. London: Faber and Faber, 1977.

Bergson, Henri, *Creative Evolution*. Trans. Arthur Mitchell. Lanham, MD: University Press of America, 1983.

Descartes, René, *Selected Philosophical Writings*. Trans. John Cottingham, Robert Stoothoff, Dugald Murdoch. Cambridge: Cambridge University Press, 1988.

Freud, Sigmund, *Psychopathology of Everyday Life*. New York: Macmillan, 1914.

Levy, Eric P., *Beckett & The Voice of Species: A Study of the Prose Fiction*, Totowa: NJ: Gill and Macmillan, 1980.

Index

Index